LEYTON ORIENT

THE UNTOLD STORY OF THE
O'S BEST-EVER TEAM

Malcolm Graham after scoring those two goals that took Leyton Orient to the first division for the first and only time in their history. Cheers, Malc!

LEYTON ORIENT

THE UNTOLD STORY OF THE O'S BEST-EVER TEAM

By TONY McDONALD

FootballWorld

First published in November 2006 by
Football World
Tel: 01708 744 333
www.footballworld.co.uk

©Copyright Football World

Printed by Biddles Ltd, King's Lynn, Norfolk

Distributed by Football World
103 Douglas Road, Hornchurch, Essex, RM11 1AW, England
Email: tony@footballworld.co.uk

Set in Times Roman

ISBN 0-9551176-7-4

To Dad . . . My Hero.

And to all the other Leyton Orient heroes from 1961-63, who proved that miracles *can* happen, that dreams really *can* come true.

Contents

Acknowledgements

Special thanks must go especially to Susie Muir and Tony Hogg, and also to Dave Dodd, John Parke, Terry Connelly, Tim Crane, Dick Richards, Marios Flourentzou, Lisa McDonald and Mia McDonald.

And also to all those dilligent club historians who have been invaluable with our opposition team line-ups research. Especially Colin Cameron, Andy Porter and Gerry Wolstenholme who certainly went far more than that extra mile.
Not forgetting, also: Dave Smith, David Bull, Geoff Allman, Rick Cowdery, Don Waters, Roger Walsh, Des Hinks, Brendon Smurthwaite, Peter Gilham, Neil Kaufman, Ian Thomas, Rob Mason, Ian Rigby, Gordon Sawfleet, Tim Carder, Ray Simpson, Darren Griffiths, Chris Neald, Ray Simpson and Simon Marland.

Of course, you cannot produce a book of this nature without leaning gently on a few other authors whose previous dedicated work has proved more than useful as a reference, so we would also like to acknowledge the following books:
Leyton Orient: The Complete Record by Neilson N. Kaufman & Alan E. Ravenhill (Breedon Books, 2006)
Tommy Johnston: The Happy Wanderer by Neilson N.Kaufman (Breedon Books, 2004)
Who's Who of West Ham United (1895-2005) by Tony Hogg (Profile Sports Media, 2005)

We also pointed our Internet browser at the following websites (in addition to Google!):
www.leytonorient.premiumtv.co.uk
www.leytonorient.rivals.net
www.screenonline.org.uk
www.onlineweb.com
www.backdate.co.uk
www.news.bbc.co.uk

HOW DO YOU DO IT?

Gerry & The Pacemakers, April 1963

Foreword by Jeff Powell

Daily Mail Chief Sports Feature Writer

WHEN we make our periodic pilgrimages to Brisbane Road – sorry, Barry, Matchroom Stadium – my son JJ comes in for some good-natured ribbing from his pals.

Which league are you in? Who were you were playing on Saturday? How many did you lose by? All that jazz. Much of it from the fashion-followers of Arsenal and Manchester United, Chelsea and Liverpool, Tottenham and even West Ham.

'What do I tell 'em?' JJ asks me.

Tell 'em they're just fair weather supporters, pot-hunters, creatures of convenience. Tell them that unless you come from round the corner to the ground – not the other end of the M1 – you're not genuine fans.

'So why do we support the Orient , dad?'

Well, we don't live there any more but it used to be my home and home is where the heart is – and the O's are our roots.

Not only that but real football supporting is about the club you grow up with, however humble, not the glamourous League, Cup and Euro-giants hundreds of miles away.

So remind them that every dog has its day and we had ours.

Not that JJ was around to relish those two halcyon seasons, the year we went up from the old second division and our year of grace in what was to become the Premiership. All that was a quarter of a century before he was born.

So I tell him how magical it felt to be an O's fan mingling with the mighty.

I tell him how Charlton and Lewis were the sturdiest full-backs in the game. How Lucas, Bishop and Lea were the best damn half-back line a man could wish for. How Foster and Graham were the most under-rated players in England. How McDonald and White were wonders of that lost species, the jinking old-fashioned winger.

I tell him that Dave Dunmore was a god who scored goals made in heaven and that Johnny Carey was the mild-mannered genius of a manager who channelled those eclectic talents into the beam of sunlight which dazzled the East End of London for one brief but glorious spell.

And I tell him about the day Terry McDonald, the father of the author of this nostalgic reference to that enchanted time, floated in a goal from way out near the flag on the half-way line, to embarrass Manchester United and to give us hope that we might actually survive in the big time.

Of course it was not to be. No matter. We had our season in the sun and we remember those precious moments, while our selective memory mercifully blanks out the dismay of inevitable relegation.

For me personally, those two seasons were a catalyst for my career in sports journalism.

For a start, I sharpened my pen by reporting on Orient's exploits for the *Walthamstow Guardian*. Just as importantly, if not more so, my job gave me hours-upon-hours of access to the wisdom of Johnny Carey. It also opened up friendships with those players which gave me invaluable insight into the workings and mentality of the professional game.

Such relationships are rare, almost to the point of being non-existent, in the celebrity world of the Premiership and I remain indebted to them for all that help in my formative years.

Of course, all good things come at a price and mine was paid in losing bets at the old snooker hall close by the ground in the High Road. That was where we spent many an afternoon hour after training. Naturally, our promotion heroes were possessed of far better skills than I, no matter what the size of the balls concerned.

So there have been many consolations for being an Orient man through bad times and good.

Professionally, for me, supporting Orient does not interfere with my judgement of the global game which is a key element of my job at the *Daily Mail*.

If only it did!

Never mind. We enjoyed another promotion last season, albeit in the lower reaches of the League. And who knows, maybe there will be another miracle at the top one day in the future. Never say never.

Why do we support the O's?

This book, a labour of love for Terry McDonald's son Tony, will help my own son understand.

TELSTAR
Tornados, October 1962

Introduction by Tony McDonald

MY Dad scored the winning goal against Manchester United! There are not that many kids of famous fathers who could say that, but I can – thanks to Terry McDonald, who used to play on the left wing for 'little, old Leyton Orient'.

Even today, 44 years after his dramatic last-minute strike that clinched a memorable 1-0 first division victory and set the Brisbane Road ground alight, he continues to be reminded about the proudest moment of his career, and maybe his life. When the regulars in the LOFC Supporters' Club bar tire of trying to explain their team's latest setback (which invariably has its roots in a lack of money spent on the team), the conversation often comes around to: 'Tel, wot about yer goal against Man U?' One committee member, Dennis Barefield, even bows at his feet in mock hero worship as soon as he enters the room!

I'll never tire of hearing about those cherished memories and, let's be honest, the long-suffering supporters of Leyton Orient don't have too much past glory to look back on with a smile and rekindled thoughts of a lost youth. That is not meant as any disrespect to Martin Ling or the players who pull on the red shirt today. They do their best within very strict financial limits but today's loyal diehards at The Matchroom Stadium (sorry, Barry, it will never be anything but Brisbane Road to most of us long in the tooth football followers) can only dream of beating Manchester United again in a league match. They can only wonder at the prospect of outplaying East London neighbours West Ham United, 2-0. And battering cash-rich Everton, the Chelsea of their day, 3-0 in consecutive home matches.

But the Leyton Orient first division team of 1962-63 actually performed that tremendous feat . . . all in the space of one unbelievable, never-to-be-repeated 10-day spell. OK, so we all know they were relegated from the top flight at the end of that same season with the lowest points tally to date. But at least they'd been there and done that and their efforts both in gaining promotion to domestic football's highest echelon and their one-off season among the giants deserves this written tribute.

Please, indulge me here . . .

Dad was working the day Mum (Jean) gave birth to me in Stepney Green Maternity Hospital on Saturday, April 9, 1960 and was therefore unable to attend the arrival of the first of his three children. Well, if you can call scoring a goal for the Orient in their 2-0 home win over Liverpool 'work'.

Top left: Dad, aged six.

Top right: Dad's younger brother, Tony, who sadly died at the age of five. He's pictured here in July 1949, playing in the garden where they lived at 23, Harold Road, Upton Park.

Above left: Dad, his father Jim and me at Christmas 1961. Both Dad and I share the same middle name of James – after my Grandad, who died of cancer in 1973. He was a very gentle and well liked man.

Above: Dad trying to teach me a few tricks, Jan. 1961.

Left: Mum and Dad about to pack me off to the babysitters (probably Uncle Eddie and Aunt Lucy!) in December 1961. They were probably about to go 'Up West' to another big show.

Within days of my first birthday I was on the beach in Jersey with my parents and all the other players' families – the players' reward for having just avoided relegation from the second division. Another year on and we were all hopping on a plane again, this time to Majorca to celebrate promotion. Eddie Lewis tells me now that apparently I was the willing and unwitting scapegoat for some minor ornamental damage made by one or two of the other players' children around our hotel. 'Tony did it' was, I'm told by Eddie, one of the first sentences I learned on that trip!

I'm not sure when I became aware that Dad had been a professional footballer. It was certainly some time after he'd given up playing as a pro and was working full-time in one of the numerous betting shops he has managed, and continues to manage right up until today, two years beyond his official 'retirement'. We come from a family of West Ham supporters – we have season tickets at Upton Park, where Dad sits alongside his three grandsons and myself, distributing Werthers Originals much better than most of the Hammers players can pass a football. Because he worked every Saturday in the bookies (take your pick from Ray Pollock, Arthur Prince and now Coral), he could only take me to the Hammers' midweek home matches, although his cousin Dennis Farrow would ensure I rarely missed the treat of seeing Moore, Hurst and Peters in the claret-and-blue after they had 'won' the World Cup.

Dad never had much chance to watch me play football as a kid at weekends either. If he wasn't working in the shop on Saturdays, he was playing himself on Sunday mornings for various local teams, including Becontree Rovers and Clydesdale. I do recall him watching me once, though – it would have been an under-11s fixture at Belhus Park, Aveley, while playing for a side called Farm Athletic. I felt quite pleased with myself as I unleashed a stunning strike from outside the box . . . only to watch in agony as the ball struck the foot of a post. At half-time, Dad's words of encouragement didn't extend beyond a dismissive: 'You should've scored'. Ex-pro's know their stuff, you can't fool 'em, although to be fair, he never did make me feel inferior for not being blessed with anything like his footballing ability.

I realised very early on that I was never going to be good enough to follow him into professional football, or even make it to the lower amateur leagues – and I wouldn't use the excuse of my very poor eyesight either. I have since been even harder myself on my own two sons, George and Jack, while watching them play for their respective school and Sunday sides, and I've always appreciated Dad's honest assessment of any situation.

One thing Dad taught me from an early age was to embrace a wider appreciation of good football, regardless of who is playing it. At the age of 10, I can recall being bought the 1970 Brazil World Cup winners' shirt, when replica football tops were still rarely worn by kids and never by adults. He would eulogise about the great Dutch team of the early 70s, the Total Football disciples of Cruyff, Neeskins, Johnny Rep and co. When I was 12, I recall him coming home from Wembley one night and raving about the brilliant West German playmaker, Gunter Netzer, who had almost single-handedly played Sir Alf Ramsey's England off the park in a European Championship qualifier. I supported West Ham but George Best was my individual favourite.

I was very fortunate that Dad had good contacts in the game even after his own playing days had finished. My pride and joy was a superb photograph of Bobby Moore that he got my idol Mooro to sign 'Best Wishes to Tony' and which took pride of place on our living room wall. Dad took me to Wembley to see the FA Cup finals of 1971 (Arsenal's double-winning triumph) and '72 and I was treated to just about every *Charles Buchan* and *Topical Times* annual going.

As a young kid, I recall wearing a royal blue shirt with a white number '11' that had been hand-sewn to the back – bet Mum was pleased that Dad wore that number, which was nice and easy to produce from white material and then stitch onto the shirt, whereas, say, a '6' or an '8' were more awkward and would involve the most deft bit of machining to get them looking right. But thinking about it now, I must have been seven or eight by then, so the shirt would have been the blue of Wimbledon (the club he joined after Reading), and not Orient, who had just reverted to their original Clapton Orient colours of red-and-white.

Thankfully, few shirts carried the official club badge in those pre-sponsorship days, so I suffered no ridicule for wearing a shirt later worn by those crude long-ball hoofers from south-west London. I did get some funny looks, though, when I wore my old gold-and-black kit while kicking a ball around in the street or over the local park. Instead of appearing to support Wolves and pretending to be Derek Dougan or (because I was blond) Alun Evans, as most people would have guessed, I was in fact sporting the colours of Dad's last non-league team, mighty Folkestone Town! You didn't see many of those in Chadwell Heath.

You don't see many grown-up sons playing proper 11-a-side football matches with their Dads either, but this was another treasured experience for me after I'd turned 40. Dad had played a few matches for the Leyton Orient Supporters' Vets, with his friends Terry Spurgeon and Neil Cook, when one day he called me up because they were a bit short (desperate, more like). We were about to kick-off in Walthamstow when one of the lads started to introduce me to my new team-mates. 'That's our keeper, Harry Nine Fingers,' he pointed. A keeper with only nine fingers – what on earth have I let myself in for here, I wondered. Anyway, I tried not to let my inner doubts show as the helpful skipper continued the introductions: 'That's Cookie, that's Johnny,' and so on until he said, 'and that's Macca over there'. I said I knew the 'old boy' quite well, thanks . . . and it was another proud moment of mine when Dad, turning back the years, provided a perfectly weighted pass for me to score a rare goal.

In the early 90s, I made my one and only playing appearance on the sacred Brisbane Road turf when, albeit with no-one other than the participants (I hesitate to use the word players) to witness these laboured efforts, I was part of a local press team, including the *East London Advertiser's* John Smith, that played against the O's groundstaff. What a carpet of a pitch Charlie Hasler had produced for us, although it's deceptively big and very knackering if you're as unfit as me and the other beer-bellies. Dad came along to watch but I managed to persuade him to leave his seat in the main stand at half-time and come down to the dressing room and put on some kit for a cameo second half appearance. Naturally, he'd long since lost the pace to fly down the wing but he hadn't lost his touch or vision and the highlight of that day for me was seeing him beat groundsman Charlie, their keeper, with a perfectly struck shot from the edge of the box. It didn't quite generate the same wild scenes of joy as his winner against Man U but I'd imagine that the execution of the strike was no less impressive.

When I (mis)managed a Sunday team called Harbon for my sins in the mid-80s, we found ourselves so short of players one week that I managed to cajole Dad and another ex-Orient player, Colin Flatt, to turn out for us on the notorious Hainault Forest slope. Finding them a shirt each big enough to cope with their expanding waistlines was the least of my problems that morning.

Anyone who runs a Sunday team will tell you how hard it is to find referees and a manager can easily spend half his life phoning around trying to get one. Anyway, our very efficiently run club had spent a season or two cultivating a referee called Melvyn Emmanuel, a quiet, unassuming gentleman who was not at all officious in his handling of matches and just grateful to pick up his regular £15 fee by helping out a club that had a good reputation for being trouble-free.

The only downside to him was that he had no transport, but as long as one of our players was prepared to pick him up from his home in Romford and deliver him back there after the game, he would always answer the call to referee our matches. He was effectively part of the club, on a weekly 'retainer'.

This particular Sunday, Mr Emmanuel wasn't having one of his best performances with the whistle, although his nervy, erratic decision-making probably had something to do with the fact that he was being tightly 'marked' by one of our players – Dad! Like many irritating professionals you see on the telly today, he followed the poor (in every sense) official everywhere on the field and the more and more he got on Mr E's case, the worse the bewildered referee became. I sensed he was on the brink of a nervous breakdown, so midway through the second half, with us leaking goals by the bucket load, my patience finally ran out and I substituted Dad before his sustained harassment of Emmanuel caused him to abandon Harbon FC – and refereeing – for good. I think Dad had seen what was coming and had already whipped off his hip-hugging shirt in disgust before he'd even reached the touchline and the sub had come on to replace him.

I'm reliably informed by my good friend, and fellow ex-Harbon veteran Steve Blowers, that my father turned out for us in the Barking & District League Division Four on more than that one notable occasion. "I seem to remember him doing his pieces at Hainault one day after a tractor had driven across our pitch and left great, big tyre grooves in the 'turf'. Terry wasn't impressed at having to chip the ball out of those deep grooves," says Steve.

Colin Flatt didn't take the mickey out of the referee. His party trick was to embarrass the opposing players, nutmegging them mercilessly at every opportunity, which only antagonised our opponents all the more and made them try even harder. His *piece de resistance* was when he *sat* on the ball in our own penalty area during play! (I'm reliably informed by David Hyde, a good friend of Dad's who used to play up front in the same Wimbledon team as him in 1966-67, that father had once performed the same audacious, mickey-taking bum-on-ball act during a Southern League match.) Who needs these ex-professional *prima donnas* who never offer to wash the kit and stroll around like they own the place! Melvyn Emmanuel, if you're reading this . . . sorry!

Seriously, I'm very delighted to say that Dad and I enjoy a great bond. We're more like brothers – or drinking pals – than father-and-son, although I can reveal that our family ties have been to his disadvantage on a few occasions when he has been chatting up a good-looking woman in a bar and I've accidentally let slip those fatal words 'what are you drinking, Dad?' One of the funniest experiences was the time, it must have been about five years ago, in the old supporters' club bar after a home game at Orient, when a vivacious lady, who couldn't have been more than 40 (that's age, not stone!), was in the process of 'collecting' ex-Orient players and she actually wrote her phone number on a cigarette packet before giving it to Dad, who was of near pensionable age by then!

The thing is, he looks many years younger than 67, with a thick head of hair on him. I have more grey hairs than him, for God sake! I've been there, at Orient, when suspicious folk have finally let their curiosity get the better of them and tugged at his hair . . . only to confirm for themselves that he's not wearing a syrup!

Our close relationship is possibly strengthened by the fact that neither Mum, who sadly died of a brain tumour on Boxing Day, 1997, nor Dad have any brothers or sisters. (Even though they had long since been divorced, Jean and Terry remained good friends and Dad was the last to see her alive when he came with my two sisters, Lisa and Joanne, and I to her bedside the night before Mum passed away.)

Dad did have a brother, Tony, who was seven years younger than him, but he died at the age of just five. His death was completely unnecessary – he went into hospital suffering appendicitis but because they took too long to operate, his blood became poisoned and he died of Peritonitis. It wouldn't have happened today.

Dad can appear shy until you get to know him. He never spoke about what happened to his little brother for many years and I only found out about Tony when I was much older. Dad told me that his brother went into hospital for what seemed a routine treatment but never came home. He was so shocked by the loss of Tony that he couldn't speak a word for a week. We talk about Tony more now and I'm very proud that my parents named me after the uncle I, sadly, never met.

Of course, like all brothers and fathers and sons, we don't always see eye to eye. For example, Dad likes everything to be neat and tidy, in a certain order, and he hates it if ever I cause him to be late or, for instance, if I've left him waiting much longer than expected before meeting up outside the Orient ground. It's a throwback to his playing days, I guess, when players prepared for games in an organised, routine manner. My other theory is that he doesn't have three kids and a very hectic small business to run either! His impatience with me in those situations mirrors his dislike of bad drivers and the complete unpredictability of the London bus and tube networks, on which he is an authority.

In the early 60s, if you supported West Ham United, the chances are you also took an interest in that other East London team, just a few miles away in E10. I can fully appreciate how patronising it must feel to O's supporters when they hear West Ham fans declaring Orient as their 'second team', but that really was the case for many men who watched their football within the sound of Bow Bells. As a schoolboy, I can remember fairly regular visits to Brisbane Road when Peter Brabrook and Mark Lazarus raided down the wings, when Peter Allen controlled midfield and when Terry Mancini lifted the Division Three championship trophy.

A few years later, after I'd started secondary school in Goodmayes I found myself sitting next to Dave Watts, a very loyal Orient fan who became my best mate at Mayfield Boys. Every other Saturday, Dave and I would put on our green drill trousers, Doc Martens and sheepskins coats and stand on the open terrace behind the goal at the Coronation Gardens end, shouting words of advice to John Jackson, celebrating a goal by Mickey Bullock or Gerry Queen, a last-ditch tackle by Phil Hoadley or Tom Walley, Barry Fairbrother's dramatic winner in the mud against Chelsea in the Cup, a rampaging run by Bill Roffey, or maybe a sublime piece of skill by Ricky Heppolette.

Dave's elder brother, John, and their father (who I'm pretty sure was also John) kept an eye on us from the back of the terrace, so that we didn't get into any trouble. In the early 70s era of hooliganism, however, there were the occasional scrapes on away trips to places like Millwall, Swindon and Oxford, where we'd find ourselves having to run back to the Orient coaches to avoid the chasing pack of local hoolies. The marauding mob were probably all spotty teenagers anyway but to us 12-year-olds, some of them looked big and hard and not to be messed with.

We wore red-and-white woollen scarves and then, to keep up with changing fashion, a 'silk' scarf would be purchased and tied around the wrist, as you did in those days. When you think back on it now, it must have looked ludicrous to strut around with a silk scarf wrapped around your wrist but we were proud to show our allegiance, even though you could nearly be reduced to tears if two or three threatening lads ganged up on you in the street before or after the match and demanded you hand over your new, nice looking scarf – 'or else'. To have your scarf nicked from your person felt almost as bad as watching (with almost 30,000 others) Ray Graydon score Aston Villa's penalty in the final nerve-shattering game in May '74 to deny the Orient team of the day the chance to emulate the 'Boys of '62' and gain promotion to the top flight. The club has not gone as close as that – missing promotion by just a point – to reaching what is now called the Premiership.

It is a great credit to Dave and John Watts that they and their sons still support the O's with a passion today – we often bump into each other in the South Stand bar – and I can see that their unconditional love of the club will never diminish. To me, they are two ordinary guys who typify the Orient support – loyal in the face of great adversity and with general low expectations from their favourite team. Unlike many casual and part-time fans of the so-called big clubs, O's fans are there through thick and thin. Jeff Powell, in his excellent foreword, has articulated what it means to be an Orient supporter much better than I could – and why the men featured in this book deserve their place in Brisbane Road folklore.

Did I mention earlier Leyton Orient and Liverpool in the same sentence? The two clubs are pretty adjacent in the football alphabet but in terms of achievement and status they have been a world apart for the past four decades. They do still both play in all-red, though.

But for one glorious season some 45 years ago, they remained within touching distance of each other near the top of the old second division and at the end of that 1961-62 campaign the two clubs filled the promotion places.

A year later and while the Reds from Merseyside began their odyssey towards 17 more League championships (to add to the first they won in 1901), five European Cups, seven FA Cups and five League Cups, the O's rapidly returned from whence they came. Back to the real world of scrapping for results. A world among the lower reaches of the Football League where even survival itself is considered a a success.

But at least Leyton Orient got there once. They went up to join the big boys of English football at the top table. Even if they gate-crashed the feast as the h'orderves were about to be served, ended up with little more than a few crumbs to savour and got kicked back out down the stairs before dessert was dished up, it was still one hell of an experience.

Thanks to Dad, I have had the pleasure of meeting most of the surviving former players at various social functions and reunions over the last half-a-dozen years or so. They are now scattered in all corners of the country – from dear Stan Charlton on the south coast in Weymouth to big Dave Dunmore in York, and from Malcolm Musgrove in Torquay to Malcolm Lucas in Norwich – but whenever the boys get together to reminisce about the 'good, old days', the special camaraderie that served them so well in their playing days is still transparent today. The respect the others afforded skipper Stan way back then is still very evident now – Dad looks up to him almost as if he were his own father and I know how much he enjoyed the time they spent together in Stan's home town last summer.

In fact, when Stan and Dave heard that this book had finally been finished, they were keen to attend the launch at Orient . . . and were quite happy to sleep on the floor of Dad's one-bedroom flat, which is little more than a Bill Robertson drop kick from the ground. No fancy five-star hotel suites for these guys – they're tough and unpretentious and remain as far removed as you can get from the modern pampered professional. Actually, if Sid Bishop doesn't take a taxi back to Harlow, he'll make up a cosy threesome on the carpet! Not quite the celebrated half-back line of the early 60s, but quite a huddle of O's legends nonetheless!

It was eight years ago that I first nurtured the idea of writing a book to celebrate the achievements of the promotion-winning team. Via an announcement in the Orient matchday programme, I asked supporters who were around in those days to send me letters and emails recalling their special memories of watching those games and players. It was never intended to be a serious commercial exercise and, for one reason or another, the book got put onto the back burner while I immersed myself in countless other projects. However, it has always been my intention to do my bit to help ensure that the achievements of Johnny Carey's players were given the recognition and respect they deserved, so here we are at last.

The writing and interviewing process was well underway early in 2006 when we suddenly became aware that a similar book, mainly covering the first division season only, would also be coming out around the same time as this one. Incredible! No-one bothers to give these former heroes more than a brief and passing mention for more than four decades and then, hey presto, two books all about them come along at once – like London buses. Good luck to the publisher and author of A Season in the Sun – it's good to see that the players from the most golden era in O's history are now getting the recognition they deserved long ago (including a 'where are they now?' type feature in a recent edition of The Sunday Times no less).

The Untold Story has not just been written for Dad's sake, but also for his former team-mates who have always been a great pleasure to meet, chat to and now interview. It's funny, I've heard many of my father's favourite Orient stories numerous times over the years and some of them still make me smile when he re-tells them today, especially when we're in the company of some of the other ex-O's. But he was the baby of that team, and now he's 67, so it would be unreasonable to expect everyone interviewed in this book to retain crystal clear memories of everything they did and didn't do 45 years ago!

However, as each former player was contacted in turn, either in person or by telephone, the bigger picture quickly emerged. Thanks to the co-operation of the men who were part of this amazing story, I very much doubt that it would be possible to produce a book that provides a more comprehensive and illuminating insight into the two-year period in question.

The true characters of the players shine through and I hope you agree that much of what these men have to say is fascinating and entertaining. Within these pages there are moments of genuine sadness and others of great humour that I hope will also raise a laugh or three.

It was never the intention for *The Untold Story* to be simply a collection of detailed match reports and statistics with quotes re-hashed from old newspapers and programmes, important though these historical aspects are. Indeed, the statistical facts are included here for posterity, but not at the expense of what I consider to be the 'best bits' – the behind-the-scenes stories , the players' view of the part they and their team-mates played in the story, and the banter that existed among them. There can be no doubt that Dad 'opened doors' for me in the sense that his former team-mates were immediately receptive and not at all guarded in their conversations with me or in any way unhelpful. On the contrary, several of them kindly lent us pictures for inclusion in the book and all of them have been supportive and enthusiastic about the project. Almost without exception, they all enjoyed their time at Leyton Orient and have enjoyed taking this peek back into the past.

I also didn't want the book to be a whitewash view of those two seasons, and the events surrounding them, through rose-tinted spectacles. The promotion season, though culminating in a triumphant finale, was by no means plain sailing, while the first division campaign began quite brightly but soon degenerated into a long, hard gloomy winter and, ultimately, failure.

Was manager Johnny Carey really as good as many perceived him to be, or was he fortunate to inherit a good team? How much blame could be levelled at the club's board of directors for not giving Carey the financial backing to sign the new players the team clearly needed, to safeguard the club's long-term future? As events would prove, it was a missed opportunity the club has not been in a position to take since and possibly never will.

There are probably no definitive answers to any of the above questions but they are a great basis for debate, so that's what this book is also about. After a long period in which to reflect and re-play the games and all the peripheral issues in their minds, the players have given a refreshingly honest account of themselves and their colleagues in the pages that follow.

It doesn't surprise me in the least that many of the most forthright views you'll read come from my father, who is as opinionated and critical as me when it comes to watching today's football. You'll have to forgive my natural bias in giving him more space than all the others to air his personal views but I'd like to think that his criticism of Carey, for instance, is presented in an evenly balanced manner alongside the much more favourable memories and views of most of his former team-mates.

A few years back, by way of a small 'thank you' to the club for making him and I so welcome every time we go back there, Dad asked to be a match-ball sponsor for what turned out to be a particularly dire midweek encounter against, I think, Rotherham. After 20 minutes of mind-numbing stuff and one misplaced pass after another, he suddenly let out an anguished cry from his seat in the South Stand: 'I want my ball back!'

By half-time, chances are he will have retreated to the warmth and comfort of the South Stand bar, clutching a pint of John Smith's 'Smooth' in one hand and a betting slip (£5 treble involving one hopeless Scottish team, no doubt) in the other. We routinely sit at a prime position table, usually with our good friends Tony King (nephew of former O's player Len Julians), Tim Crane and/or Ted Pardoe for company, hoping in vain that the beers don't go down quicker than our football bets as the updated scores appear on the screen in front of us and we experience another rollercoaster afternoon watching Sky's Gillette Soccer Saturday show.

Win or lose, though, the day is not quite complete without a stroll around the corner to the plush, air-conditioned supporters' club bar at the end of the new West Stand, where Simon (on the door) Fellman, LOSC chairman and football club director Dave Dodd, Mike Childs, Dennis Barefield, Steve Jenkins, Lew Day and their hard-working committee colleagues know how to pour a good pint of some of the finest real ale in East London and where the welcome from avid fans like John Parke, Sid Barrett, Bill Tesner, Alan Harvey and many other familiar faces is always warm and genuine.

These lovely Saturday afternoons usually end after nightfall with a wave towards father as I head up the hill for Leyton tube station and (gout attacks permitting) he puts in a 20-yard burst to catch the 69 bus back towards the Baker's Arms, where he might well be inclined to round the day off with another drink in The King William

IV or, more likely, The Drum, which are both near to his home in Capworth Street.

On Monday morning, Dad will often rise at 6.30am to rejoin the rush-hour commuters into the City for another working day in the betting shop – or gambling arcades as they have become these days. He still takes his mum – my dear, 97-year-old gran – for her habitual tipple of scotch at the Wanstead Bowls Club every Thursday evening and some Sundays. Two years on from his supposed retirement, I remind him that he really should be taking things easier and spending more time on the golf course (he's a natural at all ball sports) or with Ted Pardoe and friends in Old Town Marbella . . . where, believe it or not, the ex-pats among the locals have also been known to talk through that goal against Man U over a cool Cerveza.

One of my favourite pictures of Dad, as a West Ham youth player at Grange Farm in August 1956.

A keen watcher of the game, Dad still demands the highest standards and is easily disappointed if the players he watches today fall short of them. Even now, when England's Stewart Downing fluffs another cross, he'll automatically say: "Phil White would never have done that'. Or when Peter Crouch heads tamely wide of the target for the umpteenth time, he'll say: 'Tommy Johnston would have broken the net with that ball'. 'Imagine if they had to play on the pitches we did' . . . 'look how light the ball they play with today compared to our day – it took three of us to get the old heavy ball across in the mud from a corner kick!' . . . the observations come thick and fast between the issuing of more Werthers Originals. The inadequacies and antics of the 21st century footballer infuriate him at times but he'll be back at West Ham and Orient for their next home matches and those that follow. You can take the man out of football – but you'll never take the football out of the man.

Sorry for the delay but I'm glad, at last, to now give him this long overdue chance to tell everybody else just how good players like White, Johnston, Dunmore, Foster and all his other team-mates were from those O's teams of the early 60s, both as players and people. I just hope Leyton Orient: The Untold Story of O's Best-ever Team gives him as much pride and pleasure as it has given me putting it together.

I'm very proud of you, Dad – and not just because you scored your great winner against Manchester United!

Tony McDonald

Hornchurch, Essex
November 2006

Chapter 1

ISLAND OF DREAMS
The Springfields, 1963

THE seeds for promotion were sewn in May 1961, many miles from Leyton, across the English Channel and just after the O's had narrowly avoided relegation from the second rung on the Football League ladder, the old Division Two as it was known then.

Manager Les Gore, battling through the latest of his numerous caretaker spells, and his players had finished the season four places off the bottom of the league and only three points above the relegation zone. Victories over Stoke City and Norwich City in their last two home matches ensured a sixth successive season of second division football at Brisbane Road for the men in blue-and-white. But it was close.

Most boards of directors would have been relieved and perhaps set about ringing the changes to avoid repeating this stressful process the following season. The last thing many of them would have done was to reward their players for finishing 19th place with a holiday . . . but that's exactly what chairman Harry Zussman and his fellow directors at Leyton Stadium did as soon as the 1960-61 season had ended.

They took the team off for a break and a bonding exercise in the Channel Islands, basing themselves in Jersey while also popping over to Guernsey to play a low-key friendly fixture.

Not only was this an unexpected treat for the players, it was a very welcome social break for their young wives and children too, most of whom had never flown before. Little did they know it then, but Leyton Orient were about to take off in more ways than one.

Long-serving skipper and right-back Stan Charlton recalls: "The directors paid for all the players and our families to go on a week's holiday in Jersey as our reward for keeping the club in the second division.

"We played one friendly while we were there, which involved flying over to Guernsey. The plane could have been no bigger than a 12-seater – there wasn't even enough room for a substitute – and it never flew above 45-feet all the way across to the next island!

"While in Jersey, Leslie Grade gathered all the players together and announced that if we gained promotion to the first division the following year, the directors would also pay for us all to spend a week's holiday in Majorca. I think he thought he was safe in saying that!"

Centre-half Sid Bishop, another loyal and long-serving O's legend, remembers it this way: "We had a collection for Harry Zussman while we were there – he and Leslie Grade had turned up to pay us a visit while we were out there enjoying

A happy scene from the team's break in Jersey – a nice reward for staying up in 1960-61. Mum and Dad are on the right-hand end of this group, with Orient's Bill Robertson and Stan Charlton alongside former Chelsea player Ian McFarlane, who happened to be on the island at the same time as the O's.

ourselves for a week or 10 days. Stan must have got word that they were coming, because he organised a collection among ourselves for the chairman, as a thank you for treating us to the holiday.

"With the money we collected in, we bought him a sealskin cigar case, which Eddie Lewis' wife presented to him. Harry, who reminded me a bit of Max Miller, thought it was wonderful gift. The next thing we knew, he announced: 'If you get promotion next year, you and your wives and families can all go to Majorca for a holiday'.

"He really thought it could really happen – and it bloody well did!

"I thought Harry opened his mouth a bit too soon. We were also promised a Jaguar car each if we got to the FA Cup final, which was a crazy thought.

"That end-of-season trip was very good for team spirit, although we were a very sociable club anyway. Leyton Orient was an easy-going place to be."

And maybe the quiet, Irish gentleman Johnny Carey was just the right man to help make that Majorcan holiday dream come true. Although Les Gore had done a good job filling in following the departure of Alec Stock in February 1959, he had never aspired to do the job on a full-time basis and the club needed to look elsewhere for a long-term boss.

Carey became available after being unceremoniously sacked by Everton in the summer of 1961, having just guided them to fifth place in the first division.

Following the departure of Ian Buchan, the Everton board appointed Carey as manager in October 1958. A star from Manchester United's post-war glory days, the arrival of Carey coincided closely with the acquisition of prominent Celtic player Bobby Collins. With Collins joining players such as Albert Dunlop, Mick Meagan and Derek Temple, Carey inherited a squad with a lot of potential, but lacking real leadership.

Joining Everton following his first five-year stint as a manager at Blackburn Rovers, where he led the Lancashire club to the top flight in 1958-59, Carey's quiet assuredness seemed the perfect antidote to an increasing lack of confidence in the club. Carey immediately put his free-flowing football principles into practice at Goodison, his motto being 'Only the keeper stops the ball'.

Lucky enough to secure millionaire Everton supporter John Moores as a club benefactor, father of four Carey used Moores' financial backing to enter the transfer market enthusiastically, acquiring such luminaries as Roy Vernon, Billy Bingham, Alex Young and Jimmy Gabriel.

Following two poor seasons, Carey's leadership saw Everton reach their highest league position since the war in the 1960-61 season, finishing fifth. However, with the increased financial backing of Moores, and the removal of the maximum players' wage, football was starting to become big business. In a new era of market forces, anything less than first place was sure to be seen as failure.

His success not enough for the growing demands of the Everton board or their fans and the club supporters, rumours of Carey's impending dismissal were rife. Joining Moores, by now the new club chairman, at a Football League meeting in London, Carey was famously informed of his departure in the back of a taxi.

It was Don Gibson, the former O's wing-half and Manchester United boss Matt Busby's son-in-law, who put Carey – from Westland, near Dublin – on to Orient.

Carey said: "Gibson told me that Orient, although poor (financially), were a club with tremendous heart and feeling. I felt that although it was probably going to be the toughest job I had ever taken as a manager, this was the job for me."

Johnny B. Goode
Chuck Berry, 1959

Apart from his success at Blackburn and what Everton perceived as under-achievement given their riches as the aristocrats of English football at the time, Carey came to London in the summer of '61 with a brilliant track record as a former player of some reputation.

Carey had been one of the outstanding defenders of his time and also one of Manchester United's great captains, the Roy Keane of his day. Amazingly versatile, he played in every position except outside-right, although his favoured position was in defence. His career from 1937-53 was interrupted by the War, however he still won the 1948 FA Cup and 1952 League title. Uniquely, he played in internationals for both the Republic and Northern Ireland, 27 and nine times respectively.

He was born in Dublin on February 23, 1919 and was first spotted while playing for local side St James' Gate by United's Dublin scout Billy Behan. At 17 he was brought to Old Trafford by United chief scout Louis Rocca for a modest fee of £250. Initially signed as an inside-left, he was in competition with another famous United player of the time, Stan Pearson, for this position.

At the age of 17 he made his debut at Old Trafford against Southampton but his career was interrupted by the outbreak of World War Two. During the war Carey served in the Middle East and in Italy and played as a guest player for various league clubs. In October 1945 he resumed his playing career with Manchester United, where he was switched to the position of full-back.

He captained the Rest of Europe side which played Britain in 1947, in a fund-raising match for UEFA, and was voted Footballer of the Year in 1949.

After making 344 appearances for Manchester United, scoring 18 goals, Carey retired from football in May 1953. He was invited by the United board to a meeting where they conveyed their special thanks to him for his services and offered him a position at the club as a coach. However, in August of the same year he opted to became manager of Blackburn Rovers instead.

Carey was, naturally, very happy to retain Eddie Baily, the former England and Tottenham Hotspur inside-forward, as his first team coach at Orient, which meant Les Gore reverting to the role of trainer which he had fulfilled under Alec Stock. Gore's trusty assistant trainer, Nick Collins, was therefore deemed surplus to requirements . . . but there was a much, much bigger name about to leave Brisbane Road.

Chapter 2

CAN'T GET USED TO LOSING YOU
Andy Williams, April 1963

THERE is no doubt about it, the main reason Leyton Orient retained Division Two status in 1961 was the continuing goalscoring feats of the legendary Tommy Johnston – the player fans voted the great O's player of all-time in a millennium poll.

The craggy Scottish centre-forward finished the 1961-62 campaign with a mere 16 goals. Mere? Well, this rampant goal-getter from Loanhead, near Edinburgh, had netted 25 in the previous season and a club record 35 in 1957-58.

Johnston had amassed an amazing 123 goals in 190 league and cup appearances.

But he reluctantly ended his second spell with the club after refusing new manager Johnny Carey's offer to coach the O's reserves on a significantly reduced wage. After all he had done for the club, Tommy had every reason to feel disgruntled by this insulting offer but he never complained about the treatment he received and moved on to Gillingham with commendable dignity and grace.

Tommy was still around E10 when the traditional Reds versus Blues practice match took place in early August but before the end of September he had moved on to join Gillingham, where he scored 10 in 36 appearances that season.

Apparently Carey deemed 34-year-old Johnston too old for first team football at Orient, which was strange given the big man's phenomenal strike rate. In fact, Tommy had scored 23 league goals in 38 matches for Blackburn Rovers between 1958 and '59 . . . when Rovers were managed by Carey. And he'd just finished the season as O's leading scorer for the fifth time in six seasons (he was joint top with Eddie Brown and Joe Elwood in 1958-59), having scored the goal in the final home match against Norwich City that had preserved O's second division status.

What no-one can take away from Tommy, however, are his club records and reputation as the greatest goalscorer in Leyton Orient's history, that still stand to this day

Tommy, who is now 80-years-old and lives with his wife Jean at Sanctuary Point, New South Wales, Australia, enjoyed a particularly great friendship with the late Phil White, the tricky right-winger who provided countless quality crosses for him ever since Tommy arrived from Newport County early in 1956 for £5,500. His eight goals in 15 games at the end of that season proved the catalyst to winning Third Division South.

Terry McDonald, who later played on the opposite wing and also gave Johnston good service from the flank in his final two seasons in East London, undoubtedly

Pick that out! Tommy Johnston heads another unstoppable goal at Liverpool on November 21, 1959 following a cross from Terry McDonald. This seven-goal thriller ended in a 4-3 defeat for the O's.

spoke for their mutual friend Phil too when he said: "Without a doubt, Tommy was the best header of a ball I've ever played with, but it shouldn't be forgotten that he was also very good on the ground. You knew that he would spray a pass out to you and then get himself into the penalty box. My job then was either to get the ball across to him early or beat the full-back first before crossing.

"All I tried to do was drop the ball into a zone in the box and you knew Tommy would be there to get on the end of it. When Tommy was playing, that was my job . . . it became quite easy and very enjoyable as well.

"The timing in his heading was unbelievable and I've never seen it from any other centre-forward. But, as I say, he was a very good all round player – left-footed, but he kept the ball well and never gave it away."

Although Tommy was the club's main man throughout most of his time at Orient, he remained a very well liked person around the club.

Terry adds: "He did everything – bet, drink, whatever. He was a great icon at Orient and we all enjoyed being in his company and playing with him."

Although Tommy never kicked a ball for Orient in the promotion campaign, he had already played an influential role in developing some of the younger players who did.

Terry believes that Johnston had a big say in him becoming an O's first team regular soon after the little winger signed from West Ham United on a free transfer in the summer of 1959.

"I think Tommy had a lot to do with me getting in the side after I finished my stint in the army. Him and Les Gore were like that," he said while crossing his fingers, "and Tommy knew who he wanted around him in the team.

"When I first went to Orient I came under the influence of the senior pro's like

October 1961 and the Orient players take a break in training at Southport (where they were preparing for the League Cup tie at Blackpool) to listen to manager Les Gore (far right). Pictured (left to right) are: Tommy Johnston, Terry McDonald, Errol Crossan, Malcolm Lucas, Cyril Lea, Stan Charlton and Derek Gibbs. Front row: Ken Facey, Ron Newman, Frank George, Sid Bishop and Alan Sealey.

Tommy, Phil White and Ken Facey. Tommy would say to me: 'Aye, are yer coming for a beer?' He liked people who enjoyed a beer and a bet, just as he did. He used to appreciate other young players like Ronnie Foster and Dennis Sorrell too."

Dave Dunmore played alongside Tommy in only the last 11 matches of the 1960-61 season before he left the club for good but it was long enough for the new signing from West Ham to appreciate the value of his strike partner. Dunmore, who played at inside-right when he first arrived from Upton Park in March '61, said: "Playing with Tommy was good for me – he laid the ball off well, was a good header of the ball and I enjoyed playing up front with him. And he was one of the lads too."

Leyton Orient had much to thank the great Tommy Johnston for, on the field and in financial terms. He initially left O's in a £15,000 deal with Blackburn Rovers in March 1958 – "a big mistake," he later admitted – and returned in February 1959 for £6,000. He finally left O's for a second time to join Fourth Division strugglers Gillingham for £3,000 in September 1961.

After Tommy's book, *The Happy Wanderer*, was published in 2004, he kindly sent a copy over from Australia to Terry McDonald, signed and with the dedicated message: 'To the Wee Man, we had some great times. Bet you still can't play baseball! Fond memories. Tommy'. The Wee Man appreciated the gesture.

If Tommy had stayed another year with the O's, it could be argued that promotion would have been achieved a little easier than it was. On the other hand, perhaps Carey knew just what an impact Dave Dunmore was about to make as the new number nine and talisman.

Chapter 3

ON THE REBOUND
Floyd Cramer, April 1961

THE 1961-62 promotion season really began to hot up – literally – at Walsall on the first Saturday in September. In a match played in 85 degrees heat, Orient put the home side well and truly in the shade to register an emphatic 5-1 win over a Saddlers side that had a decent home record.

Malcolm Graham, given the chance to form a new strike partnership with Dave Dunmore following the departure of Tommy Johnston, announced himself as a new star by netting a hat-trick, while Dunmore also got off the mark and cultured inside-right Ronnie Foster completed the rout and his own impressive start to the new season.

It's funny how odd things stick in the players' minds, though. Apart from the sweltering heat, left-back Eddie Lewis remembers: "Behind the goal at Walsall they had a laundry. Whenever a shot went behind the goal and hit the laundry building wall, it would rebound back into play – I'd never seen anything like it!"

This is how the season unfolded (for the full team line-ups for both Leyton Orient and their opponents, please turn to the back of the book) . . .

In keeping with tradition, a week before the opening league game at Newcastle a practice match involving all Leyton Orient first teamers and reserves was played at Brisbane Road. It featured 'The Blues', who were the likely first XI, versus 'The Reds', those challenging for a first team place.

With newly-appointed manager Johnny Carey looking on, it's fair to assume that there was a little added edge to this pre-season 'friendly' encounter. For the record, the game ended in a convincing 6-0 win for the Blues. The teams lined up as follows:

Blues 6 (White 2, Lewis, Lea, Dunmore, Graham)
Reds 0
Blues: George, Charlton, Lewis, Lucas, Bishop, Lea, White, Foster, Dunmore, Graham, McDonald.
Reds: Cochran, Wright (Quinnall 45), Harris, Facey (Ginnis 45), Russell, Sorrell, Newman, Taylor, Gibbs, Johnston, Elwood (Cheesewright 45).

August 19, 1961
Newcastle United 0
Leyton Orient 0

Newly-relegated Newcastle gave their fans nothing to cheer and O's were definitely more grateful for the point from this dour goalless opener. Lucas earned the plaudits for a good marking job on Ivor Allchurch, while Charlton also did well to contain speedy winger Liam Tuohy.

Going forward, McDonald just missed with a far-post header in the first minute and then shot wide in the dying seconds. Closest the Magpies came to scoring was when Bishop headed out from underneath the O's crossbar.

August 21, 1961
Leyton Orient 1 (Foster)
Southampton 3 (O'Brien, Mulgrew 2)

George O'Brien gave Saints the lead in this fast and furious Monday night game with a run and low shot on 28 minutes, before Foster rose to head home a Terry McDonald corner in the 55th.

Southampton regained the lead seven minutes later when Tommy Mulgrew headed in a cross from Terry Paine, who provided another centre from which Mulgrew completed the scoring. Lea denied Saints a fourth, but earned a booking, for rugby-tackling O'Brien (who later joined O's).

August 26, 1961
Leyton Orient 2 (White, Lucas)
Middlesbrough 0

Only four minutes had gone before McDonald's cross from near the corner flag was stroked home by fellow winger White. With the forwards struggling to make an impact, it was left-half Lucas who surged forward, received Foster's square pass and sealed O's first win of the season with a 30-yard rocket that gave keeper Robert Appleby no chance.

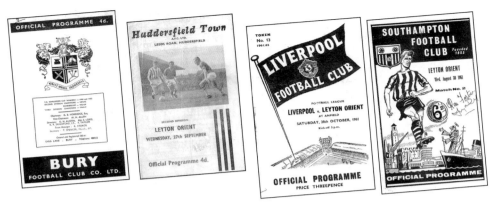

August 30, 1961
Southampton 1 (O'Brien)
Leyton Orient 2 (Foster, McDonald)

This midweek game came to life in the second half, when George O'Brien gave Saints the lead in the 52nd minute.

Foster equalised 14 minutes from time with a fine turn and finish from 20 yards, before McDonald struck the long-range winner, high into the Southampton net, with just five minutes left.

September 2, 1961
Walsall 1 (Younger)
Leyton Orient 5 (Graham 3, Foster, Dunmore)

A major turning point in the season on a sweltering day at Fellows Park, where O's turned on the style in 85 degrees heat with some slick passing football.

Having just settled new contract terms, both Graham and Foster made their point in this brilliant away win. Graham set up Foster to slide the ball beyond keeper John Christie after five minutes. Just before half-time, Foster turned provider by laying on a chance for Dunmore, who got off the mark following a deep free-kick from Lewis, who had previously twice cleared off his own line.

The second half was Graham's, who scored a hat-trick in just 12 minutes. The first came via a Lewis pass on 63 minutes which he finished from a tight angle. In the 75th minute Graham latched onto a square pass from Dunmore which he lashed into the roof of the net, before completing his hat-trick in the heatwave two minutes later.

Bill Younger's 80th minute effort was hardly a late consolation for Walsall.

September 9, 1961
Leyton Orient 2 (Swallow OG, Dunmore pen)
Derby County 0

An injustice for Derby, who could have scored three in the first half and lived to regret it. There was a stroke of luck about O's opener in the 37th minute.

Dunmore tried to find White but his intended pass was intercepted and then toe-poked into his own net by in-rushing left-winger Ray Swallow.

McDonald won the penalty when he was challenged by Tony Conwell, who then handled the ball as O's left-winger was set to score. Dunmore made no mistake to beat Ken Oxford from the spot.

September 11, 1961
League Cup, 1st round
Stockport County 0
Leyton Orient 1 (McDonald)

The unbeaten away run continued with this Cup win, secured when McDonald scored the only goal in the 23rd minute.

After seeing White's shot rebound from the legs of Trevor Porteous, the blond left-winger followed up himself to fire the winner.

The fourth division side showed good spirit, though, and Charlton twice had to clear with keeper George beaten.

September 16, 1961
Bristol Rovers 2 (Hooper, Jones)
Leyton Orient 1 (Dunmore pen)

Rovers gained their first points of the season to end O's undefeated run. McDonald missed two good chances and it was Lucas who brought out the best from keeper Howard Radford, who made two fine saves.

But Rovers led at Eastville from the sixth minute, when Peter Hooper scored easily from close range after Geoff Bradford and Norman Sykes both saw their shots blocked. Sykes had another effort foiled but the ball broke loose for Robert Jones to make it 2-0 on 69 minutes.

O's pushed hard in the closing stages and got their reward from Dunmore's penalty after Ray Mabbutt – father of future Spurs captain Gary – fouled Graham.

September 20, 1961
Leyton Orient 3 (McDonald, Foster, Graham)
Huddersfield Town 0

Under the Brisbane Road lights, O's rediscovered their best form to easily brush aside the Terriers. Orient were so in command that they even forced errors from England left-back Ray Wilson that led to two goals.

McDonald (24 mins) and Ronnie Foster (26) made the most of the home team's early pressure and the game was wrapped up when Graham (52) added a third.

September 23, 1961
Preston North End 3 (Thompson, Biggs, Humes)
Leyton Orient 2 (Foster, McDonald)

O's came to life in the last 10 minutes, in which they scored both of their goals, but by then bottom-of-the-table PNE were already three in front at Deepdale.

Winger Peter Thompson struck a great volley past George in the third minute. Preston scored a second when Alf Biggs cracked home David Sneddon's cross on

Terry McDonald scoring against Preston keeper Alan Kelly at Deepdale.

50 minutes and looked home and dry when Jim Humes headed their third after an unlucky deflection.

McDonald revived O's when he intercepted a poor backpass by Biggs intended for keeper Alan Kelly to score from 12 yards, while Foster's neat header piled further late pressure on Preston. McDonald and Foster both had shots brilliantly saved in the dying seconds as PNE grimly hung on for their first home league win since March.

September 27, 1961
Huddersfield Town 1 (Bettany)
Leyton Orient 1 (White)

O's were just four minutes away from ending Town's unbeaten home record. Terriers were reduced to 10 men after 30 minutes when centre-half Bob Parker was carried off with a shoulder injury.

Nine minutes later O's took a deserved lead when White's deep, curling cross found the net via the far post. Lucas enraged the large crowd when he clashed with keeper Harry Fearnley in a duel for a loose ball. Police had to be called to patrol behind George's goal as the O's keeper came under fire from missiles.

Another flashpoint was when referee K.E. Walker booked McDonald for a heavy tackle. There were two minutes left when John Bettany netted the Town equaliser.

September 29, 1961
Leyton Orient 1 (Dunmore)
Plymouth Argyle 2 (Williams 2)

This experimental evening fixture – the first-ever Friday night league game to be held at Brisbane Road, to avoid clashing with West Ham and Spurs who were both at home the next day – attracted the biggest Brisbane Road crowd to date (13,598), but a shock home defeat saw O's drop to fifth place.

Stand-in inside-right Frank Williams scored both goals – the first inside the opening minute after a mix-up in the Orient defence, the second just before the interval.

Orient stepped it up in the second half and Dunmore might have scored with only keeper Dave Maclaren to beat before he did with his last-minute consolation effort.

October 4, 1961
League Cup, 2nd round
Leyton Orient 1 (Gibbs)
Blackpool 1 (Oates)

Top flight Blackpool were making their first-ever visit to Leyton Stadium, albeit without the rested Stan Matthews. Despite teeming rain the pace of the game never slackened and Orient gave a brilliant account of themselves against Blackpool's first division strength.

Orient spent most of the time on attack but failed to turn clever midfield play into goals. It was 0-0 at half-time but Blackpool opened the scoring 10 seconds into the second-half and there was an element of luck about the goal. Oates lifted a ball from near the corner flag that dropped into O's goalmouth and a transfixed defence stood helpless as the ball rolled unchallenged into the goal.

But Orient earned their share of luck and got their reward when Derek Gibbs, who wandered from wing to wing to escape the attentions of Gratrix, dropped a high ball into a congested Blackpool goal area. Gordon West stabbed a fist at the spinning ball, which angled into the net.

October 7, 1961
Leyton Orient 3 (Foster, Graham, Dunmore)
Stoke City 0

A game of two halves if ever there was one. Three up and cruising by half-time and playing the kind of football worthy of their third place in the table, O's then took their foot off the gas.

They had taken the lead after three minutes, Foster nodding home Graham's cross from four yards, before Graham himself made it 2-0 on 33 minutes with an angled shot past Jimmy O'Neill.

The contest was effectively over when Dunmore nipped between O'Neill and Tony Allen to make it 3-0, but there was nothing more to cheer in a disappointing second half. Lewis had a late effort ruled out for offside.

October 14, 1961
Sunderland 2 (Clough 2)
Leyton Orient 1 (Dunmore)

Despite playing the better, more stylish football throughout, two goals by Brian Clough boosted Sunderland's promotion hopes in front of a big Roker Park crowd.

Gibbs missed three chances to put O's ahead before Dunmore did in the first 10 minutes, applying a deft header to Foster's cross.

George couldn't hold Clough's low, hard shot in the 26th minute and the ball spun over him before trickling into the net.

Ronnie Foster stooping to head a goal against Stoke City.

The equaliser came against the run of play. But the Rokermen's comeback was complete in the 51st minute when Cloughie slammed home the winner after good work by Harry Hooper.

October 21, 1961
Leyton Orient 1 (Graham)
Rotherham United 1 (Perry pen)

Two of the top teams in the division failed to impress the crowd, which included Billy Wright, who was reportedly sent by England manager Walter Winterbottom to run the rule over Orient's Foster, who had recently been called up for the FA XI at Sunderland.

O's took the lead on 49 minutes, Graham finishing off good work from Lea. But Lea was involved in Rotherham's equaliser when he was adjudged by referee E. Norman to have fouled Bill Cassidy in the area. George got his hand to Peter Perry's spot-kick but couldn't prevent the 80th minute equaliser.

O's almost paid the ultimate price for earlier missed chances when, on the stroke of full-time, Ken Houghton dribbled round George but shot against a post.

October 28, 1961
Liverpool 3 (Hunt 2, Leishman)
Leyton Orient 3 (Dunmore 2, Foster)

An enthralling match to savour between two teams destined for the top in front of a large and captivated Anfield crowd, who applauded the East Londoners off the field. O's took the lead three times but had to settle for a point that Liverpool snatched after a slip by the otherwise brilliant George.

Dunmore put O's in front by eluding Ron Yeats before striking a thunderous 30-

yard right-foot drive into the roof of the net. Tommy Lawrence didn't even see it coming. Roger Hunt equalised on 34 minutes but within a minute the visitors regained the lead when Foster whipped in McDonald's corner on the half-volley from close range.

Orient had the normally dominant Reds ruffled with some delightful, neat passing football but were rocked back on their heels when Hunt's soft 50th minute header squirmed through George's hands and Liverpool were level again.

Dunmore remained a menacing threat, though, and restored O's lead with a superb, firm header on 75 minutes . . . only for left-half Tommy Leishman to nod Reds' final equaliser four minutes later.

Orient missed a great chance to snatch both points, though, when McDonald hit the post with a sidefooted effort from six yards in the dying seconds.

It was very hard on Orient whose brilliant football even drew warm applause from the Spion Kop diehards who feared that their mighty Merseyside marvels were going to be defeated. Lucas was singled out for praise in breaking up Liverpool's midfield play and setting up counter-attacks.

For the first time in eight years, Republic of Ireland manager Johnny Carey was not present on the bench for his country who were in Prague this weekend for a World Cup qualifier against Czechoslovakia. Carey resolved his dilemma by remaining with his club's players on Merseyside, where they prepared to face first division Blackpool in the League Cup, two nights after the epic Anfield thriller.

October 30, 1961
League Cup, 2nd replay
Blackpool 5 (Parry 2, Charnley 3)
Leyton Orient 1 (McDonald)

O's stayed on Merseyside over the weekend and despite playing more of the cultured football that had impressed so many at Anfield, they could not contain the first division threat of Pool's two Rays – Charnley and Parry.

Parry struck twice before the interval before Charnley grabbed a second-half hat-trick. McDonald's goal proved academic for O's, who gave Newman a rare outing at inside-left for the injured Graham.

(Note: The programme for this Cup-tie is very rare and usually sells for a three-figure sum. It cost me £150!)

November 4, 1961
Leyton Orient 2 (Dunmore 2 – 1 pen)
Charlton Athletic 1 (Lawrie)

Once again, O's struggled to produce their best form at home and were lucky to escape with both points. But for (Stan) Charlton, Lewis and the agile George, O's could easily have been two behind by the break.

Instead, two minutes after the re-start, White held off lanky John Hewie before crossing to the near post, where Dunmore nipped in between keeper Willie Duff and

John Sewell to snatch the lead off the underside of the bar at the Windsor Road end.

Sewell conceded a penalty when he handballed Lea's throw-in, with Dunmore netting his second from the spot.

It looked all over for basement boys Charlton until two minutes from the end – right-winger Sam Lawrie latched onto a backpass by Lewis and backheeled the ball into the net, while Dennis Edwards headed over with only George to beat.

November 11, 1961
Leeds United 0
Leyton Orient 0

With Elwood in for groin injury victim Foster, O's should have taken both points from struggling Leeds in the driving wind and rain at Elland Road.

Dunmore hit a post, White wasted his chance and Graham missed a golden chance to win it 10 minutes from time when he shot over the bar from close range with his 'wrong' (right) foot.

Manager Carey missed this match – he was at Norwich to watch transfer target George Waites, the winger who had left Orient the previous summer.

November 18, 1961
Leyton Orient 4 (Dunmore, Elwood, Sitford OG, White)
Brighton & Hove Albion 1 (Nicholas)

Who says the O's forward line needs strengthening? The irrepressible Dunmore, who ran centre-half Roy Jennings ragged, put Orient ahead on 15 minutes after Bishop's freekick rebounded from the shin of Bob McNichol.

With Foster fit again, Elwood kept his place at the expense of Graham – and the Irish terrier latched onto McDonald's 25th minute pass before cleverly chipping the second over the onrushing Charlie Baker. Tony Sitford capped a nightmare first half with a panicky backpass beyond his own keeper on 37 minutes and the left-back was then beaten in the tackle by White, who made it 4-0 from the edge of the area just before the break.

It was a very classy first half performance by rampant O's but Brighton were much improved in the second period and deserved more than Tony Nicholas' 82nd minute consolation effort.

November 24, 1961
Scunthorpe United 0
Leyton Orient 2 (McDonald, White)

O's put an end to Scunthorpe's nine-match unbeaten home record and leapfrogged United into second place, to lead the pursuit of leaders Liverpool, who had recently dropped a home point to Scunthorpe.

The first goal of this Friday night thriller came in the 11th minute, when McDonald easily headed home White's cross.

United forced seven corners in 20 second half minutes and it was during this period of sustained United attack that Bishop and Lewis, in particular, stood firm.

The killer blow was struck by White in the final minute, when his shot trickled over the line after Ken Jones failed to hold it.

December 2, 1961
Leyton Orient 2 (Dunmore 2)
Norwich City 0

Cliff Richard was at Brisbane Road to enjoy this one, but it was dashing Dunmore who called the tune all afternoon. He led Barry Butler a merry dance and, after Elwood saw three great chances go begging, with reserve keeper Geoff Barnsley twice saved by the woodwork, DD struck in the 27th minute.

From a close-range, indirect free-kick, he received a short pass from Lea before cleverly chipping the ball beyond 10 yellow-shirted defenders at the Buckingham Road end.

Former O's winger George Waites tried his luck on both flanks, but got no change out of either Lewis or Charlton.

It was all over in the 75th minute, Dunmore roaming to the left where he received Lewis' long ball. After brushing aside Roy McCrohan and eluding two other defenders, the powerful No.9 unleashed an unstoppable shot past the injured Barnsley.

Before this game, Lucas was boosted by the news that he'd been called up to captain the Wales Under-23 team against Scotland at Wrexham.

The league game scheduled at Bury on December 9 was postponed due to a heavy fog. Instead, the O's players went to Old Trafford to see Manchester United play Fulham. No-one was more disappointed than 18-year-old inside-forward Harry Gregory when the game at Gigg Lane was called off . With Joe Elwood ruled out with a bout of flu, Harry had been poised to make his league debut. At that stage of the season, Gregory had scored 18 goals for the Combination and 'A' teams – but he had to wait almost another year before finally making his first team bow.

December 16, 1961
Leyton Orient 2 (White, Elwood)
Newcastle United 0

With George out with a heavy cold, Orient give a first team debut to 32-year-old former Chelsea keeper Bill Robertson, who made two solid, point-blank saves from No.9 Ivor Allchurch and outside-right Gordon Hughes as Newcastle piled on the first half pressure.

But with the O's defence in inpenetrable form, the fast Geordies couldn't break through. Orient's first came after 31 minutes, when White appeared at the far post to head Dunmore's arcing cross between Billy McKinney and the near post.

Newcastle were waiting for a freekick to be awarded to Foster in the 57th minute, when quick-thinking McDonald took advantage of the ref's decision to play on and he set up Elwood, who converted easily. White scraped the bar with a rasping drive 20 minutes from time.

December 23, 1961
Middlesbrough 2 (Harris – 2 pens)
Leyton Orient 3 (Foster 2, Dunmore)

A frostbound Ayresome Park pitch welcomed O's to the north-east, where Dunmore gave the visitors an early lead.

Boro equalised on 27 minutes after Lewis handled to stop a certain goal and Bill Harris converted the resulting spot kick past fit-again keeper George.

Man-of-the-match Foster headed O's back in front five minutes before the break, then added his second soon after the re-start. The defence, superbly marshaled by Bishop, came under intense pressure and another handball led to Boro reducing the deficit from a second penalty by Harris.

December 26, 1961
Leyton Orient 1 (Dunmore)
Swansea Town 0

O's biggest crowd of the season to date – 14,500 – for this 3.15pm kick-off (West Ham switched their home game v Blackburn Rovers to 11.00am to accommodate Swansea's demand for an afternoon start in Leyton) saluted another brilliant Dunmore performance that had alerted first division clubs to his form.

He dominated Swansea and Wales centre-half Mel Nurse on the icy Brisbane Road surface and capped another fine display with the only goal after half-an-hour. Receiving Lea's pass six yards out, Dunmore slashed the ball beyond the helpless John King.

Lea and his fellow Welsh warrior, Lucas, gave their compatriots no leeway and were equal to any of Swansea's roughhouse tactics.

Terry McDonald watches as Dave Dunmore's nets the Boxing Day winner against Swansea.

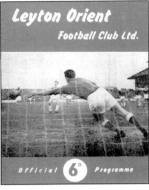

December 30, 1961
Swansea Town 1 (Donnelly)
Leyton Orient 3 (Dunmore 3)

O's were in seventh heaven after their seventh consecutive win to keep the pressure on Liverpool. And once again, it was that man Dunmore who did the damage – big-style!

On a day when O's had only 25 percent of the game and created just five chances, Dunmore scored one header, drove home two more for his hat-trick and then forced the save of the day from Noel Dwyer.

His first came on 11 minutes when he got the better of Roy Nurse who couldn't deal with a long ball from Charlton. George withstood most of what Town threw at him, except Peter Donnelly's 31st minute header.

January 6, 1962
FA Cup, 3rd round
Brentford 1 (Summers)
Leyton Orient 1 (Foster)

In a petulant cup tie, George Summers gave lowly third division Brentford an interval lead after scoring from close in.

Foster equalised on the hour but it was a face-saving strike against a Bees side that had injured centre-half Peter Gelson playing on the tight-wing for the last 40 minutes with right-winger Summers limping for the last 20.

Perhaps Brentford were even more fired up after admitting their annoyance that O's manager Carey had insisted on an earlier 2.15pm kick-off time, because he declared that the Griffin Park floodlights weren't up to standard.

January 8, 1962
FA Cup, 3rd round replay
Leyton Orient 2 (Foster, Elwood)
Brentford 1 (Higginson)

This was better entertainment for a big 22,690 crowd than the dross served up at Griffin Park, but O's still made hard work of beating their struggling third division opponents on a greasy surface.

In fact, it wasn't until Elwood dashed on to a poor backpass by Jimmy Gitsham, to keeper Gerry Cakebread in the 85th minute, that O's secured a fourth round glamour showdown with first division leaders Burnley.

Brentford capitalised on a gale-force wind to put O's under first half pressure and got the break on 25 minutes, when centre-half Tom Higginson scored with a low shot past George. But just as he had done on the Saturday, Foster rescued O's on the hour – this time, while laying flat out on the deck, he deflected Lucas' shot into the net for the equaliser that set up Elwood's thrilling finale – and a mouth-watering fourth round tie.

January 13, 1962
Leyton Orient 3 (Dunmore pen, Graham, White)
Walsall 0

The home attendance topped 15,000 but they had to wait until the hour mark for O's to open the scoring at windy E10.

Foster looked set to score until Jimmy Dudley fouled him in the box, and Dunmore was on target from the spot. Four minutes later, the recalled Graham – back in for Elwood – headed home a cross from Newman, who replaced McDonald on the left wing.

Orient could have scored five but grazed the woodwork several times before White drove an unstoppable shot that keeper Alan Boswell could only turn into the net at his near post.

January 20, 1962
Derby County 1 (Curry)
Leyton Orient 2 (Dunmore pen, Graham)

An important away win against fellow promotion challengers, this was a bruising, hard-fought encounter in which Dunmore was again the central figure.

After Bill Curry had given Rams a 17th minute lead, Dunmore was booked by referee Jack Moore for retaliation following a series of fierce challenges from Derby centre-back Les Moore, who left the O's No.9 nursing a thigh injury.

Dunmore had the last word, though, sending Reg Matthews the wrong way to equalise from the spot in the 65th minute after Jack Parry had handled a Graham header. The big No.9 then set up Graham to crack home the second from 12 yards on 72 minutes.

February 3, 1962
Leyton Orient 2 (Graham, McDonald)
Bristol Rovers 3 (Jarman, Williams, Mabbutt)

After the heroic exertions at Burnley in midweek, lack-lustre O's saw their 16-match unbeaten run ended by relegation-threatened Rovers, who completed a surprise double over them.

GLAD ALL OVER

Dave Clark Five, 1963

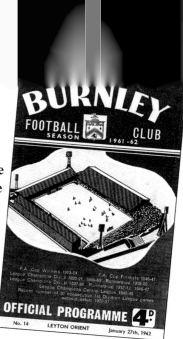

ORIENT have enjoyed some memorable FA Cup triumphs against more illustrious opponents, notably London giants Chelsea in 1972 and 1978 and, most recently, Premiership Fulham in 2006. But probably the toughest David v Goliath assignment they ever faced came early in 1962.

That's when high-flying Burnley were – along with Tottenham Hotspur – the most powerful force in English football, leading the way in their bid to regain the first division title they had won two years earlier and which had slipped into the hands of double-winning Spurs in 1961.

After overcoming Brentford in an awkward third round tie that required a replay at Brisbane Road, few gave the O's – 250-1 Cup outsiders – any hope of success when the fourth round draw pitted them against Burnley at Turf Moor. The Clarets, sparkling with star master schemers such as Irish international Jimmy McIlroy and Jimmy Adamson, were huge pre-match favourites and when the fog came down and caused the first game to be postponed, it seemed as though it had merely delayed the inevitable Burnley home victory.

Not that the Lancashire club were anything less than hospitable to their visitors from East London.

Skipper Stan Charlton says: "After the game was fogged off, the Burnley captain Jimmy Adamson came out to our coach and, just before we left for the station, he gave us a plate of hot meat pies he'd managed to scrounge from the boardroom.

"Our coach had to get us to Manchester, from where our train was leaving that night. One of our club directors, Leslie Grade, went on ahead of us in another vehicle and pulled the communication chord while the train was still in the station, so that we wouldn't miss it."

When the fog in Burnley had lifted and O's returned north a second time, they gave the first division league leaders and second (5-1) favourites for the FA Cup the fright of their lives.

Standing tall in their unfamiliar all-white strip (which soon turned brown in the mud), the Orient braves gave the near 38,000 crowd a treat. Understandably, they came under persistent pressure for long periods of this pulsating cup-tie, especially during one 20-minute bombardment in the first half. That said, the only on-target effort on goal that O's keeper Frank George had to save was a header from Gordon Harris.

DA DOO RON RON
Crystals, 1963

Johnny Carey's tactics – defend resolutely in numbers and look to hit the hosts on quick breakaways – worked a treat and when they broke forward on a rare foray in the 56th minute, they made the most of it.

Cyril Lea ran clear on the right, swung over a high cross for Malcolm Graham to nod back across goal . . . and there was fragile inside-right Ronnie Foster, four yards out, to sidefoot the ball to the left of keeper Adam Blacklaw's despairing dive. Orient were in dreamland.

Inevitably, they had to withstand another onslaught from the men in claret-and-blue shirts but as the O's defence stood firm, Burnley had to wait until just seven minutes from time before grabbing their controversial equaliser.

It was outside-left Harris, who for once escaped the attentions of Charlton, who smashed home Burnley's goal, via a post, from John Connelly's right-wing cross but afterwards Orient director Arthur Page told the *Daily Express*: "He definitely handled the ball when he scored their equaliser. The ball was well past him when he pulled it back with his hand."

As Burnley pushed hard for the winner in the dying minutes, George made a brilliant save to deny Brian Miller's header, while McIlroy was just wide with a half-volley. But had the Clarets grabbed a last winner, it would have been cruel luck on Orient, who had one or two half-chances to win it themselves.

Johnny Carey said afterwards: "We might even have popped another in when we were leading. It would have been robbery and a complete injustice to Burnley if we had, but the chance was there once or twice."

Stan Charlton added: "I don't know how the lads kept going. We were all completely exhausted by the end."

His opposing number, Jimmy Adamson, gave his sporting verdict: "They certainly gave us a scare – I have rarely seen a team fight so hard."

Although disappointed that a famous victory had been snatched from their grasp so late in the game, the draw was very good news for the Orient club coffers – it meant a lucrative all-ticket replay at Brisbane Road the following Tuesday when everyone correctly anticipated a new record crowd at Leyton Stadium.

PRESS COMMENT

Leyton Orient, with one of the lowest average gates in the second division, won the right at Burnley last night to stage one of the greatest matches in their history. And for 26 minutes they looked like achieving their greatest triumph.

Daily Mail

Burnley ran full tilt into a rock-solid wall last night and came desperately close to knocking themselves out of the FA Cup.

Daily Mirror

A sensation? To most people, yes. But to the shoestring club Orient – no. It was almost exactly as they planned it.

The Express

● RONNIE FOSTER (left) rushes in to side-foot the ball home for Orient's goal against Burnley last night.

THE GREAT WALL
OF THE ORIENT!

By FRANK McGHEE
Burnley 1, Leyton Orient 1

BURNLEY ran full tilt into a rock-solid wall last night and came desperately close to knock-

Late goal just saves Burnley

rest were either blocked, scrambled clear or hit so wide and high they didn't matter.

All Burnley's superiority, territorially and individually, was wiped out.

In a fifty-seventh minute

CONFESSIN'
Frank Ifield, 1963

IT was the biggest night in Orient's history .. . a 31,000 record sell-out crowd had come to see if the gallant O's could do what they were seven minutes away from doing at Turf Moor and beat mighty Burnley.

The incentive to progress was massive, for Everton were laying in wait as fifth round opponents following the previous day's Cup draw. Everton, the club that had sacked manager Johnny Carey the previous summer.

This was very serious business as far as all the players were concerned too. O's right-half Malcolm Lucas turned down the chance to captain Wales Under-23s against Ireland. Burnley's Irishman Alex Elder also withdrew from the same international, while the visitors' England quartet of Ray Pointer, John Connelly, John Angus and Brian Miller – all said 'no' to the World Cup squad get-together planned for midweek.

Off the pitch, Orient had to take unprecedented steps to cope with the demand for tickets. They suddenly discovered thousands of new 'fans' who were prepared to queue round the ground from early on the Sunday morning (the replay was on Tuesday) to buy tickets.

And to meet that demand, club secretary George Hicks and his helpers were up half the night at his home sorting out tickets. Hicks, who had help from his wife Lilian and 16-year-old son Marshall, said: "I'm the only member of the office staff, we keep down the expense that way.

"I was up in my front room at home until one o'clock this morning getting the tickets sorted out with nine of my friends."

The tickets even incorporated a special dye depicting the inside of the stadium, to deter would-be forgers.

And the club was taking no chances that anyone would try to gatecrash the party. Aware that "thousands of fans" had vaulted the concrete boundary wall over the years to watch the games for free, the club arranged for a barbed wire fence to be erected behind the terracing and above the low boundary wall at the Coronation Gardens end.

They brought in police to set up road blokes where only fans with tickets were allowed through.

And at the Windsor Road end of the stadium, where some 20 houses backed on to the north terrace, the club appealed to those house-holders not to allow opportunist supporters to nip through their homes and back gardens before climbing over the

Those were the days! Fans queuing around the ground for Burnley Cup replay tickets.

wall and into the ground. "I'm sure we can trust the residents to play ball," said secretary Hicks.

The first fan to queue for a ticket was outside the main gates at Brisbane Road 15 minutes before midnight on that Sunday. By 4am he had several hundred for company and by 10am, when 26 turnstiles opened for business, four separate queues were snaking in orderly lines right around the ground. It was reported that Orient had sold 22,000 tickets in three hours – which was bizarre given that only 14,737 had bothered to turn up the previous day to see Bristol Rovers end O's unbeaten 16-game run stretching back to September. "We've got fans we didn't even know we had," beamed bemused but delighted chairman Harry Zussman.

Prior to the replay, Orient had let Cup fever get the better of them when Bristol Rovers came to town. In contrast, Burnley had boosted their first division title challenge that same day with a crushing 7-1 defeat of Birmingham City, three days before the replay in East London.

The ticket touts were loving it every bit as much as happy Harry Zussman and his fellow board members. Ground tickets that normally cost three shillings were being sold for 10s, and stand seats for £4.00.

But, according to the local press, Orient's one-ticket-per-person policy was flawed – spivs went round three or four times and immediately 'went into business'.

For Orient players earning somewhere between £20 and £30 a week then, there was the opportunity of a nice bonus for them too, as reward for forcing one of England's top teams to a mouth-watering replay.

Terry McDonald revealed: "One of the Orient directors, Charles Bent-Marshall, wanted to buy tickets from the players when we played Burnley in the replay. He used to drive a great, big car and owned a car showroom, selling Wolsleys and other nice cars, in Leyton High Road. A nice bloke, he wouldn't say boo to a goose. Although why he couldn't get hold of tickets from the club himself, I don't know.

"But instead of selling them to Charles, Ronnie Foster and me got in touch with Clive Lewis, who was Best Man at my wedding, and sold our tickets to blokes that he knew well who worked in the docks near Canning Town. Clive worked there himself – I think it was Victoria Docks – and he told us there was a lot of demand for tickets from East End dockers. Clive, Ronnie and me went across the river in a rowing boat – armed with about 20 tickets each!

"I think the players had the option to buy four tickets apiece but we got hold of more, although whether that was because other players didn't need all theirs, I can't remember. I would have given my Dad a ticket, I know that.

22,000 Cup tickets in three hours

By JOHN BROMLEY

OVER 20,000 fans "invaded" Leyton Orient's barricaded ground yesterday to snap up tickets for tomorrow's FA Cup fourth-ound replay against stadium and only fans with tickets will be allowed through.
● Barbed wire—"it co us four quid"—alon three sides of the groun will prevent ticketless far from leaping over the wal —as they have done fo previous big matches.

"But by selling the others around the docks, I reckon we got double the cover price on each ticket, which would have been about 10 shilling in each case."

McDonald's frank admission that he and Foster sold tickets on the black market is anathema to genuine supporters who miss out on these special occasions, although in this case it was very unlikely that any of the O's regular 14,000-odd faithful failed in their efforts to buy a ticket for a 31,000 record capacity, although it might have denied fans of nearby clubs West Ham, Tottenham and Arsenal from seeing Orient play what was the biggest game in their history until that point.

Let's be honest, there were always many other players quick to cash in on the big Cup occasions. The fan in me says that I just hope every genuine Orient follower reading this, who wanted to be at that famous game in February 1962, did actually get in to see it.

Players selling tickets certainly didn't deprive anyone planning on travelling down from Burnley, who returned around 250 of their original 2,000 allocation.

And where did comedian Arthur Askey come into the equation? He was a good friend of Orient's impresario directors Leslie Grade and Bernard Delfont whose agency employed Askey and a number of other well known celebrities of stage and screen who were regular guests in the Leyton boardroom and, occasionally, even the dressing room. With a capacity crowd crammed inside Brisbane Road on this big night, Askey was brought in to lark around on the pitch before the game, entertain the crowd and get them to pack together tightly to create more room on the terraces.

Leyton Orient hadn't seen anything like it. Even the players' pre-match routine had been changed especially for the glamour occasion, with Carey hoping to ease their nerves by asking his men to report for light training . . . on the morning of the replay. Phil White was excused the previous day's session while he nursed his sore throat but the right-winger was declared fit to start the game as the manager named an unchanged team from the side that had battled like warriors at Turf Moor a week earlier.

When the barbed wire was put up, the surrounding streets were manned by police blockades and Windsor Road residents were turning away everyone who knocked at their front doors in search of a back route to the terraces, Arthur Askey and 31,000 held their breath for another night of high drama.

WOODEN HEART
Elvis Presley, 1961

Orient started where they left off at Burnley, fighting for every ball and not content to merely hold their own against more illustrious opponents who were brimming with full internationals. In fact, Orient actually outplayed and outclassed the Division One leaders for most of the 90 minutes and created no end of chances.

The O's had everything – poise, purpose and pure class. They had it all, except that vital ingredient that can decide just about any football match. Luck.

This thrilling replay hinged on two almost identical incidents involving the woodwork adjoining both posts.

With five minutes to go, Ronnie Foster flighted a cross from the right that Dave Dunmore – the outstanding performer on the night – headed towards goal. It looked to have overworked Burnley keeper Adam Blacklaw beaten all ends up . . . only for the ball to crash against the underside of the crossbar, allowing centre-half Tommy Cummings to slash the ball away for a corner.

Dunmore had been majestic, especially in the first half when he was roaming freely and effectively to both wings, dropping back into midfield to mop up loose balls and then getting on the end of chances in the penalty box.

On 30 minutes he rose to head Terry McDonald's cross towards the corner of the net, but Blacklaw made one of a number of brilliant saves to deny him again.

Two minutes later, Dunmore's left foot volley whizzed inches wide, followed by a rocket show from Malcolm Graham that almost embedded itself in Blacklaw's midriff.

Dunmore again brought out the best in the Burnley No.1 when he struck a high, rising shot and then saw another cracking effort skim the bar. McDonald also went close following a Phil White corner when his shot rebounded back off the grounded keeper. Foster, whose goal had earned the replay, could only direct his close-range header straight at Blacklaw. Three times Burnley defenders kicked the ball off their own goalline.

O's did everything but score and, as often happens in these cases, the team under the cosh snatches victory on the counter attack. If Burnley, who had to wait until the 54th minute to trouble Frank George, considered themselves unfortunate not to have won the tie at the first attempt, they couldn't believe their luck when they stole victory in the replay.

With 13 minutes gone in the second half, Sid Bishop conceded an uncharacteristically soft corner and from England winger John Connelly's resulting flag kick, burly, 6ft left-half Brian Miller appeared unmarked in the box to head an undeserved winner.

Even Burnley's goal had a touch of luck about it. As Miller's header looped over George, the O's keeper seemed to slightly impede left-back Eddie Lewis, who was guarding the near post and looked poised to clear the danger, only for the ball to strike the underside of the bar and sneak agonisingly over the line. Miller got lucky where Dunmore was denied.

A poignant picture in one newspaper showed Frank on his knees in the six-yard box and Eddie bent over, with head bowed and hands on both knees. It was a photo that encapsulated the utter despair felt by every home player at that moment. Although Frank had difficulty recalling the agony of that decisive, killer goal when I spoke to him recently, for Eddie it invoked vivid memories.

Speaking from his home in South Africa, he said: "Miller headed the ball towards where I was standing by the post and I was just going to head it clear when Frank dived and stuck his finger in my eye. I pulled my head out of the way and the ball went into the net but if he hadn't dived for the ball, I would have headed it clear. I think it took me about five minutes to regain my sight."

It was incredibly harsh on the O's who deserved all the respect and sympathy they got in the aftermath of a memorable performance. Burnley boss Harry Potts said afterwards: "I was very relieved at the result. Orient played magnificently."

The Clarets' chairman Bob Lord added: "Orient will be a credit to the first division. We will be glad to welcome them there next season."

Yes, for once, the old cliché about a Cup defeat allowing the losers to focus on their league efforts had never sounded truer. Burnley hadn't seen the last of the O's, although their dreams of a League-and-Cup double floundered when Ipswich Town snatched the championship, three points clear of them and Tottenham, and Spurs beat Jimmy Adamson's boys, 3-1, in the FA Cup final.

By the end of the season, it was Orient who would be celebrating . . .

Eddie Lewis clutches his face, Frank George is helpless and Sid Bishop looks on...it's the Burnley winner.

O's WUZ ROBBED

1962

THIS match didn't start, it exploded into fiery action that knocked baffled but brave Burnley out of their super soccer stride.

In the first 90 seconds Dave Dunmore, the centre-forward Spurs and West Ham let go, made two chances.

First he sent a high cross to Terry McDonald, who couldn't quite get his head to it.

Even before the great roar had echoed into the night air Dunmore was at it again. This time, trying a difficult angled shot, he sliced his kick.

| L. Orient | 0 |
| Burnley | 1 |

By LAURIE PIGNON

Burnley's freak win

PRESS COMMENT

While Frank George could have sat in the front row of the stands, an admiring spectator of his team's unrelenting effort and skill, Burnley's Adam Blacklaw was a green-jerseyed fury of action for practically the whole match.

Peter Lorenzo, Daily Herald

For many exciting spells in a game that will long be remembered, Burnley were outplayed and outclassed.

Roy Peskett

Dynamic Dave Dunmore made Burnley's England man Ray Pointer seem a learner. Dunmore – how he reminds me of Tommy Lawton! If there's a better centre-forward in England, I'd like to see him.

Laurie Pignon, Daily Mirror

'It was the greatest robbery since Cup was stolen in 1895'

The speed and elegance of these Leyton men, who as the season started were **unconsidered and lightly regarded, looked like adding up to the greatest soccer show of the year, an East Side story that would become a legend for all to learn.**

Desmond Hackett, Daily Express

February 9, 1962
Leyton Orient 0
Preston North End 2 (Spavin, Smith)

A second home Friday night encounter of the season resulted in another defeat, O's third at home in six days. This time the midweek Cup classic with Burnley had clearly drained them, although the outstanding Dunmore continued where he left off against Burnley and caught the eye of the watching England scouts.

Preston completed a league double over Orient with goals by Alan Spavin (19 mins) and Jimmy Smith (89).

Orient fans among the 19,000 crowd vented their anger and frustration on referee Harry Horner by throwing orange peel and a white ball at him as he left the field at half-time. The official needed a police escort of 12 to see him off the field at the final whistle as hundreds of home fans swarmed onto the pitch to remonstrate with him.

February 17, 1962
Plymouth Argyle 2 (Newman, McAnearney)
Leyton Orient 1 (Dunmore)

A massive contingent of visiting fans contributed to Plymouth's biggest home gate of the season. O's – with Norman Deeley making his debut in place of McDonald at outside-left – missed three scoring chances in the first half and generally looked the better side, but goals by John Newman and Jimmy McAnearney gave Argyle an undeserved lead.

Dunmore continued his brilliant run of form, setting up good openings for both Deeley and Graham, before scoring himself. O's deserved at least a point from Home Park.

February 24, 1962
Stoke City 0
Leyton Orient 1 (Dunmore)

Orient got back on the winning trail and ended Stoke's run of seven straight home wins at the Victoria Ground since Stanley Matthews rejoined them last October.

It was Dunmore who yet again did the business for the visitors, who made several changes. White was ruled out on the morning of the match, so new signing Deeley switched to the right wing and Foster moved to the left, where he was joined by the recalled Elwood (in for Graham). Taylor made only his second league appearance at inside-right and veteran George Wright was handed his only outing of the season as Charlton's replacement at right-back.

Despite the huge shake-up, O's dominated and should have won more easily than the score suggested, with Stoke keeper **????(name)** O'Neill earning all the credit for his heroics to deny Elwood.

But there was no stopping Dunmore's 25-yard drive that gave O's their deserved winner 15 minutes into the second half.

March 3, 1962
Leyton Orient 1 (Deeley)
Sunderland 1 (McPheat)

Skipper Charlton returned with a heavily strapped knee but it was the O's defence who were in distress when Willie McPheat chested in a third minute cross to give Sunderland a shock lead.

Orient couldn't have any complaints, though, about new signings Deeley and Gordon Bolland who both shone on their home debuts. Former Chelsea inside-forward Bolland looked worth every penny and more of his £5,000 fee as he supported Dunmore and struck the bar with one effort.

It was Deeley, the former Wolves winger, who as well as providing a string of telling crosses, brought O's level with a 55th minute cross-shot that floated over Jim Montgomery from way out on the right flank.

March 9, 1962
Rotherham United 2 (Weston, Houghton)
Leyton Orient 1 (Lucas)

Lucas, who had just earned his first full cap for Wales against Ireland, scored a consolation long-range goal seven minutes from time under the Friday night lights at Millmoor, but by then Rotherham had dominated most of the game.

Don Weston, who had hit an upright with one drive, gave Rotherham the lead after 32 minutes when he netted from close range following a pass from Alan Kirkman. Weston also forced a great save from Robertson just before half-time as the home side piled on the pressure.

They made it 2-0 with 20 minutes to play, when Ken Houghton tapped home from a corner by Kirkman, although it was O's who dominated the closing stages. After Lucas had halved the deficit, Deeley struck a post from three yards in the last minute.

March 13, 1962
Bury 0
Leyton Orient 1 (McDonald)

A brilliant 25-yard strike in the 22nd minute by McDonald, who cut in from the left when there appeared to be little threat to Chris Harker's goal, earned O's two vital points in this Tuesday night encounter at Gigg Lane.

McDonald returned to the No.11 shirt after a four-match absence as White made way, while Graham came back in for Taylor after missing the previous three games. Bolland simply switched seamlessly to inside-right.

But it was another solid defensive performance by O's that ensured the win as the Shakers pressed hard for an equaliser. Several good chances were squandered and even when talisman Dave Hickson finally got the ball in the net nine minutes from time, it was disallowed for a push on the impenetrable Bishop.

March 17, 1962
Leyton Orient 2 (Graham, Lewis)
Liverpool 2 (A'Court 2)

An uncharacteristic late lapse by Charlton cost O's the extra point they deserved from this impressive fighting performance against the established league leaders, who were satisfied with the draw.

Inside the last minute, the skipper declined to blast the ball aimlessly out of play when he won possession down by his own corner flag . . . but his intended pass was cut out by the lurking Jimmy Melia whose flighted cross was slammed into the net by left-winger Alan A'Court, the most effective of Liverpool's forwards.

It was very harsh on Orient, who had dominated 70 percent of the play and made light of Dunmore's absence through injury. Lea and Lucas dominated midfield, while Bishop played Ian St. John out of the game.

Graham made up for two glaring earlier misses by netting O's opener, one of their finest goals of the season, just seconds before half-time. McDonald collected a goalkick from Robertson and fed the ball to Graham, who pushed it beyond Ron Yeats before unleashing a 30-yard screamer just inside the far post.

O's seemed to be cruising to a much needed win when Liverpool emerged from their defensive shell to equalise on 80 minutes. A rare defensive mix-up in the O's goalmouth allowed A'Court, who gave Charlton a difficult afternoon, to slam home a close-range equaliser. Graham responded by heading a centre from Bolland (filling Dunmore's centre-forward role) just over the bar.

Orient got their reward, and what they assumed would be the winner, seven minutes from time when Lea tapped a freekick sideways for left-back Lewis to thunder his 30-yard shot superbly past Jim Furnell.

March 24, 1962
Charlton Athletic 1 (Kinsey)
Leyton Orient 2 (Deeley, Graham)

A vital two points, especially given the fact that Dunmore struggled with a recurrence of a thigh injury he aggravated just five minutes into this derby game at The Valley.

Deeley rounded off smart build-up play by McDonald to open the scoring on 19 minutes, while Graham unleashed a ferocious 25-yarder to make it 2-0 seven minutes later.

Brian Kinsey cut the deficit with a header three minutes before the interval and O's defence had to be at its best to withstand some constant second half pressure. Third placed Plymouth kept up the pressure on Orient by winning 3-1 at Rotherham.

March 31, 1962
Leyton Orient 0
Leeds United 0

With Dunmore again sidelined, the last thing O's needed was another injury to add to the list which also included Foster, White and keeper George. But Lewis received

a bad knock to his thigh in the early minutes and spent most of the match hobbling around up front, while Taylor dropped deep in place of the stricken left-back and had to mark his young fellow Scot, Billy Bremner.

O's had three good chances to bring this dreadfully dull game to life but Deeley shot tamely wide, Bolland (who gave Jack Charlton a tough time) went close with a raking shot and McDonald's effort brushed Tommy Younger's crossbar.

Fortunately for the O's, Leeds – second from bottom – seemed content merely to defend and never threatened to score the first goal in two matches between these teams.

April 7, 1962
Brighton & Hove Albion 0
Leyton Orient 1 (Foster)

A vital win that put a three-point gap between second placed O's and their nearest chasing club, Plymouth.

This game at the Goldstone Ground saw young local-born David Clark make his league debut at left-back, replacing the injured Lewis.

Foster celebrated his return to the side after a month out through injury by netting the winner in the 28th minute – he followed up sharply after McDonald's shot had only been parried out.

April 14, 1962
Leyton Orient 0
Scunthorpe United 1 (McGuigan)

Scunthorpe struck an early blow from which O's never recovered. The game was all of 30 seconds old when Lucas got caught in two minds and chose the wrong option.

His misplaced pass was intercepted by Scunthorpe inside-left John McGuigan who arrowed his shot past a helpless Robertson. The fifth placed visitors, who closed the gap on O's in second spot to just three points, rarely threatened the home goal again as most of the remaining chances fell to Deeley.

He saw two headers well saved by Ken Jones, while his shot – from a McDonald cross – went inches wide of the post.

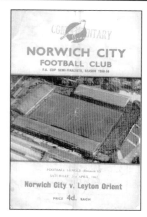
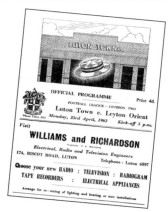

Dunmore didn't look fully fit on his return from injury but Lea dominated midfield and promoted more calls for a first full Welsh cap.

The only good news for Orient today was lowly Bury's 2-1 defeat of Plymouth.

April 20, 1962
Leyton Orient 0
Luton Town 0

A Good Friday early evening kick-off and the nerves showed again as O's went a third consecutive home game without scoring.

Well, actually they did score what looked to 21,292 fans like a perfectly good goal seven minutes into the second half. Dunmore lunged for a header but missed the ball, which dropped for McDonald. The little winger brushed past Brendan McNally to send his left foot past Jim Standen . . . only for the linesman to raise his flag.

Referee J.R. Loynton admitted afterwards that while McDonald had not been in an offside position, he said that Dunmore was . . . and had been 'interfering' with play.

Orient dominated throughout, with Deeley going agonisingly close with a shot and three headers. Dunmore was also just wide with a 20-yard shot that had Standen well beaten.

April 21, 1962
Norwich City 0
Leyton Orient 0

A dull game where the Os did not look like a team in the promotion race. Both teams were woeful in front of goal with no finishing sting in either attack. Defences dominated throughout and spectators were streaming away from Carrow Road long before the final whistle.

If anything, Norwich had slightly the better of some exchanges. But their inside-forwards came a cropper against O's tough tackling half back line. Bishop was outstanding, not giving Scott an inch in which to manoeuvre. Unfortunately for Orient, the Norwich defence maintained an equally tight grip at the other end.

Deeley, Dunmore and Taylor all fritted away good goal-scoring chances in the first half. Bolland and McDonald were guilty of similar offences after the interval.

This was the third successive match in which Orient had failed to score.

April 23, 1962
Luton Town 1
Leyton Orient 3 (Gibbs 2, Lucas)

Gibbs made a timely return – six months after his only previous league appearance of the season – to score two great goals that put O's promotion bid back on track.

After spending most of the campaign playing right-half for the Reserves, steady Gibbs slipped easily back into the inside-right spot as Foster also returned to the side and Graham remained out of favour.

His first goal couldn't have come at a better time. O's were one down in the eighth minute thanks to Bob Martin, Dunmore had seen his penalty saved by Jim Standen 11 minutes later and they looked like extending their goalless run to four games.

Gibbs equalised with a volley and then, 10 minutes into the second half, he converted a McDonald cross to put Orient ahead. Luton thought they had levelled a minute later when Brendan McNally found the net from a quick freekick, only for the referee to order it to be re-taken.

Goal of the match was Lucas' in the 77th minute. Charlton's freekick was helped on by Gibbs to Lewis, whose lofted cross was cracked home by the diminutive Welsh international from 25 yards.

The game had a bizarre twist to it in that injury-hit Luton fielded TWO goalkeepers. While regular No.1 Standen wore the green jersey, former England keeper Ron Baynham was forced into a makeshift centre-forward's role! Baynham didn't score but he did clash heads with Charlton, who spent the last five minutes clutching a sponge to his nose, which wouldn't stop bleeding.

Gibbs had returned from the wilderness to inspire Orient's final push for promotion. Now it all came down to the final game at home against Bury.

But first Sunderland, O's only rivals for the second promotion spot behind champions Liverpool, had to travel to mid-table Rotherham United. The East London club held a two-point advantage over Sunderland before their game in hand.

Maybe. Just maybe, Rotherham could do Orient a big, big favour . . . ?

Chapter 4

CAN'T BUY ME LOVE
Beatles, 1964

MONEY, it seems, can buy just about anything in football these days – just look at Chelsea for compelling evidence of that. When you've got a Russian billionaire backer and the means to entice the world's top players, it's inevitable that silverware will follow.

But hard cash – all £800 of it in crispy notes – couldn't buy Leyton Orient the result they so desperately needed to help secure promotion to the first division in 1962.

For the first time, it can be revealed here how the O's made a bizarre attempt to illicit the help of another team to enhance their own promotion hopes.

Let's make it clear, though, that the O's were not the instigators of a bribes scandal for which several Sheffield Wednesday players found themselves thrown into prison in 1964. Orient didn't attempt to 'buy off' their opponents to secure two precious league points as this nail-biting season drew to its conclusion and their date with destiny beckoned.

There was no attempt to influence a referee or other match officials either.

No, the financial inducement didn't even revolve around a match involving Leyton Orient – they knew they would have to try and beat their last day opponents, Bury, by fair means.

The £800 incentive was the carrot the East London club dangled before the players of Rotherham United, who were playing O's promotion rivals, Sunderland, the night after Orient had kept their own hopes alive by winning at Luton on Easter Monday.

And the unexpected golden cash carrot came straight from the top . . . from O's director Les Grade.

After the crucial 3-1 victory at Kenilworth Road, Grade approached skipper Stan Charlton and leading goalscorer Dave Dunmore and presented them with a brown paper envelope stuffed full with notes . . . and a mission to drive to Rotherham, where they were to meet with Millers' skipper Roy Lambert at the Millmoor ground before their home game against Sunderland.

The O's duo's instructions were to offer the £800 cash to Lambert on the proviso that it would be split among all the Rotherham players . . . provided they beat Sunderland that night.

Like a couple of undercover Secret Service agents, Dunmore and Charlton set off from London incognito, with DD at the wheel of his Vauxhall Wyvern, and the two Orient stars arrived up in South Yorkshire in good time to make their rendezvous.

Stan reveals the incredible full story: "After winning at Luton on Easter Monday, the next day Dave and I went to Rotherham, where Sunderland were playing their vital penultimate match. We drove up there in Dave's car with £800 in cash that had been given to us personally by Orient director Leslie Grade, to offer to Rotherham as an incentive to try *even harder* against our main promotion rivals. As far as I knew, it was Leslie's idea – I don't even think anyone else at the club knew anything about it.

"We arrived at Rotherham's ground about an hour before kick-off and met the Rotherham captain, Roy Lambert. We explained that there was £800 in it for him and his team-mates if they beat Sunderland and, after telling his players, he said they thought it was a 'great idea.' We arranged with him to hand over the cash after the match – as long as they won the game, as we hoped they would."

Charlton and Dunmore maintained a low profile, though. After their discreet chat with Lambert near the main entrance at Millmoor, they attempted to blend in with the crowd.

"Dave and I went 'undercover' in the crowd, trying to disguise ourselves a bit by wearing a hat, ear muffs and scarf, and we actually stood behind the goal to watch the match. We can't have disguised ourselves too well, though, because a couple of fans came up to ask for our autograph!"

Dave added: "Stan and I went and stood behind the goal, but one bloke came up to us and said: 'How are you doing, Stan?' I don't think we did a good job of disguising who we were!"

On this occasion, not even Roman Abramavich could have got what he wanted. Money couldn't talk then, just as it didn't two years earlier when Bristol City tried – and failed – to offer Orient players a bribe just prior to their vital game at Brisbane Road and were desperate for points to ease their relegation fears.

Terry McDonald revealed: "One of the Bristol City players – I'd rather not name him – approached three or four of our senior pro's near the dressing rooms before the game and offered us £20-a-man – a week's wages each – for us to throw the match. Manager Les Gore must have got wind of it, because he warned us all that if anybody took any money from Bristol, he would report those concerned to the Football League.

"To be honest, you couldn't even give Bristol City the game anyway – they were that poor – and we ended up beating them easily (two goals by Eddie Brown and one by McDonald sealed a comfortable 3-1 win).

"That's the only time I'd heard of money being offered as a bribe during my time in the game," added Terry.

Back to the scene at Rotherham, Stan explained: "As it happened, we didn't pay Roy Lambert or the other Rotherham players a penny, because they lost the match 4-1 and Brian Clough scored a hat-trick for Sunderland!

"The joke afterwards was that Sunderland must have 'got at' the Rotherham keeper!" laughed Stan.

Dunmore added: "I don't think Cloughie had more than three kicks of the ball in the whole game, but it was enough for him."

So it had been a fruitless journey north and only the petrol money to show for their troubles.

Stan recalls: "Dave suggested we should keep a hundred pounds each for our trouble, claiming that his car needed a new clutch. "Well, I'd had the motor for about 10 years," said Dave.

But when we got back to London we had to hand all the money back to Leslie Grade!"

When Charlton and Dunmore returned from Rotherham that Tuesday night, everyone at Orient knew that even victory in their final game, at home to Bury four days later, wouldn't necessarily guarantee them promotion along with second division champions Liverpool. Sunderland remained the only stumbling block to O's reaching the top flight for the first time in their history and although they were tied on 52 points with the East Londoners going into D-Day, they had a potentially decisive superior goal average – .039 to be precise – compared to the O's.

It meant that provided Sunderland won their last match at Swansea Town and collected two more priceless points, they would follow Liverpool up. If both them and Orient drew, the Rokermen would still be promoted in second spot.

It wasn't £800 in used readies or Dave Dunmore's Vauxhall Wyvern with the slipping clutch that was required now. To beat Bury and make those promotion dreams come true, Orient needed a fast, reliable but inexpensive MG.

What they needed more than anything else was the best MG in the business – Malcolm Graham.

Chapter 5

IT'S NOW OR NEVER
Elvis Presley, 1960

MALCOLM Graham was still in dreamland, pinching himself to check that what was happening to him really was for real, as Leyton Orient director Leslie Grade ushered him into a quiet room, away from the jubilation in the home team dressing room.

He had just scored both goals in the 2-0 victory over Bury that turned 'Cinderella' Orient into an elite club and the Yorkshireman was happiest among his team-mates, sipping glasses of champagne.

But Grade and his colleagues were eager to toast the hero who had shot their club into the football big time and Malcolm – 28-years-old at the time and now 72, admits recently from his home in Barnsley: "I had just been carried off the field on the shoulders of supporters. It was such a wonderful feeling to have scored the goals that took us up and I had tears of joy running down my cheeks after my second goal went in.

"Then Leslie Grade sat me down in the directors' room and asked: 'What do you want, Malcolm?'

Graham had been left out of the side for the previous two games, although he scotched rumours that he had asked for a transfer.

"I didn't know what to say to him, my head was still spinning with all the emotion and excitement of it all. Do you know what I eventually said to him? All I could think to say was: 'I'd like another glass of champagne, thank you!'

"Looking back now, perhaps I should have said: 'Can I have the rented clubhouse we're living in (at Buckhurst Hill) to own ourselves?' He was so elated by our success and the fact that we were going up into the first division that I think he might even have agreed to it!"

Malcolm, who now lives at Barnsley with his wife Margaret and daughters Tracy and Nicola, says he feels fitter than he has at any time in the last 15 years, when heart surgery and problems with his knee forced him to give up work before retirement age.

As we chatted and his memories of that unforgettable day rekindled the sparkle in his eyes, it is obvious that he still cherishes the events of Saturday, April 28, 1962 as much now as he did when he became the Orient promotion hero more than 44 years ago.

He was able to confirm that reports he wasn't even sure of starting that dramatic final game were untrue. "I had been in and out of the side a bit leading up to the

Bury game but I was told by Johnny Carey a few days before it that I would be playing. It wasn't just sprung on me, like they wrote in some papers."

The stocky, blond-haired Graham took the No.10 shirt at the expense of thigh injury victim Ronnie Foster in what was an otherwise unchanged team from the one that had pulled off a crucial 3-1 win at Luton five days earlier.

Despite understandable nerves and a touch of anxiety in their play, Orient didn't have to wait longer than the 14th minute to go in front and bring the first big cheer of the day from the 21,678 expectant crowd. Malcolm Lucas found Dave Dunmore drifting out towards the right wing and the centre-forward's cross was back-headed on by Derek Gibbs – the two-goal hero at Luton – for Graham to cleverly nod the ball over Bury keeper Harker and into the net.

The early goal settled O's who reproduced their usual sparkling football, with Graham and Terry McDonald both going close, while Dunmore, Gibbs and Norman Deeley were also always a threat to the Shakers' defence. Keeper Chris Harker saved Bury from a hiding.

At the other end, Orient's acclaimed defence – the bedrock of their promotion campaign – was rarely troubled. The visitors' only real moment of hope came when centre-forward Bill Calder thundered a shot that produced a spectacular one-handed save from Bill Robertson.

While all was going well at Brisbane Road, the thoughts of the Orient fans turned to events unfolding in Swansea, where Sunderland had taken the lead. If the scores remained that way in Wales, a win still wouldn't be enough for the boys in blue.

Terry McDonald says that prior to the final game, he hadn't felt optimistic that results would go Orient's way. "The pressure came on us in the last game because we felt that Sunderland would beat Swansea, who were third from bottom, so we knew we had to beat Bury to have any chance of going up. Sunderland had a good footballing side, led by Stan Anderson, who was their captain and midfielder. We only took one point from them that season, so we knew how good they were.

"All we could do was win and hope. It was a good job for us that Swansea were in relegation trouble and I think they were fighting to stay up."

Right-winger Norman Deeley added: "I'd heard that Sunderland were on a £1,000-per-man bonus to beat Swansea that day."

Energy-boosting drinks hadn't been invented then, but McDonald vaguely recalls Les Gore handing tablets to players in the dressing room prior to kick-off against

Above: We're on our way . . . Malcolm Graham is congraulated first by Terry McDonald as Norman Deeley (7) turns away in celebration after the O's take the lead against Bury.

Left: Derek Gibbs' presence in the air led to the first breakthrough goal.

Bury. They were probably glucose tablets.

"I didn't take one myself but I think one or two of the players did before kick-off. I don't remember feeling too nervous before the game, though, and we soon settled down and played our usual controlled, passing football."

Second division matches rarely featured in football radio broadcasts at that time but because the promotion race was balanced on a knife-edge, the BBC provided regular bulletins from Vetch Field.

And the one that announced Swansea's second half equaliser must have registered on the Richter scale around Leyton, E10!

At first, the buzz of excitement that quickly enveloped the ground took the players by complete surprise. Mal Lucas says: "Bury were attacking us and our crowd were cheering! It was so weird but then, all of a sudden, you realised that Swansea had scored against Sunderland."

With four minutes remaining at Brisbane Road and the O's in total control, Malcolm Graham put the seal on a very famous victory with a superb individual effort.

"I remember chasing a ball near the halfway line, a bit over towards the right wing, with Bob Stokoe, who went on to manage Sunderland. I beat him to the ball, then cut inside across the 18-yard line."

Malcolm doesn't recall the rest of the details, or dribbling wide of keeper Harker, but he remembers slamming a powerful trademark left-foot shot into the empty net to spark the wildest scenes Brisbane Road had ever seen.

As soon as the final whistle blew with the 2-0 win assured, an update from Swansea confirmed that the Swans had held on to draw 1-1 with Sunderland . . . so the O's were up!

TWIST AND SHOUT
Beatles, July 1963

Within seconds, thousands of euphoric fans had swarmed onto the pitch to mob their heroes. Stan Charlton was hoisted onto the shoulders of supporters and carried towards the dressing room. "It's a blur to me now," says Stan of that iconic scene, brilliantly encapsulated by the black-and-white photograph that appears on the back cover of this book and which also now hangs in a frame within the club's new main reception area. "It was wonderful, a very proud day for me," he says now.

Malcolm Graham was also engulfed by back-slapping fans eager to show their thanks for making their dreams come true. Depending on which reports you read, it took anything between six and eight policemen to finally prise him out of the clutches of the crowd and get him down through the players' tunnel and that celebration party in the dressing room.

Derek Gibbs, whose vital goals at Luton proved crucial leading up to the Bury game.

One by one the Orient players appeared in the directors' box to salute the fans, who had transformed the pitch into a sea of bodies. 'We Want Carey . . . We Want Carey," they chanted. Their wishes were granted when the 43-year-old manager, who had steered their team to promotion in his first season, emerged – unusually hatless – above them in the stand and waved back at them in appreciation. But, typical of Carey, he didn't milk the moment for himself. Instead, he pointed proudly towards the players around him before his balding head disappearing out of sight.

He probably had as much difficulty as the fans in believing that the miracle really had happened. After all, Carey had gone on record as saying: "Even I didn't believe we stood a chance of promotion at the beginning of the season."

In fact, when Carey first joined O's from Everton nine months earlier, he confided: "There's not a class player here. I will be satisfied if we get into the top half of the table."

Maybe he underestimated the determination and quality of the players he inherited from Les Gore – right-winger Norman Deeley, signed from Wolves in mid-February, and young inside-forward Gordon Bolland, a £5,000 buy from Chelsea who made his debut in early March, were the only two newcomers Carey added to the first team squad during the season.

Back down in the dressing room, Carey gave time to the press and pinpointed the biggest reason why promotion was achieved. "A willingness to work hard, both on and off the field. Everybody has pulled his weight," he said.

"Gradually, we began to build up the confidence of the players. And I would say this confidence is one of the main factors that helped us to get to the top. Only confident players produce their true ability."

Carey continued: "This confidence stemmed from the top where chairman Harry Zussman has proved a wonderful inspiration to everyone.

"It's unfair to pick out individuals, because our triumph was down to great team-work. But anyone will admit that our half-back line has been the best in the second division. And the drive of skipper Stan Charlton and the brilliance of Dave Dunmore in attack has prompted the lads to produce some really sparkling displays."

Carey continued to selflessly pay tribute to the other men around him who he knew deserved credit for their role in the greatest day of 'little' Leyton Orient's history. He said: "They are a wonderful bunch to work with. Trainer Les Gore, coach Eddie Baily . . . everybody in fact has played a vital role in our success. It's been team-work, team-work all the way. I am proud to be associated with this happy club."

Chairman Zussman, sporting his usual cigar and a smile as wide as the Thames, repaid the compliment from his manager. As press reporters and cameramen invaded the dressing room area, Harry opened numerous bottles of champagne, congratulated all the players and then pointed at Johnny Carey and said: "There's the man you want. We owe our success to him. He's a terrific manager."

An elated – but exhausted – Cyril Lea tries to leave the field before the mass invasion.

Bath-time celebrations after the Bury clincher. Left to right: Eddie Lewis, Bill Robertson, Malcolm Lucas, Cyril Lea, Derek Gibbs, Sid Bishop, Stan Charlton, Terry McDonald, Dave Dunmore and Malcolm Graham. Don't know where Norman Deeley got to!

Les Gore was the coolest man in the dressing room, attending to minor injuries before saying: "It's a great day for the Orient. I think the lads have performed miracles."

Ever-sporting Stan Charlton, a member of the team that had won promotion to the second division six years earlier, typically found time to remember the forgotten heroes during the post-Bury celebrations. He told reporters: "When you write your report, don't forget to mention the other players who have been in the first team – Frank George, George Wright, David Clark, Phil White, Ronnie Foster and Joe Elwood. They've all played a major part in our success."

Charlton and Carey were right, of course. O's success was all down to great team-work. But that final day of the 1961-62 season surely belonged to one man above all others.

Six years ago, the Leyton Orient Supporters' Club invited Malcolm Graham and his family down to Essex for their annual Star Man Dinner, which is always attended by several former favourites. Malcolm still remembers the reception he got and the occasion itself with great fondness and one moment in particular made him realise just what he had done all those years earlier.

Recalling that night of nostalgia at the Prince Regent Hotel, Woodford Bridge in 2000, the last time he returned to his old club, he said: "I went to the bar to buy all my family a drink when this gentleman – he would have been in his early-60s, I suppose – stopped me from handing over my money and insisted he would buy the round instead. He told me that he had in fact been the one who carried me off the Brisbane Road pitch that day after the Bury game ended, and he was telling me how much pleasure it had given him.

"It's wonderful to know that it still means so much to people at Orient."

Graham the Hero of Decisive Orient Win

By MAX MARQUIS—Leyton, Saturday

Leyton Orient 2   **Bury** 0

This game was not for the fainthearted. Every Orient player must have known that a single miskick could have cost the club promotion; every supporter suffered the double agony of watching his own team struggling against an apparently malignant fate while listening intently for the slightest snippet of news from the Swansea-Sunderland match.

Stan Charlton, the Orient captain, is swamped by jubilant fans after the victory over Bury.

BRAVO, JOHNNY CAREY

PRESS COMMENT

I won't disbelieve anything now that the little chaps (Ipswich, Leyton and Dundee in Scotland) have beaten off the £ symbols of soccer and proved that this is a team game and that you can buy the best player in the world and still not succeed if the team's heart is not in the right place.

Brian Scovell, Daily Mail

Match-winner Malcolm Graham wept, chairman Harry Zussman smoked a foot-long cigar, impresario Bernard Delfont gasped "Show-bizness was never like this." And Johnny Carey said thoughtfully: "Yes, you could say I am pleased."

Peter Lorenzo, Daily Herald

The memory that will stick most in my mind is of Orient supporters leaping high in the air as the news broke that Swansea had equalised against Sunderland.

Norman Giller, The Express

MIRACLE DAY
Ipswich champs—Orient join toffs

WELL—they've done it! Ipswich, the team nobody gave a dog's

★ VERDICT by Maurice Smith ★

that I, doesn't stand for Learner, believe me, you members of the First Division.

WONDERFUL LAND
The Shadows, 1962

SPRING 1962 was a great time for everyone associated with LOFC – not just the first team promotion heroes.

In a week that saw the completion of a terrific treble, the 'A' team clinched the Seanglian League title while the Reserves made sure of winning the midweek Combination League championship by drawing with Coventry City, two days after the Bury promotion-clincher.

They would meet star-studded Spurs – winners of the Saturday reserve section – to decide the overall Combination League champions in a one-off match at Brisbane Road the following October.

The Reserve team regulars in 1961-62 were: Albert Cochran, George Wright, Jeff Harris, Ken Facey, Dave Clark, Alan Russell, Derek Gibbs, Billy Taylor, Mike Hollow, leading scorer Harry Gregory, Joe Elwood and Roger Wedge.

Others who appeared were: Dennis Sorrell, Ron Newman, Len Cheesewright, K. Carter, A. Gilbert, R. Deeks, D. Harris, C. Wilkinson, G. York, J. Smith, B. Smith, T. Hopkins, R. Dinnis, D. Nagle. K. Craydon, C. Pritchard and A. Sharplin.

Orient also beat Ashford Town, 3-1, to win the Seanglian League Cup, while a 4-1 success over Spurs added the Winchester Cup to the O's trophy sideboard.

Youth team players who featured included: L. Hutley, J. Briggs, J. Coppin, G. Gasgoine, Michael Thompson, B. Fitter, D. Sykes, Terry Price, J. Albaster, W. Lampshire.

Young pro's Roger Wedge (4 goals) and Harry Gregory (3) led the team to a 14-2 FA Youth Cup, first round thrashing of Crittals Athletic.

GRAHAM MAKES IT UP THE O'S

Leyton Orient 2   Bury 0

MARCONI'S first-ever wireless message could hardly have caused more excitement than the second half news which reached the Leyton terraces, by way of transistor sets all over the ground, that Swansea had equal-

Chapter 6

YOUNG ONES
Cliff Richard, January 1962

Chart-topper Cliff Richard was part of the Orient scene.

IMAGINE if Robbie Williams had turned up in Leyton to join Martin Ling and the lads at their promotion party in May 2006! What, you didn't notice him there?

As we know, it's only the so-called 'glamour clubs', like Chelsea, Manchester United and Arsenal, who attract A-list celebrities today (quite frankly, who needs these hangers-on anyway?).

But in May 1962, when newly-promoted Leyton Orient were the toast of London football, Brisbane Road was *the* place to be for a number of leading stars from the world of pop, screen and stage.

Cliff Richard, who had another massive number one hit for six weeks with *Young Ones* a few months earlier, was the big name celebrity guest at the Leyton Town Hall, where the players, management and supporters of his favourite club were celebrating its finest achievement with local dignitaries.

Cliff, who had emulated Elvis Presley as the biggest selling pop artist in the UK that year, was singing and dancing among the players, their wives and girlfriends, as well as with joyous fans.

Harry Gregory remembers Cliff attending the end-of-season celebration bash. "My wife, Carol, was with me and Cliff was her idol at the time!"

The amazing thing is, it really wasn't such a big deal for megastars like Cliff (and his group The Shadows, who also had two No.1 hits in 1962), Arthur Askey and other well known celebs to be seen fairly regularly at the Orient, even in the club's second division days.

It would be nice to think that they were attracted along by the skill of Dunmore, the midfield dynamism of Lea and Lucas or the defensive resilience of Bishop. But the fact is, they came along as guests of Orient board directors, Bernard Delfont and Leslie Grade, the younger brothers of Lew Grade and a famous family steeped in showbiz history. They became very successful and wealthy big players in the entertainment industry, although none of them ever forgot his East London roots.

It's perhaps worth considering just how influential and well connected these two Leyton Orient directors were, as well as the effect they had on the players who Leslie and Bernard would later come to treat like their own stars . . .

The Grade brothers – Lew, Leslie and Bernard Delfont.

Bernard Delfont was born Boris Winogradsky on September 5, 1909 in Tokmak, a small town in the Crimea. In 1912 the Winogradsky family left Russia and settled in the East End of London. He left school at the age of 12 and followed his brother Louis – who had made a name for himself in Charleston dancing competitions as Lew Grade – into the music halls.

At this point he changed his surname to Delfont to avoid confusion with his brother. He formed a double act with comic Hal Monty, billing themselves as The Delfont Boys. In 1937, Delfont gave his last appearance as a dancer at the Chiswick Empire and followed his brother Lew into business as an agent and impresario.

In 1949 he started in theatrical management and acquired a series of theatres in the West End. He took over the London Casino and presented such stars as Lena Horne, The Inkspots, and Laurel and Hardy. He joined forces with the impresario Val Parnell and as a result was able to buy the lease on the Prince of Wales Theatre and to stage many of his shows at The Palladium.

His second experience with television came as a stage producer when he was asked to cast the BBC summer season variety show *Carefree*, with music by Eric Robinson and his Orchestra, for producer Richard Afton.

Within months of the launch of ITV, the Saturday evening variety showcase *Bernard Delfont Presents* (ITV, 1956-58) premiered under Lew's ATV production banner. The song and dance show *Young and Foolish*, a Val Parnell and Bernard Delfont Presents production (ITV, 1956) for ATV, followed. Then, starting in 1959, came *Bernard Delfont's Sunday Show* (ITV, 1959-62), a summer season variety spectacular bridging the gap between seasons of Parnell's *Sunday Night at the London Palladium*. Delfont's on-stage performers ranged from popsters Adam Faith and Tommy Steele to a troupe of Bengal tigers (the latter courtesy of Chipperfield's Circus).

Although *The Royal Variety Performance* had been staged for over 40 years, it wasn't until 1960 that it was allowed to be televised; the theatre owners being nervous that too much exposure would deter audiences from going to see live variety. Soon to become the major TV event to be associated with Delfont, the first *Royal Variety Performance* (aka *The Royal Variety Show*) was presented on Sunday May 22, 1960 across the entire ITV network. The two-and-a-half-hour production, under Jack Hylton, starred comedians Harry Worth, Charlie Drake and Benny Hill, pop singers Cliff Richard and Adam Faith, American actor Robert Horton (co-star of popular western series *Wagon Train*), and the flamboyant pianist Liberace, among the 60 or so top-line entertainers.

The following year, the second TV production of *The Royal Variety Performance* was presented by Delfont, under his 'personal supervision', and featured quintessential Frenchman Maurice Chevalier and American performers Jack Benny, George Burns, and Sammy Davis Jr., among the large cluster of international celebrities. Following the second televised show, the annual presentation alternated between the BBC and ITV, and always made the top TV ratings.

Delfont was also instrumental in getting the comedy duo of Eric Morecambe and Ernie Wise started with their first ITV series, *The Morecambe and Wise Show* (1961-68; aka *Two of a Kind*).

Meanwhile, eldest brother Lew Grade's ATV (the largest ITV franchise) had proved a great success. He became associated with immortal names like *The Muppets, Jesus of Nazareth*, the soap series *Crossroads, The Saint, Persuaders, The Prisoner, The Champions, George and Mildred* and Gerry Anderson's puppet hit *Thunderbirds*. His ITC (Independent Television Corporation) production subsidiary brought him international acclaim and a passage into the movie world, where his company produced the box office blockbuster *Return of the Pink Panther*, plus *On Golden Pond* and *Sophie's Choice*.

Lew and Leslie Grade – the youngest of the three brothers, who had been discharged from the army after contracting typhoid while stationed in North Africa – formed their agency, Lew and Leslie Grade Ltd, in 1951. The company had offices in London, New York and California and as well as controlling the largest UK agencies for actors, writers and directors, they also represented variety artists and music performers like Tom Jones, Lulu and The Animals, in addition to overseas stars like Frank Sinatra and Judy Garland.

In the 60s business soared and Bernard Delfont established himself as the country's leading theatrical impresario. With Lew now one of the most powerful figures in British television and Leslie running the country's biggest agency (booking other big stars such as Laurence Olivier, John Gielgud, Ralph Richardson, Abbott and Costello, Jack Benny, Dorothy Lamour and comedians Arthur Askey, Bob Hope and Danny Kaye), the brothers had the most powerful grip on British showbusiness in all forms.

To the public Bernard will probably be remembered best as the smart gentleman who always greeted The Queen as she stepped out of her car on to the steps of The London Palladium for *The Royal Variety Performance*.

Leslie Grade, in particular, became a Leyton Orient fanatic and as well as attending all home matches, he would also accompany O's chairman Harry Zussman to most away games. He got to know the players well and became a very popular figure at the club, treating the team to the best seats at the Royal Variety Command Performances and many other West End shows with which his family were associated. Grade and Delfont were massive names in the world of entertainment. They were mixing with Frank Sinatra and Cliff Richard – they didn't need to concern themselves with the fortunes of Johnny Carey's men. There were no TV cameras at Brisbane Road for them to pose in front of. Celebrities hadn't yet attached themselves to football clubs then, as they are prone to do today.

Terry McDonald backs up the point when he says: "It didn't seem a big thing to us to see different celebrities at home matches and it wasn't as if they were there to impress us. There was no big fuss made about meeting these big stars – the Orient directors would just bring them along from time to time and introduce us to them. There was no hype at all – we got used to seeing big-name personalities around.

"Leslie Grade was great with us and looked after us all very well. We could have gone to see *Sunday Night at the London Palladium* every week if we'd wanted to. They paid for us to see Frank Sinatra in concert as well as the comedian, Tommy Cooper, who was one of my personal favourites."

"You couldn't get tickets to see Sinatra in his prime for love nor money," added Cyril Lea.

Sid Bishop talked about the special relationship that existed between the players and its most high profile directors at that time. He said: "They would come into the dressing room before the game and say: 'All the very best, lads'.

"Leslie Grade and Bernard Delfont were at the ground quite a lot and once we got to know them well enough, we used to go and get togged-out and were given free tickets to top West End shows. People would cut a vein in their arm to get tickets for shows like *The Royal Variety Performance* – we went about four or five times.

"I was in high spirits in the dressing room before one game when I turned to Les Grade and jokingly said: 'Do we *have* to go to that bloody show again this year?' He said: 'Bernard, Bernard, listen to this saucy bugger!' It was all said and taken in good spirit.

'Hello Playmates!' . . . Arthur Askey would whip the lads into shape before a game.

"We only really saw the directors on matchdays, when were all a bit hyped up. They would come into the dressing room before a game and again afterwards, especially if we'd won. It seemed normal to me."

Bishop confirms that whilst Grade and Delfont were proud to be associated with Orient, they only ever had the club's best interests at heart and never tried to interfere in the football side of things. They never got ideas above their station. The lesser known directors on the board with Zussman, Grade and Delfont were Charles Bent-Marshall, Frank Harris, Arthur Page and H. Lea.

"I never thought that they ever tried to tell our chairman or the manager what to do or which players to pick – nothing like that," says the long-serving O's centre-back.

A popular comedian like Askey, apart from appearing on the pitch with his trademark long whip and helping to control the crowd at the big Burnley Cup tie, also brought a diversionary humour to the dressing room that helped to relax the players before matches. It was a practice that manager Johnny Carey did nothing to discourage.

McDonald says: "Askey would come into the dressing room sometimes to give us a gee-up before a big game. In his own way, he'd say: 'Now don't forget, lads . . . be busy, busy bees!' "

Bishop recalls meeting Askey in the comedian's own environment. "We were playing up at Liverpool and went to see him perform at a local theatre," says Sid. "We met him in the bar and I can remember it causing riotous laughter when little

Arf' went to stand up on the foot-rail, along the front of the bar, and slipped off it!

"Another time, Eddie Brown, myself and our wives went to see him perform in a show at the Brixton Empress. Afterwards, he invited us to his dressing room, where he pulled down a large padlocked suitcase from the top of his wardrobe and produced a bottle from it. It was his drinks cabinet!

"He offered us all a drink and he was laughing as he explained: 'You can't trust the cleaners here!'.

"Arthur never talked football, though. He preferred to talk about showbiz."

Dave Dunmore once shared a taxi with Askey. "He'd got into a cab with me and another player when we were playing at Cardiff – I don't know whether something had happened to our coach or what – but as we were going along the road he came out with his trademark 'Hello Playmates!' line.

"Norman Vaughan and Helen Shapiro were also at the ground when we won promotion," added Dave.

Stan Charlton recalls: "There were always big name showbiz stars around the club, including Cliff Richard, Norman Vaughan and Pat Boone. A few weeks after Pat had been to the ground and returned to America, he arranged for 17 hats – like the kind he usually wore – to be sent to the ground, where we were all pictured wearing them, along with our club blazers, in front of the main stand."

Young striker Harry Gregory said: "Mike and Bernie Winters also came to the club and I had my photo taken with Norman Vaughan. I was present with a few of the other players when he filmed the Cadbury's Roses TV commercial – 'Rosie's grown on you!' – at the Orient ground."

Stan Charlton continued: "The directors paid for all the players and our wives to attend the *Royal Command Performance* in the West End and during the interval Arthur Askey bought us all a round of drinks.

"The free tickets to all the shows were great – but it cost us a fortune to hire the fancy dinner suits!"

Phil White could sometimes make his team-mates laugh even without trying. His good friend, Terry McDonald recalls that the tricky right-winger wasn't always as enthusiastic as his team-mates about the offer of regular free tickets to enjoy the biggest shows 'up West'.

"We were all given free tickets to take our wives to see the Royal Command Performance but we had to hire dress suits to wear for this special occasion. But Whitey told Les Gore that he didn't want to go – he complained that he'd have to spend a fiver hiring a black suit from Moss Bros.

"Phil did eventually agree go to the show and, what's more, he turned up wearing the lot – including a white silk scarf and black patent shoes. He looked like George Raft! Most of us didn't bother to wear our the silk scarves but Phil made us all laugh when he pointed out that as he'd spent so much hiring the gear, he had to wear it all!"

NIGHT TRAIN

James Brown, 1962

Apart from his genuine passion for Leyton Orient, Leslie Grade was also a very generous man. Although he mixed in very high social circles through work, he was never aloof and was given to bizarre and unexpected acts of generosity that the O's players warmly appreciated and still fondly remember to this day..

Malcolm Lucas recalled the trip to Derby County in January 1962 – and not just for O's 2-1 victory courtesy of goals by Dave Dunmore and Malcolm Graham. Lucas said: "We were travelling up to Derby by train and Les Grade was wearing one of those reversible cardigans that he'd just bought – it was fantastic looking. Off the cuff, I just said to him: 'That's a very nice cardigan, Mr Grade.

"He said: 'Do you like it, Malcolm?'

"I said: 'I do.'

"He continued: 'If we win today, you can have it.'

"I told him that I hadn't meant to give him the impression that I wanted him to give me his cardigan – I was just admiring it and nothing else was said about it before the game. Anyway, we played the game and won it – Malcolm Graham got the winner.

"We were all back on the train and on our homeward journey when Mr. Grade came along to where I was sitting and gave me his wonderful cardigan. I told him I'd only been joking with him before, but he insisted: 'It's yours.'

"It was brand new – lemon coloured on one side and light blue on the reverse. I never wore it to the club – I kept it for important social do's – but it was a wonderful gesture by him and so typical of the man."

Phil White also benefited from Leslie Grade's generosity in a similar way to Mal Lucas. Terry McDonald said: "Similar to what happened to Malcolm with his cardigan, we were travelling up to Scunthorpe and Leslie Grade told Phil that if he scored that day, he would give him his smart, new Crombie overcoat. Whitey did score and on the train home afterwards he was well pleased to accept the coat as his reward."

Promotion hero Malcolm Graham added that some Orient players would occasionally visit Aquascutum's flagship store in Regent Street, renowed for their detailed tailoring and classic trench coats (one of these would set you back around £600 today and was an upmarket designer label before there was such a thing) . . . and everything they picked was put on Leslie Grade's account.

"We would go up to the West End and try on all sorts of nice suits and coats. If we wanted anything, it was all simply added to Leslie Grade's account that he had with the shop. It was great, we didn't have to pay for a thing," says Malcolm.

Bernard Delfont (who became an Orient director in 1961) and Leslie Grade resigned from the Leyton Orient board in 1967 but youngest brother Leslie remained a good friend to the players who had given him such pleasure on the field in the early 60s, long after he and they had left the club.

Eddie Lewis, who became a top coach after he emigrated to South Africa in the 70s, said: "I used to get on ever so well with Leslie. He came to me one day and said: 'You've got two beautiful daughters, so can I give you these clothes I bought in America?' He'd bought them for his daughters but they didn't fit. They were the most beautiful dresses and suits you could wish to see.

"Anyway, we got chatting and I was saying to him how fed up I was with the English weather and that I needed to find some sunshine in my life. He suggested that I should try South Africa and said that he would 'sponsor' me for a job there.

"He wrote to a mate of his in Johannesburg, who ran 50 cinemas, but Leslie's friend told me that Jo'burg was too big and that he'd get me an insurance job on the coast in East London instead."

Goalkeeper Frank George recalled a fleeting sight of a rapidly aging Leslie Grade while he was in central London one day delivering, long after his playing days were over. Frank said: "After I packed up football I worked self-employed for a mate delivering parcels for a print finishing company. Leslie had an office in central London and I'd parked my 35 hundred-weight van just down the road from where he was standing. I noticed Leslie just as he getting into a car a little way up the road.

"He was very old by then and I wasn't 100 percent sure it was actually him I'd seen. His car pulled away before I had the chance to say anything to him, but I spoke to a woman who was waving Leslie on his way. She confirmed that it definitely was him.

"I explained to her that I'd known Leslie many years before, from his previous involvement with Leyton Orient, and she suggested that the next time I was around that way I should call in to his office for a chat. 'He'd be absolutely delighted to see you again,' she told me.

"So the next time I was working in that part of London, some two months later, I went into Leslie's office to say 'hello' to him. But I couldn't. The woman I'd spoken to on the day I'd last seen Leslie told me the news that he'd died a couple of weeks earlier, which was really sad. He was a lovely man."

Leslie Grade served as a director on the Leyton Orient board from 1959 until 1967. A year before his departure, when the club was on the brink of closure and it held its famous 'bucket collection' among supporters, Leslie gave a further £5,000 of his own money to help save the club he loved.

Leslie Grade suffered a major stroke, which disrupted his career in middle age and he died in 1979. His elder brother, Bernard Delfont, who was knighted in 1974 and two years later was made Baron of Stepney, died on July 28, 1994. Lew Grade, who was rarely seen at the Orient, was knighted in 1969 and in 1976 was made a life peer. He died on December 14, 1998.

However, football remains important to members of the famous Grade family. Leslie's son, Michael, regularly attended Leyton Orient home matches with his father in the early 60s, before he began working as a trainee sports reporter for the *Daily Mirror* in 1960. Six years later he joined the family theatrical agency founded by his father and uncle and progressed into television – initially as an executive at

Chairman Harry Zussman (centre) with (left to right) secretary George Hicks, manager Johnny Carey, trainer Les Gore and Leslie Grade.

London Weekend Television in 1973 and then as Controller of BBC ONE in 1984.

In 1988 he went to Channel Four as chief executive and remained in that post until 1997, when he joined First Leisure Corporation. A year later he was awarded the CBE.

Michael, now 63-years-old, was appointed Chairman of the BBC in May 2004. He is also a director of Charlton Athletic.

Chapter 7

SUMMER HOLIDAY
Cliff Richard, 1963

GAINING promotion to the first division was never going to be a life-changing experience for the players of Leyton Orient in the summer of '62 but they were still handsomely rewarded for their achievement.

Remember Harry Zussman's bold promise on the tour of Jersey a year earlier? He told the players: "Win promotion and we'll pay for you and your families to have a week's holiday in Majorca!"

Whether it was a tongue-in-cheek offer or he genuinely believed then that his team could transform itself from second division strugglers into first division hopefuls, he didn't care. After their annual end-of-season tour to Holland, where they played a few friendlies in Deventer, they returned to London to pack their suitcases and sun-tan lotions.

On the players' part, they appreciated how well they were being looked after by the club's most prominent and charismatic directors. Leading scorer Dave Dunmore acknowledged: "For the players to be able to take our families out to Majorca in 1962 was brilliant and I don't know if any other clubs of Orient's size would have done that at the time?"

After attending the LOFC Supporters' Club annual dinner-and-dance at Plantation House in Bishopsgate on May 12, then dancing to teen idol Cliff Richard at the Leyton Borough Council civic reception at the Town Hall two days later, the players and their wives and young children were ready to sample the sangria and soak up the sun beckoning on the Spanish holiday isle.

Well, all except Malcolm Lucas. It wasn't his imminent wedding to fiancée Jenny that kept him from joining his Orient team-mates on their reward holiday. His recent success in breaking into the full Wales team had come at a price, as he explained: "I couldn't go to Majorca because I had to join the Welsh squad for their South American tour of Brazil and Mexico (where I roomed with the legendary John Charles).

"I knew I was going with the Welsh party before we clinched promotion and I was disappointed to miss out on the camaraderie of being with all the other lads.

"But the most disappointing thing to me is that we won promotion to the highest division of English football and yet we received nothing from the Football League to recognise our achievement in finishing second to Liverpool. There was no medal or little memento for the players like there is now.

"Today, a team can finish sixth in their division, win the play-off final and get a

Some players with their wives and children on the beach in Majorca, May 1962. That looks like Dave Dunmore, Norman Deeley, Eddie Lewis, Stan Charlton and Malcolm Graham at the back.

trophy and medals for doing so.

"We had our end-of-season dinner with the supporters but knowing that I wouldn't be going to Majorca with the rest of the Orient players left me feeling a little bit sad really. A medal would have been a nice pick-me-up."

Still, there was a consolation due.

Before flying out to Majorca, the upbeat mood of the players had been further boosted by the payment of promotion bonuses, based on each players' appearance record during the 1961-62 season. With Sid Bishop and Cyril Lea having appeared in all 42 league games, and full-backs Stan Charlton and Eddie Lewis missing only one match apiece, the Orient board had a bit to cough up as the players took it in turns to collect their envelopes from club secretary George Hicks' office before enjoying their summer holiday treat.

Eddie Lewis said: "Harry Zussman and Leslie Grade were both great. They promised us all a bonus if we won promotion. Some time before the end of that season they came to Stan Charlton and me and asked what we thought about them offering the players an incentive to get the club promoted.

"We said 'great' and at the next training session after we'd won promotion, we all got an envelope with money in it. I received five hundred pounds, which was a lot in those days, but I don't think Johnny Carey thought the players should have been given a cash incentive to go up. He was against it but we got paid out by the club anyway."

Malcolm Graham backed up Lewis' take on Carey's reluctance to lavish too much on the promotion team.

"Johnny Carey was a bit of a disciplinarian in that way," says Malcolm, "and I

After firing O's to the first division with 22 goals, Dave Dunmore deserved a rest. DD and Big Bill Robertson seen relaxing with their wives in Majorca.

think the directors might have rewarded us even more had he not put them off doing so."

Lewis added: "I think Carey's reward for taking us up was to be given a brand new 105 Rover car by the directors."

Terry McDonald said: "In the build-up to the Bury game, there was no talk among the players of us going away to Majorca a few weeks later if we won promotion. We were focused on winning that game and nothing else came into our minds. Thoughts of going abroad came afterwards, when we went to collect our bonuses.

"We were paid so much per game, based on our number of first team appearances, and it was also dependent on us winning promotion. I played 36 games and I think I got something like between four and five hundred pounds. We were on about £30 per week then, so that was still a lot of money. I can't remember what I spent mine on, or if we went somewhere to celebrate, although I suppose we must have gone somewhere.

"We all collected a brown envelope each from the main office, or what we used to call the 'Little House on the Prairie', which was situated on the corner of Brisbane Road and which later became the supporters' club bar. George Hicks handled the pay-out."

Terry McDonald (far left) has been to get the ball while the others wait on the beach in Majorca. Phil White (far right) must have been expecting colder weather, but Malcolm Graham, Johnny Carey, Bill Robertson and Eddie Lewis have come prepared in their swimming trunks.

Like most smaller Football League clubs, Leyton Orient has known more than its share of financial hardship throughout its turbulent existence – and no-one was more acutely aware of those struggles during the 50s and 60s than Stan Charlton. The stalwart full-back remembers when money was a stumbling block to a big move he was poised to make in the mid-50s.

He said: "In 1955 I'd been on the verge of going to Spurs for a transfer fee of £15,000 but because the Orient still owed Tottenham 11 grand on a previous purchase of Billy Rees, I had to stay and they signed Maurice Norman instead. Alec Stock, who was our manager at the time, reassured me by saying: 'Don't worry, I'll find you a better club than Tottenham!'

Stan eventually moved to Arsenal instead, although he returned three years later, in December 1958, and ended up playing a total of 408 games in two spells for the O's.

As captain, he would naturally have a better feel for the state of the club's finances than anybody else on the playing staff. In the programme for the home clash with Swansea Town on Boxing Day, the club reported it was losing in the region of £300 a week on average home gates of 11,000, which they claimed was around 4,000 fans short of the break-even attendance figure. This, despite the O's holding second position behind Liverpool in the promotion race.

Charlton said: "I once approached Johnny Carey about money, on behalf of the players who wanted to know if they could have an increase. He invited me into his office at the ground, where he opened the club's account books to show me the state of the financial plight. It soon became clear to me that Leyton Orient was operating in the red and there was no money available to pay the players any more than we were getting at the time.

"The club was so hard up at one stage, they told the players that we couldn't draw our money out of the bank until the following Monday, when Harry Zussman paid us out of his own pocket. The directors did well to keep the club going the way they did.

"I remember us drawing 1-1 at Newcastle in the League Cup, when Jim Iley scored for them from a penalty. Frank George had been carried off injured, so I replaced him in goal and faced the penalty, about two minutes from the end. I managed to get my fingertips to the shot, touching it onto the post, but the ball just rolled over the line.

"Zussman said to me afterwards: 'Thank Christ you didn't save it – we need the money from the replay!' I was sick that I hadn't managed to keep out the penalty but all Harry was thinking about was the replay revenue.

"The players would have been happy with £50 per week, even though we knew that Everton were paying their boys between £200 and £300 a week at that time. It was said that Alex Young paid as much as £100 in tax, which goes to show just how much he was on!

"When the players' maximum wage was lifted, our pay went up up by only £10 a week. As well as our basic weekly wage, we could earn an extra £1 per thousand supporters based on the attendance figure. There was also a bit extra depending on our league position, although, to be honest, the players were better off financially in the second division than we were in the first division!

"The most I earned throughout my time at Orient was £43 10s per week, just before I left in 1965. I didn't earn much money from the game but I played for the love of football and got so much enjoyment from it."

Dave Dunmore echoed Stan's thoughts when he added: "What we were paid never bothered me. I could always have done with more, but who couldn't?"

Phil White was one of those – like fellow wingers Terry McDonald and Norman Deeley – who loved to gamble on the horses and dogs, so always seemed to pay careful attention to his weekly budget, as Carey once discovered.

McDonald explained: "Our wages used to be paid on a weekly basis and we'd collect a brown envelope, with our pay slip in it, from George Hicks' office.

"One day Carey came in and sat us all down in the dressing room to explain a change of club procedure. He said: 'From now on, you've all got to open a personal account at the local Nat-West bank across the road in Leyton High Road, because your wages will be paid directly into there.' He then added: 'Now does anybody have any objections to that?'

"Phil immediately stuck his hand up. 'Yeah, me,' he says.

"Carey said: 'What's the problem, Phil?'

"So Whitey says: 'What I can't understand is why you've got to pay our wages *into* the bank, if we've then got to go over there and draw them all out again? And we've also got to pay charges on it.'

"Carey (looking a bit exasperated) replied: 'But Phil, you don't *have* to take it all out.'

"Phil must have thought about how hard he was finding it getting by on £20-a-week, so he finished off by saying to Carey: 'I bet I have!'

"It was a classic scene and yet another occasion where Whitey made us all fall about laughing."

Frank George also had an amusing Phil White story that revolved around the players' earnings. Frank recalled: "Until the maximum wage was lifted, I was on £15 a week. Then there were seven of us who got an increase to £25 a week while the rest were on £20 at that time.

"One day I was in the café near the Orient ground with Phil, having a bit of grub, when he suddenly said to me: 'I know the names of six of the players who are on the top wages at the club but, for the life of me, I don't know who the seventh is.'

"I said: 'Oh, don't you? If you think about it, you might come to the correct conclusion.'

"He just couldn't think who it could be, as he thought long and hard and continued sucking away on an ice lolly. He asked me if I'd given any thought to who the seventh 'big earner' might be. In the end I couldn't stand it any longer, so I told Phil: 'Well, it happens to be *me!*'

"He was so shocked when I confirmed that I was, in fact, the seventh player on £25-a-week that he nearly swallowed the rest of his ice lolly in one! And when we got back to the ground after lunch, he then told everybody else about what we'd discussed. Phil was so funny, though," laughs Frank.

Harry Zussman had become a wealthy man through his shoe business empire in Shoreditch, East London – "he named the company, Delia Shoes, after his daughter," says Sid Bishop – and no-one should be in any doubt that his financial clout and generosity did much to help the Orient through tough times.

The Jewish businessman was a larger-than-life character with a penchant for big cigars and he was rarely seen without a hat. On the day Orient gained promotion, he kept repeating the phrase: 'It's wonderful, it's wonderful, I'm so happy.'

Stan Charlton recalls an incident that suggests Zussman appreciated the diehard fans just as much as his players. "An Orient fan cycled all the way to Anfield to see us lose 5-0 against Liverpool," says Stan, "and I think it took him three days to get there!

"When the players heard about the fan's efforts, we had a whip-round among the lads after the game to raise the money for his train fare home. In the end, Harry Zussman said the club would pay for him."

But the directors were always happy to be in the company of the players and vice-versa. Charlton added: "After we came back from a game at Leicester one night, Harry Zussman and Leslie Grade were unable to get a taxi, so I drove them both home to Hampstead Heath."

Terry McDonald remembers sharing a cab with another long-term club director, Arthur Page, who was on the board at the same time as Zussman and Grade and took over the chairmanship after Harry stood down in 1967. He said: "For some reason that I can't recall, I once found myself sharing a cab with Arthur Page to Woodford – I think we might have been returning from an away game – and all he did was keep pumping me for information about the running of the club, other players and who got on with who. I had the uncomfortable feeling that he was trying to trip me up with his questions."

For all Zussman's flamboyance, though, McDonald recalls a more sombre occasion when the chairman's usual jovial persona slipped. He said: "Harry Zussman and Leslie Grade were almost always so lively and very upbeat, but I recall one time when Harry was very down.

"We had lost badly somewhere – I thought it was at Portsmouth, but it may have been Ipswich? – in the season before we were promoted, and I'll never forget Harry coming into the dressing room after that match and what he said to us. He had tears in his eyes as he sat us all down and said: 'You will send me to the grave, you're breaking my heart.'

"The directors never put the players under any pressure to get results. It must have really got to him, though, to think that we looked like sinking into the Third Division.

"But after that weekend, while were were third or fourth from bottom, he made a promise to us that if we got ourselves out of relegation trouble, the club would pay for the players and their families to go on holiday to Jersey at the end of that season. Whether that inspired us, I don't know, but things got better. I think Harry's words did possibly have an effect on us. Because we all thought that he *was* Orient, we all owed him something.

"That was a big turning point and the trip to Jersey definitely bonded us as a team in readiness for the promotion season."

The relationship Harry Zussman and Leslie Grade, in particular, had with the players at Orient can rarely have been replicated at any football club, either before or since. To most players, football club directors are a necessary evil, viewed as 'suits' who are to be tolerated but not liked. On the other hand, it's probably fair to assume that the modern-day chairmen and chief executives who live with the day-to-day pressure of running a club see their many of their players as greedy, money-grabbing individuals who care nothing for the club and are simply out to get all they can from their lucrative deals. This is especially true at Premiership level.

Malcolm Lucas said: "The directors at Orient were fantastic people and would do little things to make you feel a bit more special I suppose.

"Harry was very jovial, a lovely fella, and I never remember him saying a word out of turn to the players."

Goalkeeper Mike Pinner, who made his debut during the first division season, said: "It was the friendliest club I've even been with and that was partly down to the fact that the directors mixed with the players on all the away trips – and I'd never known that. Harry Zussman was a lovely man.

"Les Grade was probably the most nervous person I've ever seen. He was more or less chain-smoking going up and down the train carriage to and from our away matches."

Pinner's fellow keeper Frank George also appreciated the special rapport between Zussman, Grade and the players, even when the champagne wasn't flowing. He added: "Win, draw or lose, Harry always came out afterwards with some money – a few quid to go and enjoy ourselves with. In other words, 'go and have a pint of beer on me.' It might have given us only £20, but that was quite a lot of money then."

It has to be said that while the Orient players of the early 60s earned a pittance compared to the mega-millions paid to even the most average top flight players today (and, as Barry Hearn will no doubt confirm, they're not doing too badly way down the lower divisions either!), those promotion heroes were still earning significantly more than the average working class man who supported them from the terraces. It's all relative.

Perhaps, though, the players back then appreciated what they had much more and were more grateful for what they earned and knew the value of money more. In fact, players would take on additional work in the summer to supplement their contracted earnings from the club, which were slightly reduced in the close season.

Terry McDonald says: "Looking back to when I first joined Orient in 1959, the amazing thing is that you only ever signed on for one year at a time. And when you got that envelope through your letterbox saying that you'd been retained by the club, it was a very big relief.

"Nowadays, even useless players want four or five-year contracts and then f*** off after two on a get-out clause. and I just can't relate to that.

"To think that great, long-serving pro's like Stan (Charlton) had to wait for an envelope to see whether or not they'd been retained . . . it was ridiculous really. OK, so the top players probably knew they would be kept on when they were at their peak, but they never had the option of saying : 'Ok, I'll stay on here for the next three years.'

"And the insecurity was increased by the fact that many of these players were living in club houses and paying Orient rent on them. They could have easily found themselves out of work within a year and sweeping the roads!

"In the summer weeks, the players would work elsewhere to earn extra money. Actually, we were better off for eight weeks in the summer than we were in the playing season, because we had two incomes. We got paid £5 less a week than usual by Orient during the summer – but I used to earn a tenner or £15-a-week cutting lawns and clearing up at the City of London Cemetery in Manor Park. I worked there with Ronnie Foster, Ken Facey, Dennis Sorrell and Eddie Baily – and Baily had played for England! Can you believe that! When I was at West Ham as a youth, Johnny Dick helped lay their red running track round the pitch at Upton Park . . .

Jean and Terry McDonald at home in the early 60s. Mum was a great cook.

and he'd just finished the season as the club's top scorer in the first division!

"Harry Gregory, who was younger than the rest of us, also later worked at City of London Cemetery outside the football season.

"Other players, like Sid Bishop, actually did summer work at the club itself, helping to build the new extension to the main stand or repair the terraces."

You can't imagine Thierry Henry played much of an active role in the construction of the Emirates Stadium, or Wayne Rooney going up a crane to help fit even more new seats into the latest extension to Old Trafford, can you?

Nowadays, it is drummed into players that they must only eat certain foods before and immediately after games. The players of the early 60s still had their rituals and routines but their dietary requirements were not monitored like they are with today's players, who have fitness gurus and nutritionists crawling all over them.

McDonald recalled his pre-match eating routine: "If we were playing at home, at around midday I'd usually eat either chicken and toast or a small fillet steak and toast. I'd eat that three hours before a match.

"Now we've all since learned that it takes 12 hours to fully digest a steak, so that was totally wrong and clubs wouldn't dream of giving steak to their players for a pre-match meal. But boiled chicken was the main meal for most players in my day.

"Or if we were playing at 7.30 in the evening, I'd have a couple of poached eggs on toast a few hours earlier.

"The club basically left it up to the players, but we all more or less ate the same things. There were no rules as such, although I remember when we were on tour in Holland once and Johnny Carey asked for a meal of chicken and rice to be served for the players at the hotel, shortly before we played a team called Go Ahead. The waiters brought us a whole chicken each, so Carey stepped in and said: 'You're not eating all that!'

"The club obviously didn't expect any of us to go out and drink alcohol on a Friday, or the night before any game. Having said that, Tommy Johnston used to have his usual four pints of Mackeson-and-mild in the Monkhams Arms at Woodford on a Friday night. That was his regular drink.

"If we were playing away, Tommy would go out and have his usual few pints in a pub or in the hotel bar, but that's all he ever wanted – he wasn't interested in women. He'd have his drink and be back at the hotel in bed by 10.30pm.

"Our crowd – Stan Charlton, Dave Dunmore and me – we'd check into the hotel by seven and be washed, changed and out by eight. But then again, we'd all be back at the hotel by 11pm. We'd only have three or four pints and would never abuse it.

"We never got back in late or had any disciplinary problems with the manager. I can't remember any trouble of that kind. No-one would take liberties with Stan – we all respected him too much to let him or the club down."

It all came down to trust. Players back then were treated like adults and, almost without exception, behaved as such. Of course, there were no papparazi or 'gutter press' lurking to capture any indiscretions, although that doesn't mean to say that these Leyton Orient players didn't know how to enjoy themselves and let their hair down at the appropriate time.

Turning to the social scene within the club, McDonald admits: "There were little cliques, or semi-cliques, but it wasn't anything like as bad as that might sound. It's just a case of tending to go along with like-minded people.

"You had those who liked to have a beer after a game or after training. Then you had your gamblers, who wanted to go to the betting shop.

"And then you had people who just went off and played golf or went home and did something else.

"I was in with the drinkers that included Stan Charlton, Dave Dunmore, Ronnie Foster and Sid Bishop."

Another important difference, when comparing the era this book covers and today's over-pampered stars, many of whom have lost touch with reality as well as the common man, woman and child in the street who pay their wages, is that the 60s players enjoyed a good rapport with their supporters.

McDonald said: "After a home game, Stan made a point of insisting that all of us always had to pop into the supporters' club bar – underneath the old main East Stand – for a drink and chat with the fans before we went off anywhere else. In fact, some of the supporters played golf with one or two of our players anyway and there was always a good bond between us and the fans.

"Even after we were getting beat regularly in the first division, all the players would still continue to go into the supporters' club bar after the match. It was good and there was no bad feeling from the fans even after a heavy defeat. If you'd lost, they would feel sorry for you. We never thought, after a bad defeat, 'we'd better not go in the supporters' bar now because they'll all be upset and start having a go at us.' That just never happened. They knew we'd done our best and they accepted the result with good grace.

"We might run back over the game with them and talk about different aspects of it. They might have said 'you were unlucky there' or pointed out 'you got beat there', but they were never aggressive in their attitude and were very fair to us.

"After a drink with the fans, some of the players would move on to the Coach and Horses pub on Leyton High Road, before perhaps then going on to The King Harold, over the hill on the other side of Leyton station. There was another pub we sometimes used in Leytonstone High Road, but I can't recall the name of the place.

"If we had trained in the summer at Ashton Playing Fields, Woodford, where they had a running track, some of the players would call in at the Monkhams Arms for a beer on the way home.

"Sometimes, though, I'd go off in the afternoons with Ronnie Foster. He taught me how to drive around the streets of Plaistow, near where an uncle of mine, who had lent me his car to learn in, lived. It was Ron who helped me to pass my test. He'd passed earlier than me and he would have made a great driving instructor!"

Sid Bishop says: "The drinkers were the joke-makers – blokes like Frankie George and Peter Carey. We'd have a good laugh before going out to train each day. There was a very good spirit at the club and we'd all go out and graft for one another. There were no cliques on the pitch, that's for sure."

Sid, who moved with his wife Iris into the Orient-owned house at 32 Durham Avenue, Woodford (where Tommy and Jean Johnston had lived previously), was firm friends with two O's goalkeepers, Pat Welton and then one of his successors, Frank George. Frank says: "Sid lived just round the corner from us in Woodford – I remember that he was one of the first Orient players to own a car."

Naturally, players tended to mix with those team-mates who lived nearest to them. Stan Charlton said: "We lived in a rented terraced house at Woodford Green, in a banjo-shaped road called Fairway, just off Hillside Avenue. I later bought it off the club for £1,500. Dave Dunmore, Ronnie Foster and Sid Bishop lived nearby and we'd usually all go for a drink together in the Monkhams Arms on a Sunday lunch-time.

"Dave and I used to play golf together at Chigwell – sometimes even on the morning of a match. I remember someone once saying to Dave: 'You shouldn't be playing golf today with a football match to follow this afternoon.' But Dave just replied: 'Playing golf on a Saturday morning is easier for me than shopping with the missus!'

"After our home games, most of the players would have a drink in the supporters' club before going on to either the Coach and Horses in Leyton High Road, or The King Harold. The manager there would let us in through a little side door at about 5.15pm, even though he didn't open the bar to the public until six o'clock.

"Another pub we'd used to go in occasionally years earlier was the Three Blackbirds, near the Bakers Arms in Lea Bridge Road. One day a group of us were there when Alec Stock suddenly walked in. He asked me what I wanted to drink and I said: 'Orange juice, please boss.'

"He said: 'A man who doesn't drink a pint is a man who plays without bite'.

'Okay then . . . I'll have a pint!' I said."

Mal Lucas, who moved from his initial digs in Leyton to Barking, was part of a different small crowd during his O's playing days. He explained: "I didn't really socialise with the other players who were the gamblers, drinkers and card players – I didn't drink. "

Naturally, the two Welsh midfielders became good friends – after all, they both came from nearby villages in North Wales, played for the same amateur club and it was Lea who recommended his younger compatriot to Orient.

"Cyril (Lea) was my regular room-mate," says Malcolm, "but I also got on well with Joe Elwood. We went out a lot together. Joe was always very quiet but we got on great.

"Eddie Lewis and his wife, Shirley, were also good friends of mine and Jenny's – in fact, Eddie was my Best Man. I'm a bad boy – Eddie has written to me a couple of times but I haven't got round to replying yet!"

Cyril Lea, they say, wasn't one to squander his money on booze. A dedicated pro, he was living in digs just off Leyton High Road when he first met his wife, Val, while she was working in Leyton Library.

Harry Gregory and Gordon Bolland, who are of a similar age, socialised together with their respective wives, Carol and Angela, in the Buckhurst Hill area, where

Malcolm and Margaret Graham also lived.

Norman Deeley admits that his wife and children found it difficult to settle in Essex after moving down from the West Midlands. But the diminutive Deeley, who rented a house in Hillside Avenue, Woodford, was popular with most of his team-mates.

DECK OF CARDS
Wink Martindale, 1963

Yes, Norman Deeley – Wolves' two-goal Cup-winning legend from the 1960 final – settled in quickly among the 'drinkers, smokers and gamblers' in the ranks of the O's dressing room.

Terry McDonald recalled the first time the players met 'Little Norm', following his move south in February 1962. The team were already aboard their train at Paddington Station, about to set off for their game at Plymouth, where Deeley would make his O's debut in a 2-1 defeat.

McDonald, who was named 12th man that day (no subs then), says: "I remember Norman arriving with Johnny Carey to meet the rest of us on the train. Norman turned up wearing a straw hat, which looked funny to Phil White and me as we saw them walking along the platform towards us.

"Before you knew it, Norman and Phil were playing cards with me and Dave Dunmore at the back of the train. We normally played three-card brag.

"Anyway, after Deeley lost one hand, he got up and threw his straw hat straight out of the train window! It was the first time we'd met him – he hadn't even been to the ground or anything, Carey brought him straight onto the train."

Deeley recalls: "Carey took me to the pictures – just him and me – somewhere near Paddington. I can't recall the film we saw. We were just passing the time before we met up with the team at the station."

"I liked Norman, he was a nice bloke, and I'd like to see him again," continued McDonald. "He was a character with lots of stories to tell. He was an all round sportsman and gambler – but Whitey outgunned him at snooker.

"They used to play at Jelks' billiard hall, opposite the Coach and Horses in Leyton High Road, after training. The players spent many afternoons there playing snooker and pool, having a smoke and a beer.

"Whitey was always the thorn in Deeley's side – Norman just couldn't beat him. Phil used to give him a two-blacks start and even though they'd play all afternoon, Norman still couldn't beat him.

"Once, Phil made a 99 break against him . . . while wearing his Crombie overcoat and a scarf! They played up in the top room, the attic, and it was freezing cold. Phil won without even bothering to take off his coat. He was that good a player.

"Phil would say to me: 'Right, we're gonna play Dunmore and Deeley and you're gonna win.'

"I said: 'Leave off!' because I didn't really play a lot of snooker or pool. But Phil positioned his first two balls perfectly over the pockets and they couldn't move 'em.

He'd left me to just go round, bosh . . . and clear the table.

"Whoever lost had to pay for the table – and £7.50, which is what it would come to by the end of the afternoon, was a lot of money then.

"Norman was a good bloke who liked to socialise, although you never saw him laugh much. He was quickly accepted into the club by the other players."

Harry Gregory, the youngest of the first team squad, enjoyed being around the senior pro's and says he was always made to feel welcome, never isolated. He recognised Norman Deeley and Phil White as kindred spirits – they both liked a bet and a cigarette and enjoyed the craic.

Gregory says: "I remember being in the café opposite the big, green snooker hall in Leyton High Road, when Deeley was in there with Whitey, eating his liver and chips. Some bloke challenged Deeley, saying: 'Go on, Norm, see if you can eat the lot in two mouthfuls . . .' Whitey didn't believe it was possible, but Deeley bet him a fiver . . . and won! It was unbelievable."

Malcolm Graham remembers sharing a hotel room in Plymouth with Norman the night before Deeley's debut at Home Park. "It was funny," says Malcolm, "but I think Norman must have had a few drinks before he went to sleep that night, because he went to bed with his suit still on . . . and slept in it all night!"

Loyal and long-suffering O's supporter John Parke added further weight to the Deeley travels light story. Parke and his friends often travelled back from away matches on the same train as the players and he said: "I remember once asking Norman where his overnight bag was, because he didn't appear to have one with him. He simply just pulled his toothbrush out of his top pocket and said 'there it is!'."

After his pro playing career finished in 1966, Terry McDonald has spent the rest of his working life in betting shops, mostly as manager and even, briefly, as owner of McDonald Racing in Snaresbrook High Street during the 80s. Staying with the gambling theme, he said: "Bill Robertson won the fixed odds football accumulator two weeks running and the firm – William Hill or whoever it was – closed his account. He used to like backing Rangers and Hibernian every week in his seven or eight-match accumulator bet."

"Dave Dunmore and I used to go dog racing at Hackney on Thursday afternoons and West Ham on Friday nights. The only horseracing track we used to go to was Alexander Park – or 'Ali Palli' as it was known – in North London. The circuit was shaped like a frying pan and we'd meet up there with the Tottenham lot – Bobby Smith, Les Allen and Johnny Brooks."

Phil White also managed a bookies after leaving football. McDonald says: "Occasionally, I'd go with Phil to the dogs at Stamford Bridge, which is near where he used to live in Fulham.

"When I phoned Phil, years after we'd both left Orient, I asked if he'd been over to Stamford Bridge to see Chelsea play, because they were his team. He said: 'No, I've not been back there since the dogs packed up!'

"Phil loved a bet but he was a shrewd punter, sharp with figures. He knew how to bet and if he had a tip or fancied a horse or dog, you'd naturally listen to him."

McDonald and White kept in fairly regular touch with each other through the years, although Terry has a rather sad tale about Phil that apparently affected the former right-winger deeply.

McDonald explained: "After Phil and his family moved from Fulham to Wimbledon, he became manager of the William Hill shop in, I think, Surbiton.

"He was very conscientious when it came to his job, but he was also quite a nervous person in certain situations. One day, while Phil was taking a quick lunch break up the road, the shop was hit by a sting, where the inexperienced female cashier that Phil had left in charge of the shop accepted some winning bets that came to a lot of money.

"What happened was, somebody had placed a bet that came to something like two grand – and bear in mind I'm talking about the late 60s, so that was a hell of a lot of money to lose. She should really have phoned the area office for their approval before accepting the bet, although they would probably have taken it anyway. It was just a case of the girl, or Phil if he'd known about it, covering their own back by making the call to the area office to let them know.

"But the problem was that she had not only taken this large bet, but had accepted it FOUR TIMES . . . on different slips. It was the same bet four times, so the pay-out came to a massive EIGHT GRAND! From memory, I think the bets that copped were £1.00 forecast doubles or trebles at a dog meeting somewhere.

"Phil couldn't believe that the cashier hadn't even mentioned these bets to him until he was routinely checking through all the bets himself later. He didn't realise what had happened until it was too late.

"He told me afterwards that he was very worried Hills would sack him over it, but they never did. They realised he was a very good manager, who never made a rick. In fact, they told him after this happened not to worry about it.

"Phil took everything to heart, he was a big worrier, and he would have taken those losses by William Hill on his own shoulders – even though it wasn't his fault and it wasn't his money either. To be honest, I think Hills would have accepted the bet, and the risk of £8,000 losses without laying it off, even had they known about them before the race in question.

"But that wasn't the point as far as Phil was concerned. He still blamed himself for not being fully aware of the situation and he thought it was all down to him. He said he couldn't sleep at night and he told me: 'I've got to pack up, it's on my brain all the time.'

Phil was a sensitive bloke and he always blamed himself for not having known that those big bets had been placed in his shop. He took it personally, as if they had done him."

Julie told me at her Dad's funeral that he never really recovered from what happened in the betting shop that day and the big losses the company incurred. Phil started having heart problems and his health deteriorated."

Although players of the 60s earned more than the average man and woman, they remained in touch with the communities in which they worked and lived. Malcolm Graham remembers travelling from his rented home in Buckhurst Hill to Leyton Stadium by bus. "I used to have to change to another bus at Whipps Cross roundabout, before continuing on to Leyton. I was pleased when, after a period of having to catch buses, I could buy a little Mini to drive around in!"

As well as rubbing shoulders with their heroes in the bar at the ground, in local pubs, on the golf course, down the snooker hall and even on the bus, fans who lived in Leyton would undoubtedly have seen them eating in cafés in the High Road, just a short walk from Brisbane Road.

Stan Charlton tells a funny story that perhaps sums up the 'Cinderella' tag that has always attached itself to the O's. He said: "The players would often pop into the Coronation Café on Leyton High Road for something to eat in the morning before training at the ground. The cafe was run by an Italian – we all knew him as Albert – and he was always having a laugh with us.

"One day he said to me, in all seriousness: 'What, no training today, Stan?' I told him we had been training, but he continued: 'I suppose you have been practicing walking up and down all the steps in the ground, for when you have to go up and receive the Cup from the King?'

"I corrected him by saying: 'We don't have a king in England, you fool. We've got a queen!'.

"But, quick as a flash, old Albert came straight back at me: 'Well, it'll be a king by the time you lot win it!' We had to laugh."

YOU'RE DRIVING ME CRAZY
Temperance Seven, 1961

For footballers to own their own motor car in the 50s and even early 60s was something of a novelty.

Stan Charlton said: "I was one of the first Orient players to have a car in the late 50s. I rode a motorbike – a Panther 350 – until I bought my first car, a second-hand 1939 Vauxhall 10.

"One day I was driving Dave Dunmore and Norman Deeley back from the Bank of England cricket ground when, for a laugh, Dave decided to put his leg across the front of the car and push his foot down on the accelerator. Norman was so scared we'd crash that he held a knife to Dave's throat to make him lift his foot off the pedal!"

Why Deeley was carrying a knife is unclear. Dunmore joked: On Deeley holding a knife to his throat in the back of the car: "Maybe he liked peeling apples!"

"We had some laughs with Norman. One day, very soon after the Great Train Robbery, Sid (Bishop) drove a few of us – Terry McDonald, Ronnie Foster and myself, I think – to King's Cross station in his black Humper Snipe, which looked a bit like a police car at the time.

"We were about to catch the train to an away game and we had Deeley sat in the middle at the back of the car, with a cloth covering his head. He kept it pulled over his head as we walked him through the station, as if we were police officers escorting a criminal. That turned a few heads!"

The good news about the complete lack of press intrusion is that players could take matters into their own hands if they felt some punishment needed to be administered.

Charlton admitted: "One night, after the Orient end-of-season presentation dinner, Phil White, myself and our wives were driving along Embankment when we stopped at traffic lights and I noticed two young lads in a flashy MG giving our ladies the eye. By their actions, they were actually trying to entice them into their car. When they did it again at the next set of lights, I got out and thumped one of them!"

Car scrapes and other off-the-field incidents would also go unreported.

Charlton continued: "After getting promotion, I bought an A35 Van. I was driving it across Clapham Common late one night, after having had a few drinks, when I crashed. I hurt my chest and badly damaged one eye. The wound to my eye needed stitches – the surgeon who patched me up said I was lucky not to lose the eye.

"Anyway, I was a bit concerned that I might be breathalysed by the policeman who got into the ambulance with me as we were taken to St James's Hospital. Luckily for me, the copper salvaged an Orient team picture, with me in it, from the wreckage of my van and when I confirmed

LEYTON ORIENT
FOOTBALL CLUB
—— LIMITED ——

Telephone :
LEYTONSTONE 1368

SEASON 1962-63

Training Rules
and Player's
Instructions

No...*19*

Leyton Orient Football Club Limited

Registered Office and Ground:

Leyton Stadium, Brisbane Road, London. E. 10

Secretary - - - G. A. HICKS

Player's Admission Ticket

Admit ....

The front and back covers of the little blue players' 'Training Rules and Player's (sic) Instructions' booklet that each of them was given at the start of every season. This one relates to the 1962-63 season and had to be shown on entry to the ground.

Rule 16: 'Players are prohibited from attending dances or playing golf within three days of any football match.'

who I was, he told me that he used to play for the Met Police team. I got away with it.

"I was still recovering when I turned up for pre-season training with a big bandage over one eye and wearing a pair of dark glasses. Phil White reckoned I looked like The Invisible Man! The things we used to do!"

Terry McDonald revealed that he was once forced to miss a match over the Christmas period after injuring himself during some 'high jinks' in the supporters' club bar after a match at Brisbane Road. "They had the Christmas decorations hanging from the ceiling and as I went to kick this 'hanging ball', some silly woman pinched my bum and I slipped and cracked open my head on a table. I missed the next game with a back injury but I think the club told me to say I did it falling down the stairs at home!"

CRYING
Roy Orbison, 1961

Orient's archaic treatment room – adjacent to the home team dressing room at Brisbane Road – wasn't the best place for injured players to be.

Although trainer Les Gore and assistant Nick Collins always did their best to patch up the wounded and get them fit again as quickly as possible, neither were qualified physiotherapists and, to be fair to them, the medical facilities were some way short of state-of-the-art. It was really no different at most small clubs in those days.

In fact, the facilities and the treatment process was so basic that in the case of more serious injuries, some of the Orient players actually secretly visited a near rival club for treatment to their more serious injuries.

Malcolm Graham, Malcolm Lucas and Joe Elwood all confessed that they used to drive to West Ham United's Boleyn Ground, where they knew they would be in safer hands with Hammers' well known club physio Bill Jenkins, who had a good reputation in the game as a leading club physiotherapist.

One such occasion was after Lucas suffered a broken leg during the home 2-2 draw with Birmingham City in December 1962. Malcolm admits: "I was running through and their keeper hit me. I felt a pain in my leg but they just told me to 'go up front, out of the way', which is what I did. There were, of course, no subs in those days.

"After the match they just wrapped my leg up.

"I was a bit naughty really, because if I had an injury I used to go to West Ham and get treatment from Bill Jenkins. I knew a lot of the West Ham lads. I used to go around to Bill's house and then to the ground for the actual treatment.

"When he looked at my leg, he told me it was broken. He advised me to go back to Orient and tell Les Gore that I'd been playing at home with my children when one of them had fallen on my leg. This gave me the excuse to go up to Whipps Cross hospital to get it x-rayed – and the x-rays confirmed Bill's diagnosis that my leg was in fact broken.

"Bill advised me to tell the staff at Whipps Cross not to encase my leg in plaster, but to apply just a light strapping . . . which enabled him to carry out his remedial work on it afterwards, to ensure I didn't suffer any muscle wastage in the leg. The doctor at the hospital agreed to Bill's request and I used to go to West Ham on a daily basis.

"Orient never knew that I was having regular treatment at West Ham. They were lovely people at Orient – Les Gore and Nick Collins – but in that day and age, it was usually the case that physios were ex-players. All they tended to do in terms of treatment of injuries was what they'd seen done before, but I didn't feel they knew enough, which is not a nice thing to say. But you couldn't get much better than Bill Jenkins and I'd go to him after any injury.

"I'd have a little bit of treatment at Orient first, then afterwards I'd pop over to see Bill at West Ham for more treatment. There were times when I'd be in the treatment room at Orient and they'd notice a red mark on my leg and wonder how it got there. I'd say: 'Yeah . . . I think I must have put on a bit too much Ralgex.' And Les would say to me: 'I keep telling you not to do that!' laughs Malcolm.

"There are now so many players feeling the effects of carrying and playing on with injuries in their careers many years ago. A lot are suffering arthritis today. If you got a knock then, they'd just give you a cortisone injection, so that you could play. There were a lot of occasions when players weren't fit to play but they did – you let your heart rule your head a lot of the time."

Terry McDonald agreed with Lucas' assessment of the medical facilities – or lack of them – at Orient, and says: "Les didn't know too much about physiotherapy and I think Nick Collins, knew even less!

"If you got a bad bruise or knock on your leg, they would put a red-hot poltus on the affected area to draw the bruising out. It was gooey stuff inside a plastic package and they would lay a cloth across your leg before putting on the poltus. The cloth was meant to keep the heat on your leg for about half-an-hour or so.

"I remember they once put it on Alan Sealey and the poltus was so hot that it took the skin clean off his leg! Sealey reckoned Nick put the hot poltus straight on his leg and had forgotten about laying the cloth down first! 'Sammy' screamed out in agony.

"Les brought Nick Collins with him from Yeovil, where Nick had been his trainer – or the man who ran out with the bucket whenever there was an injury. It was originally Alec Stock who brought in Les when he joined Orient from Yeovil and then Nick followed them too."

Harry Gregory laughed when he recalled: "If you were in the dressing room, you could hear the players' screaming out loud from the treatment room next door!"

But for Joe Elwood, who stayed at the club longer than any other player who featured in either the promotion-winning or first division squad, the absence of professional treatment and sound medical advice at LOFC became no laughing matter in the winter of 1965-66.

Joe says his back problem became progressively worse until he was left with no option but to seek independent advice from a qualified consultant. After weeks of not knowing the full extent of the trouble that would sometimes leave him doubled-up in pain after matches, specialists at Whipps Cross hospital diagnosed a prolapsed disc, for which he underwent an operation.

Joe Elwood never played for Orient again and was devastated to be given a free transfer in May '66 when the club had clearly written him off because of his injury. He recalls that Bristol City, Bristol Rovers and Tranmere Rovers all showed interest in taking him, but he was so fearful that his back would give way on him again after the operation, he returned to Northern Ireland and played on for two more seasons with the Ards club near Belfast.

"No-one at Orient could tell me what the problem really was and I had to go and get my own treatment," says Joe. "I went in to Whipps Cross for the op' and I don't think anyone at Orient even knew what I was going in there for.

"I don't want to knock the Orient, because I'm sure loads of ex-players from our era could give tell you horrific stories about the treatment they received, or didn't, as the case may be.

"I don't think all those piggy back exercises that Les Gore had us doing did me any favours. Alan Eagles was pretty big to carry on my back!

"I know we only got one-year contracts in those days but the parting from the club was a big disappointment to me."

Another regular back pain sufferer was Malcolm Graham, who also found his cure away from Brisbane Road.

"I used to suffer quite a bit of back trouble. Every Friday morning we used to put on our spikes and do sprints out on the pitch. But on this particular Friday, the day before we were due to play Sheffield United, I pulled a muscle in my back while running on the far side.

"Well, at first I thought I'd pulled a muscle but I knew it was more serious than that. It was sciatica. I felt the pain go down my thigh and I could only just about walk afterwards.

"I just managed to drive myself home, where I got hold of the *Yellow Pages* and found myself an osteopath in Ilford, run by a fella called Mr Crowder. I phoned him, and explained who I was, but he said he couldn't fit me in that afternoon. He said the only time he could see me was at half-past eight that night. I hadn't told anyone at Orient that I was going to see him and I couldn't wait any longer for my back to be treated. We had the game the next day and I obviously wanted to play.

"He was marvellous. I'd been to see an osteopath before and, as osteopaths do, he 'adjusted' me that night. Not only was I able to play the next day, but I scored! I felt great.

"I went to see Mr. Crowder at his place in Ilford several times after that and also visited him at a clinic he ran in Buckingham Place, opposite the palace, where he worked as secretary of the Osteopathic Society. To thank him for what he'd done for me, I got him a ticket for the Bury game, when I scored those two goals.

"My back trouble started when I played for Bristol City, although it stemmed from the cartilage problems I had as a youngster."

Chapter 8

IT'S MY PARTY
Lesley Gore, 1963

VERY few newly-promoted teams to the Premiership today ever dare going there without spending as much as they can possibly afford on at least a few new players to strengthen their chances of avoiding immediate relegation the following year.

Even the most cautious clubs will almost break the bank and bring in a better player or two to add quality as well as depth to their squad for the testing season ahead.

But Leyton Orient won promotion from Division Two in May 1962 and didn't sign a single new player.

Whether manager Johnny Carey went to the board of directors and asked them to loosen the purse strings and reinvest some of that additional gate money generated by the promotion run, who can now say?

After promotion was achieved with that nerve-wracking finale against Bury, chairman Harry Zussman confirmed to the press that money would be made available to Carey if he felt it necessary to bolster his squad with proven top class talent. Zussman said: "Our job is to stay in Division One, and that means buying players where considered necessary. We are not on a spending spree – but there may be some strengthening to do."

If the manager did truly believe that reinforcements were needed, he certainly didn't make any such thoughts or fears public at the time.

Immediately after the Bury game, Carey said: "My main task will be to convince the boys they are every bit as good as the other players in the first division. I am confident we can hold our own."

Perhaps those two highly impressive Cup performances against Burnley – who had been strong first division double contenders right up until the closing days of the 1961-62 campaign – impaired his judgement of his team's real strength, or lack of it?

Carey virtually said as much when he invited the Daily Mirror's John Bromley into the Orient boardroom – which doubled as the manager's office during the week – at the start of May and told him: "Our team should be in no doubt about their ability. Our games against Burney in the FA Cup are a very good example. We gave them two very hard matches.

"Let's get this straight. I am NOT overrawed by the first division. I've played in the first division and managed teams in the first division. People tend to think of sides like Spurs, Burnley and Manchester United but, you know, there are a lot of ordinary teams in the division.

"The opening 10 games or so are vital . . . there is no question of rushing out and buying new players," added a confident Carey, as ever, softly spoken and sucking on a pipe.

And Carey, who won every honour as a player, took Blackburn to the first division and laid the foundations for what Everton became in 1963, also described winning promotion with the O's as "my greatest achievement". He went on: "I have found here a feeling of being wanted. It is such a happy club that one cannot be part of it without feeling that happiness. People here are so good, so nice and seem to expect so little that if you don't do a good job, you are letting those people down."

Maybe Carey had allowed recent history to cloud his judgement of his squad. A glance back at the final league tables in recent years would have told him that ALL of the promoted second division clubs in the six previous seasons went up and stayed in the top flight for at least one year.

And if the boss needed further evidence of what could be achieved by a newly-promoted team, it was staring him in the face. Ipswich Town had just grabbed even more praise and headlines than Orient . . . by WINNING the first division championship just 12 months after getting there!

Then again, how could the manager ignore other relevant facts . . .

Despite the February arrival of Norman Deeley and Gordon Bolland, the O's still stumbled – rather than skated – over the finish line to accompany Liverpool into Dreamland. The truth was inescapable . . . Orient mustered only six goals in their last seven games – and five of those came in the final two matches, against lowly Luton Town (who finished 13th) and Bury (18th), who had nothing to play for other than pride.

A lack of firepower, especially in the second half of the season, should have been cause for concern. Orient scored 30 fewer goals than champions Liverpool and 16 less than third-placed Sunderland. In fact, the O's had the lowest goals-for tally among the top six teams, with Scunthorpe United, Plymouth Argyle and Southampton all finding the net more often.

The big difference, though, between Ipswich's second division title-winning team of 1961 and Orient's promotion side a year later was 30 goals scored, mainly thanks to Ipswich's formidable twin striker spearhead of Ray Crawford and Orient-player-to-be Ted Phillips.

Where Orient out-performed Liverpool, and the rest of the 22-strong division, was on their travels. The O's rattled up 11 away victories (two more than the Merseysiders), the same number of draws (five) and one more goal. Strangely, Orient managed fewer home wins (11) than any of the top six. And of the leading 10 clubs in Division Two, only Rotherham United recorded less wins than Carey's men in front of their own fans. Even Bristol Rovers (relegated with bottom team Brighton) managed to match O's home tally of 11 successes.

Another factor that couldn't be overlooked is that the O's went up with a relatively settled side. Five players, including four who made up the best defence in the division – Sid Bishop, Cyril Lea, Malcolm Lucas, Stan Charlton and Eddie Lewis – missed only two league games between them. Orient even had a superior goals-against record than Liverpool (40 compared to the Reds' 43).

Leading scorer Dave Dunmore was only ruled out of three matches, and Terry McDonald five. It was really only the inside-forward positions that changed to any degree, with injury-hit Ronnie Foster and Malcolm Graham missing around a dozen games each as Joe Elwood and young Billy Taylor came in for occasional appearances, while Gordon Bolland made eight starts. Norman Deeley had been a straight replacement for knee injury victim Phil White in the last third of the season.

All the quotes emanating from Johnny Carey at the time indicated that he was happy to put his faith in the players that had earned the club this big chance. But was his faith misplaced?

Within a few days of clinching promotion, Orient were being linked in the local press with West Ham inside-forwards John Dick and Phil Woosnam, the intelligent midfield creator who had began his career at Brisbane Road. But cautious Carey said: "I am not prepared to say who I am likely to bid for. We do have weaknesses but most of the first team players here are capable of holding their own in Division One."

In the end, no new players were signed before the 1962-63 first division season kicked-off in August. The only first-team squad player not retained was 32-year-old reserve right-back George Wright, who was handed a free transfer after 88 first team appearances (one goal) for the O's spanning four years. The former West Ham defender moved on to Gillingham. It was a move that Wright – a carpenter by trade – welcomed, having lost his No.2 shirt to Stan Charlton the previous season in which he started only one first team match of the promotion campaign.

Teenage wing-half John Charles was the one addition to the full-time professional ranks, thus increasing the overall playing staff to 29 players.

The club did spend some money in the summer of '62 . . . on ground improvements. A new wing was added to the south-east corner of the main stand and terrace facilities were improved. The club built six new turnstiles as ground capacity increased by 5,000 – to 36,000. The office was inundated with a record demand for season tickets as excitement built towards the new season and a new era.

Harry Zussman added: "I can see few games next season when the gate will exceed our 31,000 capacity. Of course, for matches with Spurs, Arsenal, Burnley, Wolves, Manchester United and the like, we may well go over the top."

And with an added casual comment that might raise Barry Hearn's eyebrows, the ebullient Zussman said: "For the most part I expect the average gate to be about 20,000 next season. We can tick over nicely on that. We're not reaching for the moon."

The (now sadly defunct) *Stratford Express* reported that the club was about to offer their players "a big wage increase". New contracts were drawn up that would see first team regulars earn between £30 and £40-a-week.

Terry McDonald still has a copy of his original contract covering the year period from July 1, 1961 to June 30, 1962. The four-page document, counter-signed by

The promotion team before the arrival of Norman Deeley and Gordon Bolland. Back row, left to right: Cyril Lea, Malcolm Lucas, Eddie Lewis, Frank George, Sid Bishop and Stan Charlton.
Front: Phil White, Ronnie Foster, Dave Dunmore, Malcolm Graham and Terry McDonald.

secretary George Hicks, shows the left-winger earned a basic weekly wage of £16 in the summer weeks, rising to £17 basic during the playing season. However, he received £25-per-week when he appeared in the first team. At this time, my parents and I lived in a £4,000 semi-detached house in Burnway, Emerson Park, near Hornchurch in Essex. Dad drove a new red Fiat 600, which had replaced his first motor, a 1957 black Ford Anglia.

When asked to summarise why Leyton Orient achieved promotion and his thoughts on the immediate future, skipper Stan Charlton told the press: "We know we are not the greatest footballers in the world. But few teams can match us for fighting spirit. Just look at our away record and you will see what I mean."

The programme notes for the opening game, at home to London neighbours Arsenal on Saturday, August 18, reported that the only new arrival planned was that of George Waites, who was poised to rejoin the O's from Norwich City.

There was a distinct air of naiveté (as well as optimism) in the tone of the lead programme column for that opening date with the Gunners, which boldly stated: "Mr Carey has kept his word. He said when Orient won promotion he was satisfied with the men who so loyally played their part on gaining first division status for the club . . . the players will be given every chance to prove their worth once again.

"If the necessity arises then, no doubt, Mr. Carey, backed whole-heartedly by the Orient Board of Directors, will endeavour to fill the gaps as and when they arise. The cultivation of team spirit at Orient is first and foremost, it always has been . . . it is surprising what you can achieve when you are one big 'Happy Family'.

"Orient regard it as unkind, because already in some instances they have been branded as failures in Division One – condemned to die before they have even been tried. It's unkind and unfair too. Give the O's a break!"

A very healthy team spirit was one thing, loyalty to the players who got them there was another. But when it came to the crunch, would the O's have the quality to survive among the big boys? And so began another exciting chapter in the history of LOFC . . .

History in the making . . . Sid Bishop shadowing Arsenal's Geoff Strong in the opening first division match.

HALFWAY TO PARADISE
Billy Fury, 1961

August 18, 1962
Leyton Orient 1 (Gibbs)
Arsenal 2 (Strong, Baker)

Arsenal's new manager Billy Wright's gamble in leaving out £47,000 George Eastham and playing Geoff Strong and John Barnwell as inside-forwards paid dividends in this opening day win. Gunners showed that little extra bit of class, with wingers 18-year-old George Armstrong (right) and Alan Skirton especially impressive in the East London sunshine.

Strong thumped Arsenal ahead from 18 yards and was unlucky not to score with three other shots on a busy afternoon for Robertson. Although Bishop did a good close marking job on £65,000 Joe Baker, the former Torino marksman managed to skip past Lucas to make it 2-0 from 20 yards.

Dunmore was disappointed not to be awarded a penalty after being brought down by Terry Neill. Gibbs' easy tap-in – after a mix-up between young keeper Ian McKechnie and right-back Ted Magill – was no more than a late consolation.

Bill Robertson punching clear during the big curtain-raiser against the Gunners.

August 22, 1962
West Bromwich Albion 2 (Smith, Kevan)
Leyton Orient 1 (Dunmore)

A disappointing evening for O's. Their forwards failed to click and when they did they were defied by the Albion keeper Tony Millington whose brilliant, twisting save in the 60th minute from a Deeley chip gave Albion the incentive to keep Orient at bay and maintain command.

In a game of few real openings, Keith Smith headed Albion's first in the 40th minute from a centre by Clive Clark. Derek Kevan headed a strong second from a long ball by Don Howe, before Dunmore notched Orient's goal a minute later with Albion appealing for offside.

August 25, 1962
Birmingham City 2 (Bullock, Hellawell)
Leyton Orient 2 (Graham, Dunmore pen)

O's first point in the top flight. Blues went ahead after six minutes through Peter Bullock. Graham equalised 16 minutes later after good work by Deeley.

Four minutes later Dunmore gave Os the lead with a penalty awarded for handball. He shot low to John Schofield's left, sending the City keeper the wrong way.

Birmingham's equaliser came in the 50th minute when winger Mike Hellawell carried the ball along the goalline before curling a shot over keeper Robertson and in off the far post.

August 29, 1962
Leyton Orient 2 (Deeley, Dunmore pen)
West Bromwich Albion 3 (Lewis OG, Jackson, Clark)

What should have been a glorious celebration for the O's with their first win in the top flight turned to heartbreak with a tragedy of errors.

Tragedy number one came after 18 minutes of incessant Orient pressure. Albion won a breakaway freekick on the left. Derek Kevan nodded the ball towards the far post where Lewis, trying to clear from under the bar, hammered the ball high into the roof of the net.

Orient were level when Deeley notched his first goal of the season five minutes later, racing in from the right to crash a centre from Dunmore first time into the net after Potter had saved from Graham.

O's tremendous pressure brought them 10 first-half corners and a final match log of 19. Tragedy number two came as Lewis was caught in no-man's land in the 37th minute and Lea could only knee Jackson's piledriver into the net.

Two minutes later, Robertson allowed himself to be bundled by Kevan in reaching for a freekick and Clark rammed the lose ball into the back of the net. Yet Orient, with a superb mixture of graft and honest endeavour, should have been ahead.

McDonald gave Don Howe and the Albion defence a 45 minute pounding – in one run he beat five men – yet the visiting goal survived.

In the second half Orient lost their slickness in their desperate efforts to level. Deeley and McDonald continued to be a threat but a brilliant one-handed save by Potter from a Gibbs header smashed their hopes of a quick second half goal.

Dunmore set the scene for a grandstand finish when he cracked home a 72nd minute penalty after Graham Williams brought down Deeley, but Albion held out.

September 1, 1962
Leyton Orient 2 (Dunmore, Graham)
West Ham United 0

Carey made his first change, introducing Bolland at inside-right to replace Gibbs. On a blistering hot day in which several fans fainted, Dunmore turned up the heat on West Ham when he rose, unchallenged, to head O's in front from Deeley's fifth minute corner.

East End pride . . . Dave Dunmore (9) turns away after scoring in the local derby win over West Ham. Terry McDonald, Malcolm Graham and Gordon Bolland rush to congratulate DD, while Bobby Moore, Ken Brown and Alan Sealey are the dejected Hammers in view during O's 2-0 victory.

Deeley also set up the second, a 20-yard special from Graham, five minutes before half-time. O's got off the mark in Division One but for hapless Hammers – with left-half Bobby Moore doing more effective work in O's half than their non-existent forwards – it was their third defeat in four games.

The visitors included former Orient schemer Phil Woosnam at inside-left.

September 5, 1962
Everton 3 (Bingham, Gabriel, Vernon)
Leyton Orient 0

Affluent Everton went top of the table with this emphatic win. The Toffees went ahead in the fourth minute through Billy Bingham, who scored left-footed from an Alex Young pass.

They made it 2-0 a minute before the break when Bingham's freekick was headed home by Jimmy Gabriel. Roy Vernon completed the scoring with a penalty in the 58th minute.

The margin could have been greater but for some spectacular saves from O's keeper Robertson.

Chapter 9

WALKIN' BACK TO HAPPINESS

Helen Shapiro,. 1961

IT'S more than 44 years since Terry McDonald scored his sensational last-minute winner against Manchester United, the most famous team in British football history, but the memory of it is still as fresh today as it was all those years ago.

"It has to be the highlight of my career," says McDonald, "simply because what United stand for now and what it meant to O's supporters and the club at that time. Everyone talks about beating Man U, but that completed a great purple patch which included home wins over West Ham and Everton, too.

"To be honest,we caught United at a good time when they were in transition after the Munich disaster in '58 and struggling in the bottom third of the table. They had lost their previous away game, 3-1, to Arsenal, although they ended up beating Leicester in the FA Cup at the end of the season, while Everton were crowned league champions." (In fact, United needed at least a draw against their Manchester rivals City in their last game of the season to avoid relegation. The 1-1 result at Maine Road condemned City to relegation along with the O's.)

McDonald, who was 22 at the time, has vivid memories of the build up to his favourite goal of all-time.

He said: "Eddie Lewis cleared the ball to the halfway line, where their right-back, Shay Brennan, miscontrolled it. I latched onto the loose ball and sprinted to the centre edge of their penalty area. I could see big Maurice Setters and Tony Dunne coming across to challenge me, so I drove the ball right-footed past David Gaskell into the top right-hand corner of the net at the Coronation Gardens end. There was just enough time left for United to kick off again before the ref ended the game.

"On an otherwise great day for me personally and the team, my only small regret is that there were no photographers at that end of the ground to capture my goal on film – they were all at the opposite end, waiting for Denis Law to score! He'd just come back from Italy, where he'd been playing for Torino, and was still looking for his first goal following his £116,000 move, which was a massive amount to pay for any player back then so you could understand all the attention he received."

Despite the thrill of scoring that late, late winner over mighty Manchester United, McDonald didn't take off his blue shirt and swing it above his head, or leap into the crowd behind the goal, or perform some silly, pre-rehearsed dance routine that so many of today's show-offs can't resist doing after a goal has been scored, regardless of its significance.

Terry says: "We didn't go mad after scoring in those days, although Eddie Brown – who was at Orient a few years earlier – used to 'shake hands' with the corner flag! That was about as extravagant as it got in those days. I probably received a few hugs and pats on the back from team-mates, and just jogged back into our half. That's all we did after a goal was scored.

"Obviously, there was a great mood in the dressing room afterwards. Johnny Carey was the first to come over to me, saying: 'Well done, son'. Being a former United star himself, he was especially happy we had beaten them and his old boss, Matt Busby."

Did the Stepney-born, crew-cut winger enjoy a night on the town with the other lads afterwards?

"I can't remember exactly what we did that night, but it was probably no more than our usual routine. We were a good social side and about seven or eight of us - led by skipper Stan Charlton - would always join the fans for a drink in the supporters' club after home matches. I think it was where the players' bar is today. A little later, we'd move on for more drinks at The King Harold pub . . . as McDonald would tell Denis Law many years later.

Terry explains: "I met Denis again about five or six years ago, when he was signing his autobiography, Lawman, in Waterstones, near the Coral shop where I was working in Leadenhall Market. I bought a copy, queued up to get it signed by Denis and then had a brief chat with him. I surprised him by saying I had the pleasure of playing against him several times - when he played for Huddersfield Town as well as Man U – and I referred to the part in his book where he said that United were going through a difficult time when they visited Orient "and even lost to them!".

"He asked if I'd played in that particular game. He said that Sir Matt had kept the United players behind in the dressing room for a bollocking afterwards . . . and I told him the O's players were all in the bar by then!"

McDonald's brilliant winner, and the 1-0 victory against one of the biggest clubs in the world, will never be forgotten by those lucky enough to be there. And naturally, Terry will never tire of talking about that epic occasion whenever it comes up in conversation, as it often does when long-in-the-tooth O's fans seek refuge in memories of golden days gone by.

Having celebrated his 67th birthday in November, 2006, he says: "I still get to most Orient home games and it's always great to see so many old faces still there. I was so pleased for Martin Ling, the players and the fans when they won promotion to League One last May. It's hard at this level when you are given hardly any money to spend on new players, but Martin always sends his team out to try and play football the right way – the same way we always used to try and play it.

"I like to pop into the supporters' club for a beer and chat to the fans in there after every game I attend. Some of them tell me that they were there on the day I scored against United, even though many of them were only kids at the time.

"And John Pratt, the former Spurs midfielder, told me some years ago, when I played with him in a vets' game, that he was playing for a local boys' side on Hackney Marshes the afternoon we beat United – and he heard the roar of the crowd from there when our winning goal went in!

"It's still a great pleasure to look back on it and my time at Orient in general. It was very nice to get all the acclaim and the headlines after the game, it doesn't get any better than that for me, but Dave Dunmore and Gordon Bolland also went very close to scoring that afternoon and they could just as easily have been the heroes that day. We were very much a team who played and socialised together. There were no individuals, we all had our feet on the ground."

A great advertisement for the game, an abundance of good football from both teams and a glorious finish to end all thrilling finales.

With barely a minute of this enthralling match remaining, Brisbane Road erupted when McDonald scored a superb winner. When United right-back Shay Brennan controlled an intended pass to the left-wing from O's former United player Lewis, McDonald latched onto the ball as it got away from the Irish right-back.

The flying, blond winger cut inside and ran right through the heart of the Reds' defence before floating an unstoppable right-foot shot from 20 yards, high into the far corner of David Gaskell's net at the Coronation Gardens end.

It was very tough on Gaskell, easily United's best player who had performed heroics all afternoon to deny the O's the goals they deserved, Bolland had two drives and two point blank headers from corners saved, while Dunmore's rasping, 25-yard drive was tipped over the bar by the United keeper three minutes from time. Graham and Deeley also saw fine efforts saved by the overworked Gaskell.

At the other end, Orient's half-back line did a superb job of keeping a clean sheet, with Bishop denying David Herd space – though he did force one full stretch save from Robertson – and the outstanding Lucas shackling Denis Law on his recent return from his spell in Italian football with Torino. Cyril Lea was also impressive, virtually becoming O's sixth forward at times. In the second half, Lucas got forward more, which further negated the threat of the retreating Law.

In comparison with the Burnley Cup matches of the previous season, this was played with much less haste and more attention to detail.

Sammy McMillan went closest for United when he headed against the woodwork on the stroke of half-time.

Arguably, this still ranks as O's most famous league victory of all-time, although the Orient board were disappointed that only 24,901 came to see it. Director Leslie Grade asked: "What do people *want* for their money?"

PRESS COMMENT

Leyton Orient, babes in the jungle of the first division, grew up in the flaring last minute when all East London heard the roar which said: "We've beaten United . . . Denis Law and all." Orient, at that moment, ceased to be excitable underdogs, thrilled of the thought of Matt Busby's men even playing on their East End ground, and became instead, assured citizens of soccer's big-time.

Clive Toye, The Express

Denis Law was an abstract painter on Orient's green canvas. With delicate strokes and pastel passes he was clearly the master of United's attack – but never Orient's defence. There were too many action men there.

Walthamstow Guardian

That United survived until the 89th minute was mainly due to the acrobatics of keeper Gaskell. Bolland might have had a hat-trick.

Reg Drury, Reynolds News

What a proud moment it was for Johnny Carey to receive the warm congratulations of his old boss, Matt Busby, at the end.

'Claptonian', Hackney Gazette

After consecutive home wins over West Ham and Man United, the excitement didn't end there. High and mighty Everton were also in for a shock . . .

September 12, 1962

Leyton Orient 3 (Deeley, Bolland, Dunmore)

Everton 0

Just seven days after being outclassed at Goodison Park, O's gave league leaders Everton a shock with this brilliant performance in the return clash in East London. It all happened in four electric second half minutes.

Deeley struck the first blow when he rammed home a powerful Lewis cross that eluded Brian Labone following McDonald's quick throw-in. In the 57th minute the Toffeemen came unstuck again when McDonald danced down the left wing before setting up Bolland to score his first league goal for the club. McDonald also laid on the third, his freekick being firmly headed home by Dunmore 11 minutes from time to complete a memorable night. If O's could inflict this sort of damage on classy opponents such as championship-chasing Everton, then surely they could secure their place in the top flight? After three euphoric home wins, over West Ham, Manchester United and Everton in the space of 10 days, Orient were proving their doubters wrong. And Johnny Carey, sacked by Everton 18 months earlier, would have taken immense satisfaction from this win at the expense of the 'Mersey Millionaires'.

September 15, 1962
Burnley 2 (McIlroy, Lockhead)
Leyton Orient 0

Robertson was an absolute hero, time after time he kept out the Burnley forwards. Also outstanding were wing-halves Lucas and Lea, who never stopped working at breaking down the Burnley front line but were unable to instil front line aggression in their own men. O's were two goals down before Lucas had their first shot.

Jimmy McIlroy got Burnley's first soon after Robertson had made stunning saves from Ray Pointer and John Connelly.

Adam Blacklaw began the move that brought their second goal from promoted centre-forward Andy Lockhead, who dived to head a superb goal.

Dunmore led late rallies and worried Blacklaw with two finger-stinging shots and Lucas tried again but was unlucky.

The game was no comparison to last season's floodlit classic.

September 22, 1962
Leyton Orient 2 (Bolland, Deeley)
Sheffield Wednesday 4 (Layne, Dobson, Kay, Quinn)

A rough encounter that boiled over at the end, when fans invaded the pitch to remonstrate with several Sheffield players they held responsible for treatment meted out to O's players. The most notably injury victim was Bishop, who suffered ankle ligament damage after being sent tumbling by aggressive Owls' centre-forward David 'Bronco' Layne, who also dealt forcefully with Lucas.

Both Layne and skipper Tony Kay were booked by referee Norman Matthews, while 18-year-old right-half Peter Eustace – an O's manager of the future – also inflamed the crowd after a flare-up with Graham. McDonald and left-back Don Megson also had to be separated as tempers boiled.

It was Layne who gave Wednesday the lead in the first half with a 15-yard angled shot. O's equalised three minutes before the break when Bolland headed home from McDonald's corner – a reward for intelligent play in which Graham caught the eye.

Wednesday regained the lead soon after the re-start through Colin Dobson's 20-yard cracker that surprised Robertson. Deeley equalised with his head from another McDonald cross in the 56th minute but a miss-hit shot from the fiery Kay, which

Robertson believed was drifting wide, restored Owls' lead midway through the half.

With Bishop limping out on the right wing, Charlton filling in at centre-back and Lucas having to drop into the skipper's right-back position, Orient's defence were in dissaray when Johnny Quinn rubbed salt into their wounds 11 minutes from the end.

September 26, 1962
Newcastle United 1 (Fell pen)
Leyton Orient 1 (Bolland)
League Cup, 2nd round

Orient lost keeper George with an injury 17 minutes from time but held struggling Newcastle to a hard-fought draw.

Four minutes stood between Newcastle and defeat. Only an 86th minute penalty by Jimmy Fell, which gave substitute goalkeeper Charlton no chance, saved the Geordies from humiliation.

Orient's first half shooting was inept but Newcastle's was worse, although the visitors took command of the game in the second half.

Bolland hammered O's into a 49th minute lead when he headed home a Deeley corner. Deeley's solo effort eight minutes later was disallowed. The Os would never admit defeat. They fought like tigers for every single ball and their second half superiority looked like carrying them through. Youngsters Taylor and Clark showed great form.

Newcastle's limited attacks were confidently repelled by Orient's half-back line of Lucas, Clark and Lea. But in their efforts to hold on to victory Orient gave away a penalty when Lucas punched away a Ken Hale header only four minutes from time.

September 29, 1962
Fulham 0
Leyton Orient 2
(Graham, McDonald)

Centre-half Bishop's ankle injury, sustained in the previous game, ended his incredible run of 97 consecutive league appearances and resulted in a league debut call-up for his 23-year-old, Leyton-born understudy, Clark.

Graham gave O's the lead after half-an-hour before McDonald made it 2-0, scoring direct from a corner kick a minute before the interval.

On a bad day for Fulham keeper Tony Macedo, who was caught out for both goals, the score flattered O's.

FULHAM Football Club
LEAGUE DIVISION I
SEASON 1962-1963
OFFICIAL PROGRAMME
PRICE 6d
LEYTON ORIENT
SATURDAY, SEPTEMBER 29, 1962
KICK OFF 3.0 P.M.

October 1, 1962

League Cup, 2nd round replay

Leyton Orient 4 (Graham 2, Bolland, Deeley)

Newcastle United 2 (Lucas OG, Suddick)

(After extra-time)

Despite lousy, wet conditions, this was a thrilling cup tie that only drew breath when a faulty switch caused the floodlights to briefly fail soon after the start of extra-time. The second division Magpies led after nine minutes when Lucas' attempted clearance squirmed into his own net off the rain-soaked surface.

But O's fought back quickly and equalised eight minutes later when Bolland headed in a cross from Dunmore. O's took the lead on 26 minutes after Graham polished off Deeley's good work.

Dunmore was unlucky not to clinch the tie when his shot struck a post, before the Geordies made it 2-2 through Alan Suddick five minutes from the end of normal time.

Dunmore did, though, supply both crosses from which Graham and Deeley made the tie safe in the second period of extra-time.

October 6, 1962

Manchester City 2 (Hannah, Harley)

Leyton Orient 0

Despite playing the classier football and dominating long periods of the game, O's lacked punch in front of goal and paid the price.

Bottom-of-the-table City snatched the two league points with goals from George Hannah (72 mins) and Alex Harley (86).

Dunmore came closest to scoring for the visitors but his 25-yarder rocked the crossbar.

October 13, 1962

Leyton Orient 0

Blackpool 2 (Parry 2)

A couple of weeks after skippering England in a 1-1 draw with France, Jimmy Armfield led Tangerines to this win. Ray Charnley had made his England debut in that same European Nations tie at Sheffield,

Ray Parry, the £23,000 former Bolton inside-left, was gifted with both Blackpool's goals in the 16th and 90th minute.

He made use of his chances, whereas Waites – who made his O's first division debut in place of Bolland – found himself in front of the Blackpool goal but couldn't beat keeper Tony Waiters.

At the end of the game Armfield ran practically the length of the pitch to shake hands with Orient captain Charlton. Their words were private, unlike Blackpool's manager Ronnie Stuart who afterwards commented: "Orient were unlucky not to get one goal. And if they'd got one I fear they'd have got another."

October 17, 1962
League Cup, 3rd round
Leyton Orient 9 (Waites 3, Graham 3, Dunmore 2, Deeley)
Chester 2 (Gregson, Myerscough)

O's made the most of a welcome break from the cut and thrust of first division life to slaughter lowly Chester City by a club record score (equalling the 9-2 league win against Aldershot in 1933-34).

There were hat-tricks for new signing Waites and Graham, while Dunmore added a brace and Deeley also netted.

This historic game saw Roger Wedge make his one and only appearance of the season, wearing the No.11 shirt.

October 20, 1962
Aston Villa 1 (Burrows)
Leyton Orient 0

This one was settled by a flukey goal by Harry Burrows. What was clearly intended as a swerving cross deceived keeper Robertson and found his net via a post.

The team defeated at Villa Park showed several changes from the one that played against Blackpool. Although Bishop resumed after a three-match absence, Lucas and Lewis (virus) were both ruled out, which meant a chance for Gibbs at right-half and Taylor at left-back, while Waites kept his place, replacing McDonald on the wing. It was Waites' last senior appearance before moving to Brighton the following month.

While the first team were losing at Villa, McDonald played for the Reserves who were beaten 1-0 by a strong Spurs side in the Football League Combination Cup Final (the competition for 1961-62 had seen O's win the midweek section, with Spurs the Saturday section winners). A crowd of 9,000 turned out at Brisbane Road to see Bobby Smith win it with the only goal.

October 27, 1962
Leyton Orient 1 (Deeley)
Tottenham Hotspur 5 (Allen, Bishop OG, Medway, White, Jones)

Goalkeeper Mike Pinner made his Orient debut but couldn't stop defending league champions Spurs from romping to an easy win that put them top of the table.

Pinner had a great first 15 minutes but in 21 minutes he conceded when Les Allen whipped one in with his left foot from just outside the box.

Deeley brought O's level (25 mins) with a shot from 15 yards but their chance went in the 34th minute when Bishop headed a Tony Marchi shot over Pinner's head.

Dunmore, the former Spurs player, had an impressive game but when Terry Medwin (44) grabbed a third Spurs started to show their superiority. John White (57) made it 4-1 before Welsh winger Cliff Jones (83) completed the rout.

Jimmy Greaves had a quiet game but White and Allen were prominent in attack and Danny Blanchflower outstanding. It hardly troubled Spurs that Dave Mackay was ruled out by a cold and keeper Bill Brown was limping (both played in the following Wednesday's European Cup clash with Glasgow Rangers).

Spurs manager Bill Nicholson commented afterwards: "I hope Harry Zussman, the Orient chairman, won't be upset but I describe this as a match between thoroughbred race horses and a pack of willing horses."

Ronnie Foster came in for his first game in the top flight, at the expense of Graham, while Lucas and McDonald returned to the side.

November 3, 1962
Nottingham Forest 1 (Quigley)
Leyton Orient 1 (Dunmore)

This was Mike Pinner's second outing for Orient and he gave a good display. The O's looked sharp and snapped up the few chances that Forest allowed them.

Bishop was fully fit after being out with an injury for three weeks. Hesitant Forest, unnerved by the lightening runs of wingers Deeley and McDonald, took the lead in the 39th minute. A threatening centre from Dick LeFlem (a future Orient winger) caught Pinner out of position and Quigley's neat header was good enough to score. Pinner made no more mistakes.

Dunmore, back among the League goals after eight games without scoring, looked like an England player when he levelled for O's 11 minutes later.

Orient might have won when Deeley, unmarked in front of goal with John Armstrong way out, could only push on a pass towards Foster. But Bobby McKinlay cut back to clear it.

Forest, who maintained their unbeaten home record this season, included ex-O's Len Julians at centre-forward.

November 10, 1962
Leyton Orient 1 (Gregory)
Ipswich Town 2 (Blackwood, Baxter)

In a programme editorial for this game against the reigning First Division

champions, the club denied a national newspaper report quoting manager John Carey as saying that his players 'were not good enough for the first division.' The club insisted Carey had been misinterpreted.

The teams went into this game – already billed as a relegation scrap – level at the bottom on 10 points each but it was Alf Ramsey's Ipswich who grabbed the vital points with two goals in three minutes.

Probably the only man in a blue shirt with anything to feel satisfied about was 19-year-old Harry Gregory, who marked his first senior appearance with O's only goal. Inside-forward Gregory was just 15 minutes into his league debut when he latched onto a clever, defence-splitting pass from Foster before clipping a left-foot shot over the advancing Roy Bailey to put the home side ahead.

But within another 15 minutes, Ipswich equalised through Bobby Blackwood, who controlled a Jimmy Leadbetter outswinging centre before giving Pinner no chance. Two minutes later Town – who were set to face AC Milan in the European Cup the following week – were in front when a corner from the right by Roy Stephenson was punched away by Pinner, only to be volleyed home by Billy Baxter.

Foster had a header cleared off the line while Bailey saved Dunmore's penalty after the O's top scorer had been brought down by future O's centre-half Andy Nelson.

November 12, 1962
League Cup, 4th round
Leyton Orient 3 (Foster 2, Gregory)
Charlton Athletic 2 (Matthews, Peacock)

O's League Cup run continued with this thrilling win on a difficult pitch over second division Charlton, with all five goals coming in the first half.

It was a mystery how Orient came out raring to go in the second half after such a pounding in the first in which Roy Matthews delicately lifted the ball over the diving George to score before Orient got down to work in earnest.

With Foster at his best Os were irrepressible and 'Fozzie' headed two beautiful goals with young Gregory (a future Charlton star) earning one in between. They were enough to scrape the O's through into the last eight of the competition, although the visitors pulled one back 10 minutes from half-time through Keith Peacock to ensure a nervy second period in which Charlton dominated.

November 17, 1962
Liverpool 5 (Hunt 3, Stevenson, St. John)
Leyton Orient 0

There was little between these two teams when they were promoted the previous season, but there was certainly a big gulf in class at Anfield on this torrid day of rain, sleet and snow. It was one to forget for George, making his first start of the campaign in the green jersey as cover for Mike Pinner, who was playing for England in the amateur international against Wales at Shrewsbury. Not that George could be blamed for the margin of defeat.

Roger Hunt gave Reds the lead after 10 minutes, made it 2-0 on 25 minutes and Willie Stevenson had virtually sealed the game with Liverpool's third 10 minutes before the break. The home side's dominance continued in the second half, as Hunt (62) completed his hat-trick and Ian St. John completed the rout two minutes later.

For Foster, it was his last game in O's first team – he bowed out with two goals for the Reserves against Brighton – before moving to Grimsby Town at the end of November.

November 24, 1962
Leyton Orient 0
Wolverhampton Wanderers 4 (Stobart 2, Crowe, Hinton)

Carey rings the changes – seven in all, five of them positional – but he couldn't alter O's dismal run. Right-half Lucas and left-back Taylor were pushed up as inside-forwards, with Gregory playing at No.9 and Dunmore in the unfamiliar seven shirt. Gibbs and fit-again Lewis were recalled but McDonald was left out.

Without a win in their previous seven games, Wolves got back on track with this comfortable victory in the Brisbane Road mud. Despite a string of saves from George, the O's keeper couldn't prevent another four going past him.

Ron Flowers was outstanding for Wolves, who scored through Barry Stobart (two), Chris Crowe and Alan Hinton.

December 1, 1962
Blackburn Rovers 1 (Harrison) Leyton Orient 1 (Graham)

Described as a 'pools buster', this hard-fought score-draw was gained against the odds but was nevertheless well deserved.

O's recalled Graham, after a five-match absence, and McDonald, who had missed the walloping by Wolves, while Pinner reclaimed the No.1 shirt from George.

Mike Harrison blasted Rovers ahead on 33 minutes but O's levelled in the 71st after Lea's freekick found Deeley, who pulled the ball back from the bye-line for Graham to score.

December 3, 1962
League Cup, 5th round
Leyton Orient 0
Bury 2 (Calder, Jones)

Second division promotion contenders Bury caused a surprise by ending O's League Cup hopes at the quarter-final stage, despite a third consecutive home draw in this competition that is now into its third season.

When the draw was made, it immediately evoked great memories of the promotion celebrations of seven months earlier, when Bury last visited Leyton Stadium. But this time there were to be no scenes of jubilation on a cold night.

While Pinner denied Bury many scoring prospects on the rock hard, sandy surface, he could do nothing about the two goals. Centre-forward Bill Calder got the first, clipping the ball over Pinner's head in a goalmouth mix-up. Inside-right George Jones, an 18-year-old stripling, caught onto a pass from Calder and slipped too easily past Bishop and Lea before burning the ball through the fog from 20 yards.

December 8, 1962
Leyton Orient 2 (Graham, Dunmore)
Sheffield United 2 (G. Shaw pen, Pace)

Graham was back again in the O's side with a bang, lending very active support. To the disbelief of Sheffield's dour defence he hit Orient into the lead with a superb fourth minute goal.

He made a 40-yard dash that took him past three United men and without checking his stride, lashed the ball past a startled Alan Hodgkinson from 20 yards – with his unfavoured right-foot.

United scored from a Graham Shaw penalty in the 30th minute – a woeful decision by referee Aubrey Moore who ruled that Lea fouled Keith Kettlebrough. Charlton had an outstanding game with touches of brilliance but Doc Pace gave United a 55th minute lead. Dunmore salvaged a point with a great header 20 minutes later.

December 15, 1962
Arsenal 2 (Baker 2)
Leyton Orient 0

It looked ominous for O's even before kick-off, with Lucas and Dunmore both ruled out by ankle injuries – the centre-forward having been hurt in a midweek friendly to mark the opening of Walthamstow Avenue's new floodlights at Green Pond Road. Gregory was recalled at inside-right at the expense of Taylor, while Bolland took over Dunmore's No.9 jersey.

Arsenal seized the initiative in the 10th minute, Joe Baker pouncing to score after Pinner failed to deal with the elegant George Eastham's driven cross. Baker added a second 14 minutes into the second half.

Only young Gregory seriously threatened Ian McClelland in the Gunners' goal. With fellow relegation strugglers Ipswich Town and Fulham both winning away, this defeat plunged O's even deeper into trouble, five points adrift of The Cottagers.

For McDonald, who missed a good chance when clean through in the last minute, this marked his final appearance in the first division following the signing of experienced left-winger Malcolm Musgrove from West Ham.

December 22, 1962
Leyton Orient 2 (Musgrove, Bolland)
Birmingham City 2 (Bloomfield 2)

Orient played with virtually a four-man forward line – right-half Lucas was on and off with a leg injury (it turned out the leg was fractured!) and when he hobbled onto the right-wing the O's scored two goals and narrowly missed a dozen others.

New signing Malcolm Musgrove gave the lead in attack and a three-man move ended with the left-winger having a glorious left-foot shot pushed away by keeper Colin Withers soon after his goal after just two minutes.

Seconds later Graham hit the bar with a header and so it went on until a Deeley corner, back-headed by Graham, went to Bolland who volleyed it in after 24 minutes.

Deeley showed his class throughout the game. Moving inside when Lucas took to the wing, covering magnificently, probing in defence and darting into attack. He put on a superb display for the O's but in the second half the fight drained from Orient and Birmingham's skipper Jimmy Bloomfield (destined to become Orient manager in 1968) twice scored to ensure a point each.

O's claimed they were robbed of a last minute penalty when left-back Colin Green appeared to punch the ball clear of the post.

December 26, 1962
Leicester City 5 (Charlton OG, Keyworth 2, Cheesebrough, Appleton)
Leyton Orient 1 (Musgrove)

Boxing Day in 1962 was a significant date in many ways. On a national scale, the weather took a distinct turn for the worse and many of the traditional holiday fixtures had to be called off. At the time no-one could have foreseen that this was the real start of the worst winter of the 20th century, when snow and ice would cause

 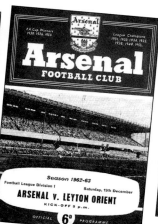 

total havoc for sporting clubs and the average temperature would remain below freezing point for more than a month.

Fixtures had already been disrupted on the Saturday before Christmas due to widespread thick fog, but, unfortunately for O's, this game at Filbert Street went ahead.

Fourth from top Leicester totally outclassed the struggling visitors on a snow-covered pitch and not even another goal by new boy Musgrove could lift the winter gloom that had engulfed the East Enders.

From the kick off, City tore into the bottom club and were gifted the perfect start after just three minutes when Charlton turned the ball past Pinner for an own goal.

City were rampant during the first period, hitting four goals without reply to effectively wrap up the points. Ken Keyworth scored the Foxes' second on 19 minutes and Albert Cheesebrough made it 3-0 two minutes later. Leicester's fourth came from Colin Appleton five minutes before half-time.

After the break, the pace eased off, but Keyworth (71 mins) added his second to make it 5-0. Musgrove, later to become the coach at Filbert Street under Frank O'Farrell, netted O's only goal past Gordon Banks in the 88th minute.

The return clash between O's and Leicester was scheduled for Brisbane Road three days later but, with five inches of snow covering a frozen pitch, the 'Big Freeze' had brought football (and much of the country) to a halt.

It also caused the postponement of the home league game against Burnley and three away league fixtures – against West Ham, Manchester United and Sheffield Wednesday. In fact, as Britain was gripped by its worst winter of the century, the O's didn't play again for another six-and-a-half weeks . . .

February 11, 1963
FA Cup, 3rd round
Leyton Orient 1 (Musgrove)
Hull City 1 (Chilton)

After a succession of postponements when groundsman Jack Tonner's best efforts were repeatedly confounded by freezing temperatures, football finally resumed. It seemed like an age since the heavy defeat at Leicester but Malcolm Musgrove scored in his third consecutive game to spare O's blushes against third division Hull City in freezing conditions.

Hull rocked Orient with a cheekily taken 28th minute goal, and defied a second half barrage to allow only one goal – the equaliser.

Played at the 10th time of asking since the original scheduled January 5 staging, this match rarely crackled on a pitch that was fast and true, aided by the night frost.

Over-elaboration robbed Orient of early chances. There were some nice touches but the football lacked the basics. Left-winger John McSeveney lashed the ball past keeper George, who almost death-dived attempting to stop the shot. The ball jarred the post and with Os defence frozen in indecision, Cliff Chilton nipped in to convert.

Charlton, never shy about becoming a sixth forward, led the rally that brought Orient's 55th minute equaliser. He found 'Muzzie' who volleyed home from 25-yards. O's came an inch short of victory six minutes from the end. A floating corner from Deeley wafted near to Dunmore, whose right-foot sped the ball goalwards.

February 16, 1963
Leyton Orient 1 (Graham)
Fulham 1 (Cook)

With only two points separating O's from second-bottom Fulham (who also had a game in hand), this was a must-win game, but Fulham were clearly happiest with the point.

George, recalled in place of Pinner, couldn't stop Maurice Cook from giving Fulham the lead.

Graham, who scored in O's last league win, ironically at Fulham way back in September, was on the mark again to equalise.

February 19, 1963
FA Cup, 3rd round replay
Hull City 0
Leyton Orient 2 (Musgrove, Gibbs)
(After extra-time)

O's adjusted better to the condition of the snow-covered pitch, which almost caused an abandonment at Boothferry Park.

Fortunately for O's the game continued and three minutes into extra-time, Dunmore set up Musgrove to score his fourth goal in five matches.

Victory was sealed by hard-working Gibbs, who lobbed the ball over the Hull keeper seven minutes from time.

More encouraging news was the return from a broken leg of Malcolm Lucas, who came through the reserves' win over Watford unscathed. Thanks to the long list of postponements, the Welsh international had missed only two league games before returning to face Manchester City . . .

February 23, 1963
Leyton Orient 1 (Elwood)
Manchester City 1 (Harley)

Another home draw against fellow strugglers was not what O's needed, although there was no faulting the effort on a muddy pitch that wasn't conducive to cultured football. Joe Elwood, making his first start of the season at inside-left in place of the injured Graham, celebrated with the opening goal on 14 minutes. It came from a Charlton-inspired raid which ended with Bolland floating across a centre which Elwood guided home with his head.

Orient showed enormous spirit and skill throughout the game and they were incredibly unlucky to come away without two points after a lack-lustre performance by City, who were saved from a drubbing by a series of impossible saves by their new young keeper Harry Dowd.

Dunmore, Bolland, Elwood and Musgrove made a series of superb strikes on target but to the frustration of the 12,464 crowd, Dowd was inspirational. In sharp contrast home keeper George had only a couple of serious shots to deal with. One of these brought City's incredibly fortunate goal after 34 minutes, when the ball rebounded off George's body to marksman Alex Harley and ricocheted back into the net.

So marked was Orient's territorial superiority that for short periods, when first Musgrove – his right ankle damaged in a 26th minute shaking tackle – and later Lea – whose right eye was hurt by the flying elbow of an unusually robust Peter Dobing – were off the field, their absence went unnoticed.

March 2, 1963
Blackpool 3 (Quinn pen, Charlton OG, McPhee)
Leyton Orient 2 (Dunmore, Deeley pen)

When your luck's out . . . O's were dealt a big blow when Lucas headed the ball clear, only for a penalty to be awarded against him. Pat Quinn converted from the spot.

There was more freakish heartache seven minutes after the break, when Charlton turned a harmless-looking shot into his own net. Blackpool extended their lead to 3-0 15 minutes later when John McPhee headed in after the first effort struck the bar.

Never-say-die O's hit back on the bone hard pitch and got their reward when Dunmore scored after good work by Deeley, while the winger himself further reduced the deficit 11 minutes from time by scoring a penalty.

Gibbs came in for Musgrove, who hadn't recovered from the ankle he injured against Manchester City.

March 4, 1963
FA Cup, 4th round
Leyton Orient 3 (Dunmore, Elwood, Deeley)
Derby County 0

Briefly relieved of their dire need for league points, O's cruised to this confidence-boosting Cup win over second division strugglers Derby.

The opening 20 minutes belonged to inside-left Bolland whose prodding and scheming brings out the best in Dunmore who continued on to make the night his own. Dunmore's seventh minute goal relieved the crowd who had seen Derby nearly score in the opening seconds when inside-left Barry Hutchinson back-flicked the ball into the O's side-netting.

Orient with a much sharper edge than Derby, went on to score two more, miss three sitters and watch Derby send the ball roaring over the bar six times.

Outside-left Elwood, playing more inside than on the wing, hit a brave 70th minute goal, while Deeley ended a four-man move with a header that brought number three on the stroke of time.

Derby wingers George Stephenson and John McCann and a rumbustuous Bill Curry were the most threatening for the Rams.

Orient, who recalled 37-year-old Robertson in goal as a replacement for the unfit George (Pinner was cup-tied), threw a defensive screen around the goal to ensure that the veteran had only one hard shot to meet. Lewis, Lucas and Bishop were the stars of the O's defence.

In the match programme, the club responded to criticism that it hadn't made any moves to strengthen the team. It was revealed that O's had made a bid – which ultimately proved unsuccessful – for Burnley's Irish international inside-forward Jimmy McIlroy.

March 9, 1963
Leyton Orient 0
Aston Villa 2 (Woosnam, Wylie)

Three points adrift of Ipswich (who had a game in hand) before this match, this home defeat, played out in a dreadful gale-force wind, driving rain and on a quagmire of a pitch, cast further gloom over E10.

Robertson kept his place in goal after missing the previous 13 league games but he still couldn't deny former Orient playmaker Phil Woosnam and inside-forward Ron Wylie.

O's gave a debut at inside-right to Bobby Mason, their new £15,000 signing from Chelmsford City, who replaced Gibbs.

At times Mason was competent. Twice he was inspired long before the O's were a goal down. Mason sent Dunmore tearing into the penalty area after a perfect through ball. Unfortunately Villa were as alive to the situation as Orient were.

In the 33rd minute Mason deliberately left a floating Deeley cross to give Bolland a heaven-sent chance which he was unable to convert.

This was a match that seldom belonged to Orient. Ex-O's skipper Woosnam was Villa's centre-forward for a day, which he made his own when he threw himself down to head home a cross from right-winger Tommy Ewing in six minutes.

That goal, and a second from inside-left Wylie (38 mins), were not un-expected. Despite the friendly wind, O's couldn't muster one direct shot at the Villa goal.

March 16, 1963
FA Cup, 5th round
Leyton Orient 0
Leicester City 1 (Keyworth)

The second biggest crowd of the season of almost 26,000 – the best since the opening day fixture against Arsenal – turned out for this all-ticket cup tie, but the majority went home suffering more disappointment as O's cup run ground to a halt.

It was a very tall order, however, because City had emerged as the team of the season and, going into the game, were locked level with Tottenham at the top of the first division table on 41 points. Apart from the opening 15 minutes, the home side enjoyed most of the territorial advantage.

Bill Robertson can't stop Leicester City going through in the FA Cup.

Lewis went closest to equalising in the dying minutes when he popped up in the box, but his goal-bound header was somehow cleared by John Sjoberg. For all their possession and pressing, though, O's couldn't score past Gordon Banks and force the replay they at least deserved after Ken Keyworth had given City a seventh minute lead with a fine header following a good run and cross from right-winger Howard Riley.

Leicester went on to lose the FA Cup final at Wembley in May, 3-1 to Manchester United.

March 23, 1963
Leyton Orient 0
Nottingham Forest 1 (Addison)

Back to the hard slog for priceless league points, but another home defeat brought relegation ever closer.

Typical of O's bad luck that has haunted them all season, Forest's 54th minute winner by inside-right Colin Addison only went in after TWICE hitting a post! Charlton hoofed away the ball that had stuck on the mud, dangerously close to a vulnerable Orient goalmouth, but Addison collected the clearance and smartly sent it back into the net via the woodwork.

The pattern of play that led up to it seemed loaded against Orient who gave a dire performance. Orient's defence was as strong as it has been and of first division standard. Unfortunately, their attack was not. O's had half-a-dozen shots that were of very small concern to Peter Grummitt whose early defiance, when Orient were at their best, was a clue to the result.

Musgrove, painfully aware that no-one else was likely to score, elected himself a second-half role of shooting on sight. Using 25 yards as a minimum range, he threatened the goal once, the terraces twice, and the right-hand corner flag once with his wildest effort!

March 27, 1963
Tottenham Hotspur 2 (Smith, Greaves pen)
Leyton Orient 0
Orient went to a waterlogged White Hart Lane in midweek with relegation staring them in the face. Although Spurs continued to march forwards, Orient put up a gallant performance.

Big Bobby Smith, picked as England's centre-forward only hours before kick-off, shook Orient a couple of times in the first 10 minutes by twice hitting the woodwork. In the 24th minute he scored with a perfectly taken right-foot shot.

But Orient refused to be crushed and took heart from the surprisingly inept other Spurs' forwards and defenders. Yet time and again the midfield touches of inside-right Bobby Mason were ruined by the sort of shooting that had only seen Orient score 29 goals in as many matches in previous first division games.

It took a 64th minute penalty to finally finish brave hearted Orient's fight for a point. Lea brought down a very subdued Jimmy Greaves and the Spurs star scored from the spot himself. It was a decision hotly disputed by up-against-it O's, and left back Lewis had his name taken for arguing with the referee.

All in all, though, the Os could look back on this rain-filled night with pride.

March 30, 1963
Wolverhampton Wanderers 2 (Wharton, Stobart)
Leyton Orient 1 (Graham)
Another familiar hard luck story. Behind to Terry Wharton's goal after just three minutes, O's were unlucky not to level when Dunmore's shot struck the underside of the bar and rebounded into play.

The visitors finally got their reward in the second half when Graham netted from Musgrove's pass. Utility man Gibbs proved his value again by coming in for Lea, whose ever-present run was ended by a badly bruised ankle.

April 3, 1963
Leyton Orient 0
Leicester City 2 (Stringfellow 2)
Leicester arrived for this rearranged Wednesday fixture buoyed by their FA Cup sixth round victory just four days earlier, in front of an all-time record crowd at Norwich, imbuing Orient with a sense of what might have been.

This was to be the 14th game of what would eventually turn into a (then) record run of 16 unbeaten games for City. By a strange quirk of the fixture list, Orient managed to figure three times in this sequence, neatly book-ending the initial run of 10 consecutive victories from Boxing Day to the fifth round tie, and now facing the East Midlands club in full flow, and genuine double contenders at this stage of the season.

Any hopes of the home side improving on their spirited cup tie showing were soon dashed. In fact, it was the same seventh minute in which City again took control, this time through rangy winger Mike Stringfellow.

Stringfellow added the second goal just three minutes before the break and that effectively was that. If Gordon Banks, in the Leicester goal, was harbouring any nerves in anticipation of his first England cap, due just three days later, then Orient were unable to take advantage, and were left six points adrift of Manchester City at the foot of the table, whilst City closed in on Tottenham at the top.

Two days after losing to Leicester, O's had to reshuffle their fixtures again when the home match against Liverpool had to be postponed because the Merseysiders had three players involved in the England v Scotland international at Wembley. Instead, O's played a Friday night (April 5) friendly at home against Scottish second division promotion-chasers Morton.

April 12, 1963
Leyton Orient 0
Bolton Wanderers 1 (Butler)

It definitely wasn't a Good Friday for O's as Bolton – making their first-ever visit to Leyton Stadium – left town with both points. Wanderers arrived with only one previous away win under their belt and the O's were given an advantage when keeper Eddie Hopkinson spent 18 minutes of the first half off the field.

But Orient were not up to the job in hand. They fretted their way through 90 minutes of poor football where accurate passes looked accidental and inaccurate ones looked well rehearsed. In this game, resignation to the inevitable seemed evident in all that they did, or rather, all they failed to do.

When Hopkinson was out of action with a gashed knee, left-back Syd Farrimond went in goal . . . and became a hero when he saved two shots from Dunmore and a point-blank effort from Gregory.

That was Orient's lot. Hopkinson returned, Bolton reshaped and took control of the game. After 63 minutes, left-back Lewis upended Bolton striker Ron Davies and left-winger Dennis Butler coolly netted from the spot. Lewis had mis-passed with a short ball to Davies and in chasing him brought him down. Eddie told the press afterwards: "I didn't play the man. I knew I had made a mistake. I tried to play football using the short ball instead of the long one. And that's what happened."

One paper who quoted Eddie said: 'Sympathy is with Lewis – the record books will show a defeat apparently caused by him. He accepts the blame which so many other Orient players should have shouldered.'

April 13, 1963
Ipswich Town 1 (Moran)
Leyton Orient 1 (Musgrove)

What, two games in 24 hours! They wouldn't hear of it today, of course, but that was the Easter programme back in those days.

Ipswich, who had climbed to fifth from bottom, were much the happier with this outcome of a poor game.

Musgrove led the line with plenty of spirit and his fine efforts were rewarded three minutes before half-time when his 20-yard drive scorched the back of the net.

Orient looked determined although lacking in flair. Ipswich were lacking and feeble in front of goal. Only dreadful shooting prevented Ipswich from getting three goals in the first-half, with Pinner beaten each time.

After 63 minutes they equalised with a rebound from the post that Doug 'Dixie' Moran chipped in. At the end both teams were grateful for a point.

April 15, 1963
Bolton Wanderers 0
Leyton Orient 1 (Dunmore)

Dunmore prolonged O's fast-fading survival hopes a little longer, although this first league win since September 29 still left them six points adrift of Birmingham City, who had two games in hand.

The battle against relegation looked hopeless but the two points from this Monday evening fixture were sweet revenge for the Good Friday defeat at Brisbane Road.

Altogether a much better game with Orient working with enthusiasm and team spirit in abundance. O's winning plan was based on cutting Bolton's under-23 international Freddy Hill out of the game. Each time Hill got the ball he was challenged first time. With Mason looking very dangerous on the right-wing, the forwards played with more fire and skill than they had in a long time.

The goal which was always promised came in the 50th minute. Elwood's back pass foxed the defence, and Dunmore's shot zipped home, touching Warwick Rimmer on the way.

Bolton rallied desperately in the later stages and O's survived a 10-minute bombardment in which came corner after corner. But Orient refused to let go.

April 20, 1963
Leyton Orient 1 (Dunmore)
Blackburn Rovers 1 (Pickering)

On a very muddy pitch Orient's forwards, with the exception of Dunmore, were kept hidden.

Mason, Musgrove, Deeley and Elwood were chosen to sustain Orient's belated revival. None of them heavyweights in their height and none of them known to make light of heavy going.

It took them 58 minutes of sheer graft to find a formula that could have brought them success against uninspired Blackburn, when at last the long ball was used. Dunmore guided a shot against Else which rolled inches past the right post.

Blackburn, unencumbered by the need to play four forwards out of position, relied on England's flying winger Bryan Douglas to do their foraging and he did well. He switched to the middle to pick up a pass and played it into in-running Fred

Pickering. The centre-forward sent the ball through the mud to where Pinner flung himself down – only for the ball to bounce from his body into the net.

Mason, who looked less at sea than the rest of the forwards, ended a useful right-wing run in the 58th minute with a long, probing cross. Dunmore sent the ball home to earn O's another point.

April 26, 1963
Sheffield United 2 (Jones, Hartle)
Leyton Orient 0
Lucas was the only visitor to really trouble Alan Hodgkinson in the home goal. Had he scored with at least one of the two commendable individual efforts before Mick Jones thumped a glorious header past Pinner after 22 minutes, it might have been a different tale.

But following the goal United's youngsters gained in confidence and pace, although Bishop kept a very tight grip on top scorer Doc Pace.

Barry Hartle caused problems for Charlton and scored in the 71st minute, following a wonderful dribble along the by-line.

To O's credit, they played some very attractive football, although they couldn't manage to finish.

May 2, 1963
Leyton Orient 2 (Graham, Bishop)
Liverpool 1 (St. John)
An unusual Thursday night fixture – and an even rarer first division win!

It was a rare goal by Bishop that sealed this last home win in the first division, the centre-half having played a one-two with Musgrove before scoring with his right foot. On the final whistle the Orient players went wild as if they had won the European Cup. They had waited a long time for this home win – since September!

Keeper Pinner's fine performance included many first rate saves.

Mason and Musgrove showed their wonderful footballing skills which, had they been part of the team earlier in the season, many doubted the Os would be where they sadly were placed in the table.

Orient's forward line moved with confidence and a hunger for goals. Graham shot repeatedly, while Elwood chased the most hopeless balls – and often got them.

Orient rattled FA Cup semi-finalists Liverpool with a furious opening which gained just reward with two goals in 90 seconds. After 16 minutes Pinner kicked out, Mason fed Graham who rounded two men and slammed a fine ground shot in from 25 yards.

Almost immediately the O's were on the attack again, and Bishop came steaming up to take Musgrove's pass and score – his only strike of the season.

Liverpool's goal came a minute before the interval when Alan A'Court, under pressure, crossed brilliantly and St. John had an easy header.

May 4, 1963
Sheffield Wednesday 3 (Dobson, Fantham, Finney)
Leyton Orient 1 (Graham)

Colin Dobson put the home side ahead at Hillsborough in 21 minutes, after which Orient began to play some useful football and had to wait only six minutes before Graham headed them back into the game with an equaliser.

The O's finished the first half slightly on top but after the interval allowed Wednesday to pile on more pressure and gradually fell into an almost constant defensive role. Bishop managed to blot out Wednesday's record breaking goal scorer 'Bronco' Layne with some admirable work.

Charlton, who had the measure of Dobson for much of the match, found the Wednesday winger too much in the second half and most of Orient's trouble began on that wing. Pinner, who should have held Dobson's first goal, had little chance with those scored by John Fantham or Alan Finney, and in the second half pulled off some first class saves to keep out the Owls.

May 7, 1963
Leyton Orient 0
Burnley 1 (Towers)

The 10,000 Orient fans jeered the first half sorties, turning the Os into 11 fighting furies under the Brisbane Road lights. The ferocity with which the fans booed Burnley matched the enormity of their cheering for Orient.

Unfortunately Burnley gave Orient a slick lesson in first-time passing, defence covering and speedy build up of movement. The fans cheered non stop as Bolland, then Gibbs winged rasping drives round Alan Blacklaw in the Burnley goal – but always round him and not near enough to test him.

George's 20th minute hesitancy to dive allowed Ian Towers carefully pin-pointed shot to put the O's one goal behind. For Frank, recalled for his first game since February, it was very little consolation and a sad Brisbane Road farewell to a six-year reign at Orient.

For Orient it was another game of careless shooting, defence blunders and heartbreaking luck. Jimmy Adamson kicked a first-half Musgrove shot off the line with Blacklaw beaten, and the keeper knew nothing about Bolland's flying 46th minute header from Gibbs' canny cross before fumbling it away.

Orient hurled nine men into Burnley's half in a desperate bid to score and for the fighting furore of the second half alone Orient deserved a point. What a tragedy the cheering and fighting came 40 games too late to save Orient, who ended their home first division reign as they began it.

May 11, 1963
West Ham United 2 (Brabrook, Scott)
Leyton Orient 0

Musgrove, chided and cheered for 10 years by West Ham fans, came back to Upton Park wearing the number nine shirt as Orient's skipper for the day.

And in three Musgrove-inspired moments doomed Orient came within an ace of repeating their September victory over their East London rivals.

Musgrove – and their best forward Bobby Mason, the visitor prepared to move the ball forward – laid on chances in 32, 44 and 79 minutes for Gibbs. Each time Gibbs hesitated, Lawrie Leslie moved smartly and the chance was lost.

Gibbs and Orient paid highly for the missed chances six minutes from the end. Martin Peters and Peter Brabrook worked the ball cleverly on to the right. Brabrook centred to the far post where Bobby Moore headed the ball back into the middle for Tony Scott to beat Pinner with a clever overhead kick.

In between these so sparse thrill moments, Hammers, without ever impressing, strolled through.

When Brabrook rose brilliantly to head home Scott's 17th minute cross after a telepathic touch by top men Johnny Byrne and Moore, they were set to rub Orient's grubby nose more firmly into the Upton Park turf.

But West Ham failed again to turn their obvious supremacy and class into goals and were slowly dragged down in pace and style to Orient's less imaginative game.

Orient plugged away down the middle, where Musgrove used his speed and know-how to occasionally ferret a way past old colleague Ken Brown, but with John Bond taming Elwood and Bolland struggling, the two man Musgrove-Mason thrust was not enough to rattle West Ham's rearguard.

May 18, 1963
Manchester United 3 (S. Charlton OG, Law, B. Charlton)
Leyton Orient 1 (Dunmore)

Dunmore flashed a warning to second division followers with a cracking ninth minute goal when he out-jumped Bill Foulkes to score with a header from Mason's cross.

And O's, much the better side against the wind and on the greasy pitch, almost made it two when defender Tony Dunne headed a cross against his own crossbar with keeper David Gaskell beaten.

After the break United were the better side but they certainly used up their quota of luck. All three second half goals were gifted to them – the first when a hard working Stan Charlton netted a freak 52-minute own goal for the equaliser and the second and third, in 81 and 83 minutes, scored by Denis Law and Bobby Charlton both coming from errors by George who was deputising for Pinner (on England amateur duty).

Lucas and skipper Charlton almost blotted United's international left-wing pair out of the game until that final 10-minute spell. Mason, Dunmore and Musgrove were other top performers as Orient bowed out of the first division as they swept in – defeated but not disgraced.

Chapter 10

IT'S ALL OVER NOW
Rolling Stones, 1964

THE cold, hard facts tell their own story of how Leyton Orient were relegated at the end of their first – and only – season in the top flight. Only six victories and nine draws from 42 games meant they were destined for the dreaded drop long before the last rites of their season in the sun were performed by a 3-1 final day defeat at Manchester United.

Orient's meagre final tally of 21 points equalled the pitifully poor record of Portsmouth two years earlier and was the lowest by any team relegated from Division One since Leeds United went down with only 18 points in 1947. Some of Orient's blushes were eased, however, in 1966 when Blackburn Rovers dropped back into Division Two with a mere 20 points.

Those thrilling, consecutive home wins against West Ham (2-0), Man United (1-0) and Everton (3-0) in the space of 10 gloriously happy days in September, with not a single goal conceded, seemed like a distant dream by the time they managed their only other league win at Brisbane Road, with the trap door to Division Two already wide open, against Liverpool in early May.

Five home draws, with Sheffield United, Birmingham City, Fulham, Manchester City and Blackburn Rovers, were nowhere near enough. Man City went down with Orient despite finishing with 10 more points and having inflicted a 4-1 end-of-season defeat on Tottenham that ended their hopes of catching Everton, who were labelled the 'Cheque-book Champions' for effectively buying the title. Everton boss Harry Catterick splashed £175,000 on five new players, then added to it during the season by signing Tony Kay from Sheffield Wednesday for £60,000 and Alex Scott from Glasgow Rangers for £40,000.

All the O's had to show for their troubles away from Brisbane Road were wins at Fulham's Craven Cottage (2-0) and Bolton (1-0), the Burnden Park success coming way too late in mid-April to have any real meaning. They managed to avoid defeat at Birmingham City (2-2), Nottingham Forest (1-1), Blackburn Rovers (1-1) and Ipswich Town (1-1).

Sheffield Wednesday, Spurs, Liverpool (who, interestingly, also changed very little from the side that had won promotion with Orient a year earlier), Wolves and Leicester City all hit four or more goals against the O's.

It wasn't as if Orient could even partially blame their demise on the big winter freeze-up that paralysed the Football League programme for weeks between December and February as one postponement led to another. If anything, their relatively small squad should have welcomed the unexpected respite – a chance for players and management to regroup, although it would have hit Orient's finances hard.

But Orient were not swept aside all the time. No-one could question the players' effort and no fewer than 10 defeats by the odd goal makes you wonder what might have been.

Malcolm Lucas, one of the most consistent performers, actually benefited from the worst British winter in years. Despite breaking his leg in the home game against Birmingham City on December 22, Lucas missed only two league matches and was back in the side before the end of February.

The Welsh international gave an honest assessment of Orient's failure to stay in Division One and his own contribution to the cause when he said: "When I look back, I think I was a little bit disappointed with myself. I thought I could have done better. I think we lost that feeling we had when we got promoted.

"Perhaps we tried too hard at times that can backfire on you. Plus teams don't always function as well when they are under the type of constant pressure we found ourselves under in the first division.

"One main difference I found playing in Division One is that when I went forward to support our attackers, there were opposition players who wouldn't follow me. So if our move broke down, I'd often find that there was a spare player behind me in space to receive the ball – and we couldn't seem to counteract that kind of situation. I'm not blaming anybody, because I possibly did the same.

"I never went into the season thinking that we would come straight back down again, although we certainly knew it would be tough. You only had to look at the teams we were up against to know that. We'd moved up to a standard where mistakes that we might have got away with in the second division, we paid the price for it in the top league.

"The shame of it was that we didn't strengthen the squad. I'd rather not say which positions we particularly needed to strengthen but if the Orient wanted to stay in the top flight, that was the time they should have looked to improve the squad.

"I'm not being nasty but there were players who were in the twilight of their careers, although I don't know if the board had the money to bring in new players. That was obviously a matter between them and Johnny Carey," added a thoughtful Lucas.

Mal's fellow Welshman and wing-half, Cyril Lea, recalls a meeting he had with Carey as Orient's first division plight worsened. He said: "We knew we were struggling and didn't have enough good players. I was captain for a spell when Stan was out injured and I remember going into see Johnny Carey and asking him if he felt there was anything more I could do to get us through this. He was always very calm and all he said to me was: 'Just keep playing your football and don't panic.'

"I said to him that I felt we needed some fresh blood to get us through but he said: 'We haven't got the money, my hands are tied.'

"I don't know why that was, because we'd had two good years when the crowd had come. Obviously I didn't know what was going on behind the scenes but, as a player,

I thought we were going to struggle because we just weren't good enough. We couldn't score enough goals against the big clubs. It's the same today. If you don't score enough goals, you don't survive in the Premiership.

"Whether he'd tried desperately to bring in new players and couldn't because of the money, I don't know. But I came out of my meeting with him feeling frustrated, because I hadn't achieved much.

"But we just didn't have it – and we didn't have the money either."

In the updated 2006 edition of *Leyton Orient, The Complete Record*, Carey and Leslie Grade are quoted as having had the following conversation after yet another defeat had nailed Orient to the basement position.

Grade: "John, how much would it take to keep the O's in the first division?"

According to the above book, Carey replied: "Mr. Grade, may I be honest with you? . . . please don't waste your money."

Terry McDonald, who was dropped after the 2-1 defeat at Arsenal on December 15 and never made another first division appearance after Malcolm Musgrove was signed from West Ham to replace him on the left wing, agreed with Lucas' assessment. He said "It was definitely a mistake not to have strengthened the squad immediately after getting promoted.

"There was too much onus on Dave Dunmore to score, although Malcolm Graham weighed in with nine goals, but there wasn't much support from the rest and the ratio of goals from midfield was poor.

"The wingers were having to defend a lot more, and we were under much more pressure as a team. We were more defensively minded, so I wasn't skipping past full-backs and getting crosses in, like I had been doing in the second division. There was a lack of possession too, because you had to work that bit harder to get the ball, especially away from home.

"People talk about how good our halfback line was – and they were particularly brilliant for us in the promotion year – but how many goals did they score in the first division? I'm not saying Malcolm Lucas was playing purely defensively. Because he was under so much pressure, he obviously couldn't get forward as often as he would've wanted to, and as much as we needed him to. I thought we often lacked support from midfield to be able to create enough chances."

Cyril Lea played 228 League and Cup games for the O's, most of them at left-half, but he never scored. He laughed when he pointed out that he went on to score a couple of long-range efforts after moving on to Ipswich.

"Maybe I should have been a bit more selfish. But Mal Lucas would push on and I would make sure that Eddie Lewis was protected, and if I needed to get across the pitch to help Sid Bishop, I'd do that too. I suppose I never got far enough forward up the pitch to score.

"I got my kicks from being part of the team and the good spirit we had."

McDonald dismisses any notion that the O's players went into the season with an inferiority complex, saying: "We weren't overrawed by the situation and the prospect of facing these teams. Arsenal were one of the top teams but there was

Up for the fight . . . Terry McDonald and Sheffield Wednesday defender Don Megson square up to each other during the brutal first division game at Brisbane Road that left several O's players nursing injuries.

really nothing in the match when they beat us 2-1 on the opening day.

"I always thought that the most unfortunate two games were those against West Brom, where we lost despite absolutely dominating both matches. We felt we were unlucky against the Albion.

"Then we won three homes games on the trot – against West Ham, Manchester United and Everton – and felt that we'd really cracked it in the first division."

After the team had gone 11 games without a win, McDonald was dropped following a 2-0 defeat by Arsenal at Highbury on December 15. He was replaced by experienced left-winger Malcolm Musgrove, an £11,000 signing from West Ham, and never played another game in the top flight.

"It was a big step up for all of us and, after the initial good start, you didn't realise how much more difficult these teams would make it for us, with their better organisation as well as ability.

"Where we had the luxury, in our promotion season, of being able to play our football instinctively and with ease at times, in the top flight we got muscled out of it. I probably had my best games against two England full-backs, Jimmy Armfield (Blackpool) and Don Howe (West Brom), but I found that most of the full-backs were stronger and more clued up compared to those I'd faced in Division Two. The most difficult right-backs I came up against in the top flight were Burnley's John Angus, George Cohen of Fulham – even though we beat them at Craven Cottage – and Tottenham's Peter Baker.

"In the first division, we had to do so much more defending as a team, even most of the forwards, which meant leaving Dave isolated. When we did go forward, we had no six-yard box goalscorer, like a Clive Allen or a Tony Cottee, and that's the easiest place to score. We never had that - our forwards were more suited to scoring from more long-range efforts *outside* the penalty area. I probably scored more goals in the six-yard box than anyone else I played with at the club!"

But don't forget the part heavy pitches played. The inside-forwards and wing-halfs had to contend with cloying mud. And come autumn, never mind winter, you would have been hard pressed to find another pitch in the Football League as heavy and so lacking in turf than the notorious Brisbane Road mudheap.

"Yeah, when you think about it, the inside-forwards had to come back deep and pick up balls up inside our own half, starting moves from there, and then try and get in the box as well. On very heavy pitches. It must have °been hard work for them.

"When I looked up before crossing the ball, I never saw three or four of our players in the box waiting for the ball, like you do when teams attack now.

Players can get up and down so much easier now on the lovely, perfect pitches they play on in the English Premiership. But I can't remember crossing a ball and someone scoring from inside the six-yard box. Goals were more often than not scored from either a header or a long-range shot. There never seemed to be any tap-ins.

"I'd love to see re-runs of all our games and see why things happened the way they did."

"They say the players of today are so much fitter than they were in our day, but all

I know is that we were knackered at the end of training. And our facilities were probably 10 times worse then."

Malcolm Graham recalls that Orient abandoned their usual passing game as the first division struggled worsened. He says: "Before things started going downhill in the first division, we liked to pass the ball around – people like Eddie Lewis especially. But then after a while, Carey got us playing a long-ball game and a few of us started to grumble about it.

"I think if we'd kept playing football, we might have done a bit better."

Apart from the return of George Waites (who returned from Norwich for £5,000 but soon moved on to Brighton) and Musgrove, a more experienced and direct winger than McDonald with a proven scoring record, Johnny Carey's only other signing during the course of the first division struggle was inside-right Bobby Mason – a controversial £15,000 buy from non-league Chelmsford City. Apparently, Orient pulled a bit of a flanker in taking the dribbling inside-forward from their Essex-based Southern League neighbours. Mason was too good for that level, having played alongside Norman Deeley in the same star-studded Wolves team of the late 50s but he wasn't the immediate answer to Orient's problems.

Even though he was disappointed to be axed from the side after 20 games and two goals, McDonald admits: "Let's be honest. If the manager and directors had been ruthless, they might have decided that half the team probably wasn't up to first division standard anyway, which would have meant a major rebuilding job and half-a-dozen new signings brought in, to have given us even half a chance of staying in the top flight. But, obviously, that was never going to happen."

Eddie Lewis is another who offers a forthright opinion on why the O's didn't hack it in the top grade. He says: "We had a team of guys who were *nearly* very good players. We gelled together and we had a great team spirit.

"If I'd been quicker, I think I could have played for England. If Dave Dunmore had been a bit more dedicated, *he* would have played for England. If Terry McDonald had been a bit stronger, he too would have played for his country."

Dave Dunmore, who led the way with 11 league goals (half his impressive second division haul), added: "I just don't think we had enough firepower, we never scored enough goals. When it came down to it, we were just playing against better all round teams and superior finishers.

"We showed enough in some games but in others we just got walked over. At the end it was a case of 'are we going to do it today, lads?'.

"We gave our best but in the end it wasn't good enough."

The facts can't argue with DD's succinct summing up.

Johnny Carey took the O's into Division One, but couldn't keep them there.

Chapter 11

JOHNNY REMEMBER ME
John Leyton, 1961

WHERE do we go from here? While some of the relegated players waited nervously to see if they would be included on the retained list for 1963-64, Johnny Carey made a swift exit and headed to Nottingham Forest, who had just finished ninth in Division One.

Yet again, the beleaguered Leyton Orient board turned to trusty Les Gore, that serial caretaker boss, who answered their latest SOS call and stepped into the breach for a FIFTH time! Much more on what the players who knew Les thought of him and his methods is to follow, but let's first look at the immediate fall-out and the sudden departure of Carey.

In the process of interviewing no fewer than 15 surviving members of the squads that spanned the two-year period of Carey's turbulent tenure for this book, it has to be said that the vast majority of them had only kind words to say about the genial, quietly spoken Irishman with the pipe. The overriding view is that he was unconfrontational, easy-going and, from a football aspect, he let the players do their own thing to a large extent. He was, and remains, highly regarded by most of the players who wore the blue of Leyton Orient during his two years with the club.

He was no tracksuit manager – how many were in those days? – and was happy to leave the tactics and coaching to first team coach Eddie Baily. "Happily, Eddie's views coincide with mine," said Carey on his introduction to the former England and Tottenham inside-forward.

Stan Charlton enjoyed a good working relationship with Carey and said: "I was very disappointed when he left – I didn't know anything about him going until it had already happened – but you couldn't blame him for bettering himself.

"Unfortunately he came to a club that had no money to spend on players. For instance, I know he wanted to sign inside-left George O'Brien from Southampton, because I'd recommended O'Brien to him. But Johnny told me that we just couldn't afford him, that the club was strapped for cash. He had to strengthen from lower leagues, hence the signing of Bobby Mason from Chelmsford City.

"I think Johnny just accepted that he'd come from a club that had more money than just about any other in English football, to one that had relatively little to spend on players. But I never heard him complain about anything – he seemed to have a good relationship with the board of directors.

"When we played Everton at Goodison Park, he received a standing ovation from the Everton fans when he appeared in the directors' box just before the start of the game. It must have given him a lot of pleasure, because I know how hurt he felt when Everton sacked him. He was so well respected that it must have come as a big shock to him.

"He named his house in Woodford 'Moore's Folly', after the Everton chairman, because he bought it with the money the club paid him when they gave him the sack.

"Carey must have done something good for us – we won promotion to the first division."

"He always seemed to have his pipe in his mouth, although he never actually smoked in the dressing room area. He was a gentleman and so laid-back.

"He made sure everybody stood up for and respected the club, as well as the people in it. We all had player passes that we were supposed to show whenever we entered the ground on a match-day. He told us to always respect the doorman when we arrived. He told us all: 'It doesn't matter how the fellow on the door knows you, or who you are, *always* show him your player's pass. That's his job, so don't embarrass him at all'.

"That comment by Carey has stuck with me ever since and, in later years when I was manager at Weymouth Football Club, I always made the players and staff show their passes to the doorman. That was typical Johnny – he respected everybody."

Dave Dunmore said: "Johnny Carey got the lads playing for him and he made everybody believe they were the best. He told me that I should have played for England but I don't know about that – there were one or two good 'uns about at the time. Bobby Smith, of Tottenham, for one.

"I was surprised when he left suddenly. He didn't say anything to me, nor any of the other players as far as I know, before going."

Dunmore gave Carey one of his happiest days as O's boss, as Joe Elwood explains: "The day when Dave scored a hat-trick at Swansea, in our promotion season, was the only time I saw Johnny Carey show any emotion. As Dave took off his shirt in the dressing room afterwards, Carey kept saying to him: 'Great game, DD.' He even helped Dave to take off his wet shirt and boots! It was so unlike Carey."

Carey's two biggest signings for Orient were Norman Deeley and Gordon Bolland, who both arrived to aid the promotion push in February 1962. Gordon admits: "I've obviously got a lot to thank Johnny Carey for, because he saw something in me. I came in late on in the promotion season and I think they brought me in to freshen things up a little bit and with an eye on the future.

"He was a lovely guy – calm and laid-back.

"A lot of people didn't like him, because he was a bit too . . . how can I put it? . . . laid-back, if you like, but I thought he was a great guy.

"Although Carey was obviously the sort of guy who wouldn't survive today in the job that he did. To be fair, how many managers from his era could?"

Norman Deeley wasn't impressed, though. Comparing the Orient manager to his previous boss at Wolves, the legendary Stan Cullis, he says: "Johnny Carey didn't measure up to Cullis' standards at all. Cullis was a hard taskmaster.

"I'd obviously been playing in a better side at Wolves. But at Leyton Orient, they wanted me to track back, like wingers do nowadays, and it upset my game. Cullis had never wanted me to come back any deeper than the halfway line, whereas Carey expected me to get back and help out Stan Charlton, which became harder for me to do by that stage in my career. I was getting on when I went to Orient . . . but Stan was even older than me!"

Deeley was dismayed by Carey's apparent inability to stop the rot as the first division campaign unfolded.

"After a fairly decent start, we were soon out of our depth and Carey couldn't do anything to turn it around. We'd be losing by four or five and all he'd keep saying to us was: 'Just keep playing'. He gave us no motivation or ideas whatsoever."

Carey gave two Orient players – England amateur international keeper Mike Pinner and young forward Harry Gregory – their first team debuts midway through the first division campaign. Mike said of his former manager: "He was a quiet man and in many respects he had the same sort of approach as Matt Busby did at Manchester United. Everybody respected him. He never pointed the finger at me or anyone as such and he would give personal advice when necessary."

Harry said: "Before my debut against Ipswich, he just told me to go out and fizz it about – he didn't baffle you with science. He just told you to play it easy, knock it around, give and go.

"He was very good to me after the game. He came and had a quiet chat and asked me how I felt I'd done."

Carey's distinguished playing career with Manchester United earned him the instant respect of all when he first arrived at Brisbane Road. Mal Lucas said: "You couldn't help but look up to him because of what he'd done in his playing career. He let people do their thing and, in doing that, you felt more relaxed. He very rarely got upset with you and always talked in that easy manner, which relieved you of pressure.

"I was very fortunate that I always got on well with him. As a man, he was so nice, terrific, a lovely fella and I couldn't say anything against him.

"As far as him being a good manager is concerned, the footballing side came through Eddie Baily and the tactics were deployed from there. Now whether that was on Johnny Carey's instructions, or he gave Baily his head and let him get on with it, I don't know for sure.

"That was the thing about Carey, though – he didn't put any restrictions on you as a player. He let you play your natural game but he never sent me out to play with any specific instructions. If things weren't going well in the game, he'd just walk around the dressing room and give you a bit of encouragement and tell you not to worry.

"He was always so relaxed and I can't ever remember seeing him lose his temper."

In many respects, Johnny Carey was ideally suited to the gentile atmosphere and solitude of the golf course. Malcolm Graham remembers: "He was a very good golfer and, as usual, he played the game while puffing on his pipe.

"We used to play at a course out in Essex somewhere, where we had matches against their club members. Afterwards they'd put on a super meal for us and Johnny always enjoyed those days.

"Years later, we had a bit of a 'do' when a lot of us got together again at the ground. Johnny was there and the first thing he remembered about me was a goal I scored at Derby, where I dribbled the ball along the touchline in the six-yard box before scoring."

Unlike most of their former team-mates, Eddie Lewis and Terry McDonald were very critical of Carey's ability in both a tactical and man-management sense.

Lewis, who went on to become a top coach in South Africa and was a member of the country's coaching team at the 1998 World Cup finals in France, said: "I played with him at Man United as a forward and he was a great player – 10 times better than me. He captained United, Republic of Ireland and also the Rest of Europe against England.

"I liked him as a man but as a manager, he never inspired me. He never got me on my own and told me anything that would enhance my game, make me a better player.

"We'd be having a team-talk and then he'd suddenly walk out. We got beat 5-1 at Leicester and the players wanted to know when we were going to discuss the situation and try to put it right, and in the end we *forced* him to have a team-talk. When it started, he asked me what I thought the problems were. But I told him that we'd like to hear *his* views on what *he* thought had gone wrong on the pitch. He didn't really know what to say to that, so he just looked at me and said: 'The five goals were all down to you!'

"His favourite saying was: 'Get the ball, fizz it here and fizz it there'. He said it so often, we called him 'Mr Fizz It'.

Joe Elwood remembers the home game against Norwich City, in December 1961, when Eddie Lewis 'fizzed it' a little too much. "When Carey told us in every pre-match team-talk he gave to 'fizz it', he meant he wanted us to play quick, incisive and accurate passes. He also told us to give our goalkeeper an early touch of the ball.

"Anyway, we'd only just kicked off against Norwich when Eddie over-hit his backpass to Frank George . . . and Frank pulled off a great save to concede a corner!

"Being a Catholic and a religious church-going man like myself, neither Carey nor I ever swore, even though swearing is a language in itself within football. but when we came in at half-time, he turned to Eddie and said: 'What were you bloody thinking off there, hitting the backpass so hard?' It was strange to hear him use the word 'bloody'," added Joe.

"In fact, Carey tried to ban any swearing around the club and he became unhappy one day with your dad while we were training at Low Hall Farm (sports ground), Walthamstow. Alan Eagles was a very hard tackler, who kicked lumps out of me in a practice match at the main ground one time. Anyway, on this particular occasion, Eagles was repeatedly kicking Terry to bits until after one bad challenge and your dad said: 'For effin' sake, Alan!' Carey went across to Terry and told him to calm down and watch his language. Your dad replied: 'It's not *you* he's kicking effin' lumps out of!'

"I think Carey was on the point of setting up a swear-box by then!" laughed Joe,

Johnny Carey quietly listens while his players have their say in the dressing room.

whose preferred choice of F-word is 'flippin'.

As relegation loomed large, Eddie Lewis was dropped by Carey and missed the last nine league games of the first division campaign, including what, for him, would have been an emotional return to Old Trafford on the final day of the season.

"He brought in Mike Hollow and, before that, a kid called Billy Taylor also had a number of games at left-back. But Billy was actually slower than me!

"I don't want to speak ill of the dead but Carey was a very lucky man to walk into Orient and take over that team, and then go on to manage Forest and Blackburn the way he did."

Frank George added: "What Eddie says about Johnny Carey is absolutely correct. As great as he was as a player, Carey couldn't talk football, so he'd get the players to talk about it. He'd puff on his pipe and, in his Irish lingo, he'd just pick out people. For example, he'd say to Dave Dunmore: 'Now Dave, let us have your thoughts on this or that.'

"But he was a lovely gentleman."

Cyril Lea said: "We could play a tight game and still get beat one or two-nil and that frustrated us if we'd played well for the vast majority of the game. We were living beyond our means really.

"I think Carey was lucky, because he came and we did well for him. He'd been a great player in his time but he was so laid-back as a manager when I felt that we needed to show a bit more urgency.

"He was a good manager in the sense that you could go out and express yourself – he never put pressure on you in that way and he never rollicked you. He was a good man and I think, with good players, he would have been an excellent manager."

As Orient's first division plight deepened, it seems Carey was prepared to try just about anything to turn the tide. Supporter John Parke recalls a bizarre team selection for the home game against Wolves in November, following the previous week's 5-0 drubbing by Liverpool at Anfield and a run of seven consecutive matches without a win.

Parke said: "A mate of mine lived next door to Carey at Woodford Bridge. He saw him the day before the Wolves game and Carey told my friend that he would be going all out to confuse the Wolves the next day – by changing around the Orient players' shirt numbers!"

Malcolm Lucas handed his customary No.4 shirt to Derek Gibbs and, instead, wore No.10 for the one and only time that season; centre-forward Dave Dunmore gave his No.9 to Harry Gregory and took the No.7 shirt from Norman Deeley, who wore the No.11 vacated by the axed Terry McDonald. Billy Taylor pulled on the No.8 that Gregory had worn at Anfield.

Whatever the manager had in mind, his shirt shake-up appeared to confuse his own players more than it did Wolverhampton's. Orient lost 4-0!

Terry McDonald is also critical of Carey's management style and admits that he and the manager never really saw eye to eye. He said: "Carey inherited a team that was on the up.

"To be honest, I think he was a big mickey-taker. He came across as aloof of everybody and what he did for Orient, I don't know. *He* didn't get them promoted – the players did. It seemed to me that he thought to himself: 'What am I doing at Orient? I should be somewhere better than this'.

"I think he looked down on a lot of the players, although he respected Stan, being an older player. He couldn't fault Stan and obviously knew that he was a 100 per cent, no thrills player, someone who worked very hard and did his job.

"All he ever said, no matter what the situation, was 'just keep playing football, boys'. You could be 3-0 up or three down, but all he ever said to us was 'keep playing football'. And that was it. Or he'd say: 'Fizz it about'. "But, from a tactical point of view, we got nothing from him and I don't think he knew the game. Eddie Baily was the only one who said anything constructive to us.

"When things were going wrong in the first division, none of the Orient players challenged his authority in the dressing room. He never really gave anyone a proper bollocking – at least Les Gore would if he felt he needed to. Les would go 'For f*** sake . . .' He'd talk to us in *our* language. He'd tell you where you were going wrong and you'd respond to his words.

"Carey never did anything to help me become a better player, that's for sure. He never got hold of me and told me what to do – never. He never told me how I could improve my game. All he would do occasionally is tell you what he thought you were doing wrong.

"He'd say things to me like: 'I never see you heading the ball', or 'when you challenge someone, you're three yards away from the ball'. I did try to jump with six-foot-two full-backs but I was never going to win those aerial battles, was I? My answer to him would be: 'Why is the ball being played to me in the air, instead of to my feet?' Was it me not showing myself or what? Just tell me! But he never could. Eddie Baily was the only one at Orient who helped me to improve my game."

Apart from being dismayed by Carey's apparent lack of tactical nous, McDonald also questioned his man-management skills.

He continued: "Carey was never a manager to put his arm round you and give you encouragement or good advice.

"The only time we really spoke to each other was when he walked along the train while we were travelling to Leicester, just after I'd been dropped from the first team. I was sitting on my own and he got his pipe out, sat down next to me and asked: 'Hello Terry, how would you like a move?'

"He took me all the way there in the snow to be 12th man. I just told him 'no thanks' to the move. He didn't even mention the name of another club but it didn't matter to me anyway. I told him I just wanted to stay and win back my first team place. I didn't want to move anywhere.

"He had a strange way of saying things and sometimes you didn't know whether he was testing you or what. Whether he wanted to hear you say 'no, I'm Orient through and through and I want to stay here', I don't know.

"Carey didn't like me for some reason and I don't know why, because he never gave me a reason or even a bollocking. Apart from him asking me if I fancied a move, we never sat down for a one-on-one discussion about anything.

"After Carey dropped me from the first team, I was playing for the Reserves when we were beaten 3-2 by Brentford. I played at inside-right and scored twice but we threw the game away. As I walked into the dressing room at the end of the game, Carey was waiting by the door, puffing on his pipe as usual. I shook my head in disappointment at the way we'd lost and he just said to me: 'I don't know why you're shaking your head – you're the biggest culprit'. I went: 'Yeah, I know'.

"I thought, 'what the hell does he mean by that?' I couldn't believe it but he could turn on you like that. We just didn't get on.

"I don't care what other players have said about him – and I know Whitey would say the same as me – but Johnny Carey did nothing for me."

In case anyone should dismiss the strong views by McDonald and Lewis as simply sour grapes from players who were dropped from the team, Sid Bishop echoed some of their thoughts on Carey. He also recalled a cryptic conversation with the manager over a possible move.

Bishop said: "We were on the train coming back from Manchester – we could have been playing at Bury or Preston, or someone like that. It had only just pulled out of the station when Carey looked over and said: 'Sid, would you like to live up here?'

"All of a sudden, things started to click in my head and I just wanted him to explain properly what he had on his mind. He repeated the question and I told him: 'Nah, I'm perfectly happy where I am now . . . Woodford Green, lovely house and two lovely kids'.

"My wife Vera used to work as a seamstress for a dressmaking company just off Brick Lane, and we were both so happy with our lot. I'd come from a bleedin' old terraced house at Tooting Broadway and she'd been brought up in Hackney Wick. We loved it in the club house we rented at Durham Avenue – I was as happy as a pig in muck at the Orient.

"Carey didn't say any more to me about it, and I never pressed him on the possibility of me moving, but he must have been referring to interest in me from Manchester United. What he was trying to say to me tied in with what Don Gibson – the former Orient player – had told me about Matt Busby, his father-in-law, having recently watched me play. Things were really buzzing for me at the time and Don said: 'Matt is having another look at you today', but I just dismissed it as football talk.

"In quiet moments on my own, I still occasionally wonder what it would have been like to have joined Man United, how I would have done up there. But it wasn't a big thing at the time – I would have only earned money from my percentage of the transfer fee. If Carey had said: 'There's £10,000 going into the bank for you,' I might have been interested. But it would have taken something very big, financially, to have moved me from the Orient."

Sid recalled another time, in the dressing room, when Carey made one of his 'funny' remarks to him.

"He was a bit of a character who would come out with funny, little Irish quips," says Sid. "I didn't understand half of them but you knew he was trying to be funny because he'd give a little grin after he'd said something.

"We came in from training once and he walked over to me, just before I got stripped off and into the shower. He said: 'Where have you been? . . . have you been out training with us?' He called Les Gore over and added: 'Look Les, there's not a bit of sweat on him'.

"I said: 'Perhaps I'm *super-fit!*'

"Carey gave me a long, hard stare, and then walked away."

Sid Bishop likes a laugh, but jokes questioning his fitness were not to be entertained.

How much credit for winning promotion should go to Johnny Carey is a point that can be debated forever more. The fact is, the team was 19th in Division Two when he arrived and a year later their free-flowing football – encouraged by Carey and coached by Eddie Baily – saw them elevated to the big-time. No Orient team or manager has been there since.

Carey always appreciated how well he was treated by Leyton Orient, although the cold, hard statistics from the first division season indicate that he under-estimated the size of the task, or overrated the ability of his own players. Maybe both?

And then you look at what Carey achieved after leaving Brisbane Road. At his next club, he built a good Nottingham Forest team that finished runners-up in the first division (1966-67), proving that he could manage well at the highest level.

But the last controversial word goes to the forthright Eddie Lewis, who said: "Les Gore could have done the same job that Johnny Carey did for the Orient."

Orient's most successful manager-coach combination – Johnny Carey and Eddie Baily.

FROM ME TO YOU
Beatles, 1963

IF Orient had an unsung hero during the two-year period we're covering, it was undoubtedly Eddie Baily, the former England inside-forward and a member of Arthur Rowe's famous push-and-run League championship-winning side at Tottenham in 1950-51.

A decade later, after Baily had quit playing and became the O's first team player-coach (a role he started on joining the O's in 1958-59), everything he learned at White Hart Lane manifested itself in the Orient promotion-winning team. Johnny Carey received much of the credit for taking Orient up in his first season with the club, but Baily was the man behind the scenes who pulled the strings on the training ground and who nurtured those players to fulfil their potential.

Clapton-born Eddie, now 81 and still living in London, last returned to Brisbane Road to watch a match about seven or eight years ago. His cockney wisecracks were unmistakable as he entered one of the lounges in the East Stand shortly before kick-off. Dad quickly introduced me to his larger-than-life former coach as he was on his way to his seat in the main stand and I seized the chance to ask Eddie if he would agree to be interviewed for this book.

Sadly, he declined with a few choice words that, anyone who knows this irascible character of London football, will recognise as the thoughts of an old man too long in the tooth to worry about going over so much old ground. What Eddie Baily – who

Eddie Baily had been a winner as a player and he won the players' respect again as a top coach.

also played for Port Vale and Nottingham Forest before joining the O's – has forgotten about football is more than the rest of us can ever possibly know. So while it's a disappointment to me that this great character wasn't up for reflecting on his very influential role in Orient's finest league success, his impact on the place can still be measured on the following pages through the players who played with and worked under him on all those mornings while training at Ashton Playing Fields, Hackney Marshes and Leyton Stadium.

Terry McDonald is in no doubt who should get much of the credit for his progress at Orient after signing from West Ham before the 1959-60 season. He says: "Baily was realistic, he never complicated the game and he knew what assets you had and what you needed to improve on. He brought more options to my game.

"He used to get me back in the afternoons for individual training, or sometimes he'd work with me, Ronnie Foster and Dennis Sorrell. That's how we got to develop such a good understanding between us on the field. Eddie would teach me the art of wing play and coach you to your assets. He impressed upon me the need to be able to dribble with both feet, about coming inside to shoot with my right foot and making it difficult for full-backs to read what you were about to do next. I was naturally right-footed but I had no problem crossing with my left, I didn't have to switch the ball to my right foot.

"That type of coaching started when I was at West Ham Boys and my coach there called Mr Walsh, who was on the FA committee at the time. He emphasised to me that you just can't expect to play well with only one foot, because you can create so many more options for myself by being two-footed. It's all about practice, practice and even more practice.

"It was the same if I played outside-right, which I did quite a few times for the Orient later on. If I came inside, I knew I could shoot or continue to build up play with my left foot. It's just common sense really and I'm amazed when I watch football today how many one-footed players there are earning a great living in the game. Players today don't try and improve on their weaknesses, or they are not confident enough to use their weaker foot. Once you've got the confidence to use it, it leads you to so many more options for your team and yourself. Obviously, while I was coming inside onto my right foot, the inside-left – Foster or whoever – would move outside to take my place. The picture opened up to us. To be honest, because I was two-footed, I always thought I could have done a good job at inside-forward."

"At Orient, we didn't do much of the weightlifting work Malcolm Allison had introduced while I was at West Ham in the late 50s. At Orient, it was all short fitness stuff, such as sprints, but most of the training with Eddie Baily was done with the football. We played small-sided games – like three versus three – with the emphasis on keeping control. Eddie's main thing was that you had to be able to control the ball. If you couldn't do that, you had big problems."

At 9st 4lbs wet through, McDonald was considered lightweight but no-one doubted his willingness to work for the good of the team, even though he was slight and lacked physical strength.

He admits: "The tackling aspect has to come into it too and, obviously, being lightweight I was never going to be too brilliant at that. But I used to do my share of working back to help Eddie Lewis.

"But Baily didn't expect me to win many tackles – he just wanted me to make it more difficult for the opposing right-back and to try and stop them playing from the back or making runs forward. When you're lightweight, that's all you could do – you can't throw yourself into tackles.

"Eddie was all for educating us in how the game should be played, he loved a ball-player. He wanted to play the game the right way – pass and move and keep the game flowing.

"He was a terrific inside-forward in his heydey with England and Spurs and the Orient were lucky to have him as both a player and then as a top coach.

"The great thing about both Eddie Lewis and Stan Charlton is that once they got possession, they gave me the ball. Then we could start to pass our way up the field. We were all doing our jobs - the game is simple."

Malcolm Lucas also appreciated Baily's influence, saying: "He was fabulous. The first time I encountered him was when I played against this 'old fella' for Orient Reserves against Tottenham Reserves. I thought I'd take care of him that day but he tore me to pieces. He couldn't beat you with skill but his touch, and his ability to play neat one-twos around players, was tremendous.

"I'll always remember it . . . he put his arms round my shoulders and said: 'Don't worry about it, son, it'll all come to you!'

"As a player of his stature, you had to give him respect. I admired what he did with the ball and I just wished I'd met him earlier in my career, then perhaps I would have played on for longer. He taught me a better appreciation of the game.

"If ever you stopped to have a cup of tea or coffee after training out at Woodford, Eddie would always be there, talking non-stop about the game. He was so vehement and passionate about football.

"If anything had to be said in the dressing room at half-time on a matchday, Eddie – not Johnny Carey – would be the one to say it. Mr Carey would smoke his pipe and be a calming influence, while Eddie was much more vocal. I'm sure he must have got on my case at times, like he did all the players, but you still respected him anyway. He played for England and Tottenham, he had the experience and the know-how, so you couldn't help but learn from someone like him."

Eddie Lewis said: "Eddie and I used to get on ever so well. He wanted us to get the ball down and play like his old Spurs push-and-run side did."

Sid Bishop knew Baily for longer than most, having played together in the same O's team before Eddie hung up his boots. He said: "I used to occasionally play cricket with him and other Tottenham players for Lennarts Cricket Club – before Eddie joined us as player-coach."

Bailey loved banter with the players and would invariably give out more than he got back.

Stan Charlton, another former team-mate of Baily's, recalls: "Eddie's favourite saying was, 'Life is just a bowl of cherries.'

Eddie Baily (centre with the ball) in the squad line-up for 1959-60 – his last season as a player, with many of those who would soon come under his wing when he became coach. Back row: Cyril Lea, Ronnie Foster, Eddie Lewis, Peter Burridge and George Wright. Third row: Les Gore (manager), Ken Facey, Sid Bishop, Frank George, Dave Groombridge, Stan Charlton and Nick Collins (trainer). Second row: George Waites, Tommy Johnston, Baily, Eddie Brown and Joe Elwood. Front: Phil White and Malcolm Lucas.

Norman Deeley said: "Eddie wasn't too bad but he didn't work us as physically hard as the training I'd been used to at Wolves."

But Charlton, who had worked under Baily for far longer, added: "He made us do a lot of running around the pitch and the players would say to him: 'Joe Davis never used to have to run around a snooker table.'

"Eddie would reply: 'Well lads, it's better than looking at the clock in some, old factory . . .'

"Eddie disagreed with a lot of what the FA's top coach, Walter Winterbottom, preached. He refused to go on a coaching course but they gave him a coaching badge anyway. He knew his football.

"I went on a coaching course that Eddie was running, and that's how I got my prelim badge.

"I rated Eddie very highly. He had a good rapport with the players – he'd put you down but pick you up just as quickly.

"I had a right go at him once during a session when he kept asking us to change positions in a certain drill we were doing. At the time I had a bit of a blind boil on the back of my neck and as I moved back to where Eddie wanted me to be, a bloody bee stung me right on the boil! I said to him: 'That's your bloody fault!' God, it was sore."

Gordon Bolland and his friend, Harry Gregory, both learned mucy from Baily. Gordon recalls: "I think Eddie had bad arthritis in his knees and he wasn't a great physical specimen, but what he said was good and tapped into all his experience.

"He was a great character, always having a laugh, but, at the same time, he earned much respect from everybody. He helped me a lot, even though I couldn't appreciate then what the staff at Orient did for me in the 18 months I was there.

"He had many words for me – including some bollockings – but also a lot of nice things. Eddie was a really good bloke."

Harry echoed those views, adding: "I was brilliant learning from Eddie, who I'd watched as a young boy in the Tottenham league-winning team of 1950-51. He was a real East Ender, who lived at Clapton Pond.

"I remember that he only had to run about five yards and he'd be sweating absolute buckets. In the end, his legs wouldn't carry him but his brain was still as sharp as ever.

"He was a great coach, teaching us how to move off the ball and then get in a position to receive it back from a team-mate."

Another forward, Malcolm Graham, was taken aback when he first turned up for training with Orient and was greeted with the sight of a . . . football! "We'd not seen one while training at Barnsley, where the physio had us running all the time. You couldn't get a ball, but we had our own ball at Leyton Orient – we had to carry it out about with us, and it was fantastic. When I went back to Barnsley at the end of my career, the same physio was still in charge of training . . . and he still wouldn't let any balls out of the bag!

"Eddie was absolutely marvellous, such a good coach. I was left-footed but I remember him saying to me: 'If you've got enough time to get the ball onto your left foot, then do it.' And it was marvellous for me to hear him say that.

"He used to have a bit of a joke with me sometimes about coming from Yorkshire but he was a good bloke. I liked Eddie."

Terry McDonald recalls a funny incident involving Baily and cricket that happened after the footballs had been put away and regular training had finished at Ashton Playing Fields running track in Woodford Bridge, which Orient used for pre-season stamina-building work. He said: "We were playing cricket one afternoon, as we sometimes did, at Ashton Playing Fields and Ted Phillips was bowling to Eddie Baily. As well as playing inside-forward for Orient, Ted was opening bowler for Chelmsford at the time, so he knew what he was doing.

"He came running in off a long run, ignoring the fact that Baily had only one pad on. The ball whistled only a matter of inches past Baily's head and he wasn't impressed. He gave Ted a look of disgust and called him a 'c***!' while the rest of us tried hard not to laugh!

"Ted Phillips did everything with power. We played a so-called friendly against a Celebrity XI. Ted hit a shot so hard that he broke the fingers of Colin Welland, the curly haired actor from *Z-Cars*, who was in goal for the Celebrities' team. Ted whacked the ball as hard as he could – just as he always did – and he was only six yards out at the time. Colin Welland was cursing, clearly in some pain, and he wanted to know from Ted why he felt the need to hit the ball so hard when he was so close to the goal.

"But Ted showed no sympathy for him. He probably didn't realise that the injured keeper was out of the police series *Z-Cars*, because he just said to him: 'I hope you're a juggler!'

In the years well before even the top clubs even considered employing specialist goalkeeping coaches, all the squad came under Eddie Baily's watchful eye. Goalkeepers Bill Robertson and Frank George were not exactly natural athletes and were usually the back-markers in all cross-country runs, as goalies still are today.

Frank admits: "I was pretty heavy but Bill was even heavier than me. I think my playing weight was 12-and-a-half-to 13-stone. I didn't like the running – I didn't think it was even necessary."

George recalled one training session, though, when Baily's methods didn't meet with the approval of Johnny Carey.

"Eddie once dreamed up an idea where all the outfield players had the ball, 10 yards outside the penalty box. He wanted me to dive at the feet of each player as he tried to dribble the ball round me.

"Anyway, Johnny Carey was standing at the side, listening to what was about to happen, when he asked Eddie what he was trying to prove. Carey pointed out to Eddie that they knew I would come out and do what he was asking me to do instinctively in a game situation, so he couldn't see why I was being asked to risk a head injury in training.

"That was one of the most sensible things I ever heard Johnny Carey say."

I REMEMBER YOU
Frank Ifield, 1962

LES Gore devoted most of his working life to LOFC, serving the club as **player, trainer, manager and caretaker manager over a 16-year period between 1939 and November 1967, when he was finally let go for economical reasons. He had playing spells away from Brisbane Road but after returning in 1951 as assistant coach, he gave the O's another 16 years continuous service.**

Without exception, none of the ex-players I spoke to in the process of writing this book had a bad word to say about this very likeable, grey-haired man who originated from Coventry.

Although he answered the Orient board's request to fill in as 'manager' on four separate occasions, between longer-term appointments, Les did actually manager in his own right between March 1959 and the arrival of Johnny Carey in 1961. Fact is, Les actually picked the team and took responsibility for it on no fewer than 187 times.

What's more, he made two very significant signings in Tommy Johnston and the player who succeeded him as centre-forward, Dave Dunmore.

Most of the O's players who knew and worked with Les certainly believed he was very capable of succeeding in the No.1 role on a full-time basis and, to them, it remains a mystery why the club ever felt the need to look beyond Gore, especially after Carey quit to accept Nottingham Forest's irresistible offer.

Malcolm Lucas added: "I think he was underrated a little bit. Les was Leyton Orient through and through. No matter what wanted doing, he was the man to do it and I couldn't say anything bad about him."

McDonald compared Gore to Carey: "I think Les understood the game and, unlike Carey, he would talk tactics with the players and work on certain things in training. For instance, we worked on one corner, where Whitey would drive the ball towards the near post and it was my job to come in from the far side of the penalty box and get my head to his cross at the near post. Mind you, I can't say I remember it actually coming off in a game!

"What I'm saying is, Les didn't just play everything off the cuff. He got you thinking more about the game too. Like if things weren't happening for us, he would sometimes suggest to me and Whitey that we switched wings, or I'd move inside and Joe Elwood would move out to the wing. Les let you get on with it and he trusted his players."

At 5ft 8ins, Gore understood the worth and the role of wingers. After all, he was one himself in the 30s with Fulham, Stockport County, Carlisle United and Bradford City, before first joining the O's as a player in 1939 (and scoring on his debut). He ended his playing days in the late-40s at non-league level for Yeovil Town and then Gravesend & Northfleet.

McDonald continued: "Ronnie Foster loved playing for Les, because he just let us go out and play our natural game. He never complicated the game and he knew what all his players could and couldn't do.

"Les could also put a good team together – he deserved more credit for us winning promotion than Carey. I think Carey admitted this, or at least that's the quote from him that I read somewhere."

Sid Bishop paid tribute to Les and acknowledged the part he played in developing his career. "He had a difficult job. Jimmy Richardson, the ex-Newcastle player, was the first team trainer under manager Alec Stock when I first came to the Orient and Les was then second in charge of the bucket-and-sponge. But with all the coming and goings of different managers, Les was asked to stand in.

"It was Les who persevered with me as a young player. He used to say certain things to me and then smile, as if to say: 'Yeah, you're getting there'. He gave me a lot of encouragement and confidence in what he said, either before the game or at half-time. In the end, he didn't have to tell me anything."

Whenever the multi-faceted Gore had to revert to the role of trainer-cum-physio, he was like most 'bucket-and-sponge' men in football in those days – unqualified but keen and there to patch up the walking wounded.

"Les didn't know too much about physiotherapy," confirms Sid, "but, then again, not many trainers did in those days."

Perhaps surprisingly, Bishop is not convinced that Gore would have become a successful manager, had he ever taken on the challenge full-time.

"I don't think he would have been tough enough for the job and, I suppose, he was also lacking a bit tactically.

Likeable Les Gore gave the club great service over many years.

Pictured during a break in training at Ashton Playing Fields. Back row: George Wright, Ken Facey, Phil White, Tommy Johnston and Sid Bishop. Front: Frank George, Terry McDonald, Dennis Sorrell and Stan Charlton.

"But Les was a good bloke who would do anything for you. He was popular with the players, because we knew we could talk freely to him. If you wanted something 'carried' to the manager, without causing a big bust-up, you could let Les know your feelings and he would put those thoughts into proper context and take them to the manager. I can't recall any specific instances but if you were laying on the treatment table and just chatting with Les, whatever was said was for the good of the club. It wasn't a case of being snidey about anything."

McDonald disagrees that Gore lacked toughness. He says: "Les wanted his players to play to their strengths but he'd give you a bollocking if you needed it – and whenever he did have a go, you knew he was right."

Players enjoyed a bit of craic with Les Gore.

Eddie Lewis recalls some advice Gore gave him with regard to a pair of new boots. Lewis explains: "I bought a pair of Italian boots in to wear and Les said: 'Who can you f****** hurt with *them!*' The funny thing was, when I did happen to kick the opposing winger, my toe *did* bend upwards – but I didn't want to tell Les that he was right about my soft boots!

"I got on well with both Les and Nick Collins," Eddie added.

The subject of boots reminded Stan Charlton of the way things used to be at Brisbane Road. He recalls: "The club bought us a new pair of boots for each season. They were called Manfield Hotspurs and we got them from Arthur Sedgwick's sports shop in Walthamstow, where a lot of London-based footballers and cricketers used to get their equipment. Manfield Hotspurs were supposed to be more lightweight than the old-style boots but they still had a bit of a toe-cap on them. The Adidas boot that came in later was much lighter."

Stan recalls a funny situation that involved Les Gore after the team had won 4-1 in an evening game at Sunderland in February 1960.

"Me and Phil White had missed the sleeper-train back from Sunderland – I think their captain, Charlie Hurley, had taken me to a local nightclub.

"At first I thought that I was the only one to have missed the train. But after I'd managed to get a lift to Newcastle station, I met Phil and we were obviously both surprised to see each other.

"Anyway, the overnight train got us back into King's Cross a little later than the one the other players were on, although they tended to stay on board for a while at the end of an overnight journey to continue their sleep in what was still the early hours of the morning.

"After Phil and I got off, we were walking along the platform at King's Cross when Les Gore stuck his head out of the window and said: 'You're up early, lads!' He hadn't realised that we'd just got off a different train and that we'd both missed the one he and all the other players were on!"

Stan believes that Gore was content to manage in a caretaker capacity and never aspired to go one rung higher.

Likeable Les Gore outstayed successive full-time managers Alec Stock, John Carey, Benny Fenton, Dave Sexton and Dick Graham while always remaining loyal and dedicated to the Orient. Les Gore teams always tried to play football in a progressive, entertaining way and the players responded to him positively. He left his mark on a lot of people who passed through the club and, as Gordon Bolland says, "he was a lovely fella."

Chapter 12

BREAKING UP IS HARD TO DO
Neil Sedaka, 1962

RELEGATION often spells the start of a decline for many clubs and so it proved for Leyton Orient, who slipped to 16th in 1963-64, 19th the following year (just two points clear of relegation) before finishing rock bottom in 1965-66, 10 points adrift of Middlesbrough.

In the space of a decade the O's had clawed their way out of Third Division South, risen to the top flight of the Football League and gone all the way back down to the third division.

Benny Fenton, who succeeded Johnny Carey in November 1963 (after Les Gore had briefly held the fort again), and Dave Sexton were both hired and fired in that time, both of them barely lasting a year, as the club spiralled into freefall and almost out of existence.

Goalkeepers Bill Robertson and Frank George, and promotion hero Malcolm Graham, all left within weeks of the O's dropping out of Division One. Derek Gibbs was also completely out of the picture.

Norman Deeley started the 1963-64 season but both him and Gordon Bolland, who signed at virtually the same time in 1962, were both on their way as Fenton struggled to get to grips with the club's ailing financial position. Indeed, the sale of Gordon to Norwich City for around £30,000 in March '64 proved a bit of a lifeline.

Phil White retired in the summer of '64 after the club awarded the veteran right-winger a well-earned testimonial.

Cyril Lea was an ever-present in '63-64 but departed to Ipswich Town at the end of that campaign in a £12,000 deal.

Sid Bishop announced that the final game in May of '64 – at home to Bury (but without the excitement of three years earlier!) – would be his finale too . . . but the durable centre-back was persuaded to delay his retirement until a further five games into the following season.

It was around that time that Lea's Welsh wing-half colleague, Malcolm Lucas, also decided that he had become too frustrated with how Fenton wanted his team to play and how his own role in the side had changed.

Lucas explained: "I asked him if we could play with a more solid defence, with Sid and Cyril holding back to allow me more freedom to get further forward, but he said: 'No. I want you and Cyril to *both* get forward.'

"I thought that if we did as he wished, then what had happened the previous season would happen again – the team would be exposed at the back. That was when I told him that if that's how he saw the game, then it's time he got me on the road."

After the sterling service Malcolm had given the O's, he was disappointed how his time at the club came to a sour end early in the 1964-65 season, when he followed Gordon Bolland up the A11 to Norwich. Orient made around £20,000 on him.

"I went to train at Orient one day and Fenton told me that Norwich were interested in signing me. I met the Norwich manager, Ron Ashman, and we agreed the deal. Until everything was finalised and while I was waiting for the transfer to go through, I went back to Orient to train as normal the next day – but there was no kit for me. Eddie Heath (O's trainer) said: 'I'm sorry, Malcolm, there's no gear for you to put on and Benny says you can't train here anymore.'

"Fenton had put the block on me. So, instead, I went to West Ham, where their manager Ron Greenwood was happy for me to train with them for a few weeks that summer, which was brilliant of him.

"West Ham had just won the FA Cup, so the place was buzzing and I knew the players socially. When we were getting promoted, quite a few of their players used to come down to Brisbane Road and support us from the stand. Their Scottish goalkeeper, Lawrie Leslie, was the most vocal of them. I also knew the players from having played against them, and from when we were at functions together, as well as those occasions when I saw one or two of them while visiting Bill Jenkins for treatment."

Malcolm reveals that he might have moved from Orient to the Hammers a year before O's promotion campaign.

"There was talk of me joining them as a right-back but then nothing happened because they changed their manager around about the same time."

Ironically, it was Benny Fenton's elder brother, Ted, who was sacked by West Ham in March 1961 when Greenwood was brought in (from Arsenal) to start a successful new era in Hammers' history.

"I was disappointed that I left the Orient, because they will always be in my heart as a lovely club. I didn't want to leave – it was just that things had changed."

Eddie Lewis and Terry McDonald, both critical of Johnny Carey's management style, were even less impressed with West Ham-born Fenton's approach following his arrival from Colchester United.

Lewis said: I injured my leg near the end of the (1963-64) season and then he suddenly put me on the transfer list once the season had finished."

At the time, Eddie reportedly said he was "knocked sideways" by the decision not to retain his services and he was quoted in one local newspaper as saying: "I have been at Orient six years and I love the club. This has shattered me." It was also reported that Eddie received £750 in severance benefit pay.

By transfer-listing Lewis, Fenton had also denied him the chance to extend his time with Orient in a coaching capacity. Eddie reveals: "When Carey left, Les Gore resumed the caretaker manager's role yet again and he asked me to join him on the coaching staff. He wanted me to take the juniors and I was really looking forward to doing that job.

"But then Benny Fenton was appointed and I was soon on my way. Les was very apologetic but there was nothing he could do about it."

Orient's loss would be South African football's gain . . .

YOU DON'T KNOW
Helen Shapiro, 1961

It was not until midway through the 1963-64 season, following the departure of Carey, another temporary stint for Gore (this time for three months) and the appointment of 45-year-old Fenton, that McDonald eventually regained a first team place – on the right wing.

Ironically, Terry's first manager when he joined West Ham straight from school was Benny's elder brother, Ted.

"Benny was more outgoing than Ted but, tactically, he never taught us anything. On the rare occasions that he did go out onto the training field and start to talk tactics or do a certain drill with the players, all of a sudden the phone in his office would ring and he'd make the excuse that he had to leave us to go and take the call. But the thing is, he'd never come back out to the pitch to finish what he'd started saying to us! I'm sure they were 'hoax' calls. Benny was a spoof – you ask Cyril Lea about him . . ."

So I did. Lea says: "I always thought Benny was a bit of a spiv. Sometimes he'd mouth off after a game and be a bit impetuous.

"I never thought he was a man I could ever learn anything from. In the end, I went a bit against him because I didn't think we were getting anywhere.

"I had a little dust up with Benny down at Portsmouth. We were winning 2-0, I think, and ended up losing 4-3. We came off and he rollicked everybody, he threatened us, and I stood up to him.

"To be fair to him, for us to be two or three goals up and lose like that was very poor and maybe we did deserve a rollicking. But you do it in the right way and say the right words, and Benny didn't do that. It got personal – I think he called us 'cheats' or something similar, which wasn't called for. A lack of effort wasn't the problem – everybody had worked hard enough.

"I think that was really the end of me with Benny Fenton. I didn't feel I could give him the same respect I'd given other people like Carey, who was a better manager.

"Benny knew it, too, because he called a meeting the next Monday to go over what had gone wrong in the game.

"He called me in and said Ipswich were interested in me. Bill McGarry had taken over there and although it was a big decision – my wife Val was from Leyton – I was keen on the move. I was at Ipswich for 14 years and had a super time at the only two clubs I played for."

Like McDonald, Dave Dunmore also experienced playing under both Ted and Benny Fenton and was equally damning in his verdict: "I played under Benny's brother, Ted, at West Ham and although I think Ted had a little bit more about him, football wise, I wouldn't say either of them were good managers."

Stan Charlton and several of his team-mates thought that Fenton had himself in mind when he had a long mirror installed in the home dressing room.

He revealed: "Benny had a four-foot, six-inch mirror put up on the wall and we

A troubled new era begins . . . 1963-64. Back row: Malcolm Musgrove, Eddie Lewis, Sid Bishop, Mike Pinner, Cyril Lea and Malcolm Lucas. Front: Harry Gregory, Gerry Ward, Stan Charlton, Gordon Bolland and Norman Deeley.

used to call it 'The Benny Fenton Mirror'. He told us that he had it put up so that we could check that we looked smart before going out to play, but I'm convinced it was really for him!"

Fenton prided himself on always being smartly attired in suit and tie, but McDonald added: "Stan's right. Benny couldn't walk past that mirror without looking at himself!"

Charlton recalls some surreal activity at one training session, soon after Fenton took charge. He chuckled at the absurdity of it all when he said: "Benny had some funny ideas. We once spent a whole training session at Ashton Playing Fields . . . practicing how to tie our boot laces and the tie-ups on our socks!"

One training session under Fenton, at Low Hall Farm, which was another training ground used by the O's, almost erupted into a fight between the manager and McDonald after the winger had been dropped from the team.

Terry revealed: "We were playing a practice game – first team v the reserves – when Frank George kicked the ball to near the half-way line twice in quick session. The ball dropped to me both times, so I trapped it . . . and chipped it back over Frank's head and into the net! I wasn't deliberately trying to take the mickey out of Frank at all – the chance was there to be taken and I simply took it.

"But Benny must have thought I was trying to be funny, perhaps make him look a bit silly because he'd left me out of the side, and after it happened the second time he came running over and grabbed me by the throat. He was going nuts at me and it took big Andy Nelson to pull him off me."

McDonald added: "As far as I know, very few of the players at Orient respected

Benny Fenton as a manager."

One who did was Gordon Bolland, who played under dapper Fenton at both Orient and, later, Millwall, where Fenton had some success with a Lions team that finished just a point away from promotion to the first division in 1971-72.

Gordon says: "At Millwall, one or two of the lads took liberties with Benny, but he did a fair, old job there and he was good for me.

"He made the lads laugh with some of the things he came out with. Like the time he was raving about a Brighton player – I can't remember his name – who, he said, could throw a two-bob bit in the air and catch it on his foot. We all stood there in amazement, unable to believe what he'd just said. After that, most of the lads started throwing coins in the air and catching them on their shoes!

"Benny didn't quite get Millwall promoted to the first division – I think we finished a point behind Birmingham (who went up with Norwich City in '72) – but he was there five or six years, so he must have been doing something right.

"He could motivate me. I was having a fairly good spell until I wanted to pull out of a game after going down with a really bad cold. I felt knackered, not even well enough to train, so Benny suggested I took a couple of days off.

"Anyway, he phoned me on the Friday night. Even though I still wasn't fit enough to play the next day, he asked me to meet him down at The Den the following morning at nine o'clock. I told him it was no good but he insisted, so I reluctantly turned up at the ground the next day as he'd asked me to.

"We were sitting there chatting in the dressing room when he suddenly produced some kit and a track suit and asked me to get changed. He told me he just wanted me to have a little stretch and a jog, to see if my breathing was OK.

"I told him that I still felt knackered and was unable to run but, to keep him happy, I agreed to go out onto the pitch. The pitch looked in immaculate condition, the sun was shining and it was a nice day.

"After a few stretches and some little runs and turns, Benny got a ball out and before long he was passing it to me and asking me to take shots at him in goal. My adrenalin started to flow and, before long, I was starting to feel good again.

"At the end of that one-on-one session, he said to me: 'I think you can play. What do you think?' I told him I wasn't sure, but I agreed to play and I think I scored in a 3-0 win.

"Benny was still as fussy about his players being tidy and looking good when I played under him at Millwall. Dennis Burnett was a bit of a rebel, though, and would sometimes play Benny up. Eamonn Dunphy was another who took a few liberties but he allowed him to go so far and I think Benny had a good rapport with his players in general."

Bolland's friend at Orient, Harry Gregory, also prospered under Fenton. Harry said: In the season after relegation, Harry had to bide his time until the start of 1964, under new manager Benny Fenton, when he began to establish himself in the side. Harry seems to be in the minority of players who thought much of Fenton.

"Benny was a good guy. He recommended me for an England Under-21 cap, although I didn't get it in the end.

"He was always immaculately dressed and expected all his players to be just as neat and tidy. His players could never get away with wearing their shirts outside their shorts, like they did in later years. In the dressing room before the match, he'd be immaculately dressed in his suit and he made sure the players all wore suits when we played away. It was natural in those days for players to wear a suit and tie anyway, not tracksuits like a lot of players do now, but Benny was fussier than anyone about that.

"He liked you to do your football boots up properly and he'd even show you how to do them up if he wasn't happy with how you'd tied them up in the first place!"

Benny Fenton was dismissed in December 1964, with the O's then bottom of Division Two.

RETURN TO SENDER
Elvis Presley, 1962

If most of the senior pro's at Orient didn't exactly warm to Benny Fenton, his replacement, Dave Sexton, was received like an icy chill blast from the Arctic when he arrived from Chelsea, where he had coached under manager Tommy Docherty, in January 1965.

Of all the managers who have passed through Leyton Orient, the history books show that Sexton has been the most successful after moving from Brisbane Road. He first became well known for winning the FA Cup with Chelsea in 1970, although perhaps his biggest achievement of his club management career was guiding QPR to their highest-ever league position (second, a point behind Liverpool, in 1975-76). He brought the first European silverware to Stamford Bridge when Chelsea beat Real Madrid in the 1971 European Cup Winners' Cup final and also led Manchester United to runners-up spot in the League (1980).

Sexton became a leading figure and highly respected coach within Football Association circles, working as Technical Director at the FA's National School of Excellence at Lilleshall between 1984 and '89.

But Orient was Sexton's first experience as a manager and the 35-year-old rookie boss clearly still had much to learn before going on to manage at the highest level and become a very experienced part of the England coaching and scouting set-up, even beyond his 70th birthday.

But back to Sexton and his unpopular year at Orient. McDonald says: "Dave's ideas on the role of wingers was totally against what I thought we were meant to be all about. As soon as their goalkeeper got the ball, he wanted me to forget about their full-back and, instead, get back and mark their midfield players.

"When we were attacking, he wanted me to come off the wing and mark one of their players, to stop them playing. I thought, 'this isn't right'. I'd always been told to close down the full-back so that the keeper couldn't throw the ball to him, so that he could start the next attack from deep in their half."

McDonald says that Sexton put too much emphasis on excessive physical training to the detriment of the players. "He used to run us like mad on Friday mornings. So much so that Dave Metchick wasn't able to play the next day because his calf muscles were killing him!

"His first game in charge was due to be at home against Swansea, but when that was snowed off, instead of letting us all go home, he had us doing a cross-country run up at Chingford golf course. He stood under the oak tree giving out tickets, so that he'd be sure everybody had done the whole run properly without cheating!"

Dave Dunmore told of similar physical excesses, adding: "It was Sexton who more or less got rid of me. He had us all doing lots of sprints and 'doggies' and wasn't happy until he saw one of us being physically sick."

Harry Gregory – who McDonald describes as "the fittest player at the club" during his Orient days – was more receptive to Sexton's demands for improved fitness and also his coaching ideas. Harry says: "Dave would show you how to work off the last man – what they call playing on the shoulder of the last defender – and he would open your eyes to that kind of thing. I thought he was brilliant on the coaching side.

"Perhaps while Dave was OK dealing with youngsters like myself, he found it harder working with the older players. Remember, Dave wasn't very old when he took over as manager," added Harry.

McDonald knew Sexton better than anybody else at Brisbane Road. "I knew him from my time at West Ham, when he was one of the senior pro's there. He got hold of me one day and said: 'What are you doing this afternoon?'

"I said: 'Nothing', so he took me with him up to the West End, to help him pick out Laura Ashley wallpaper for his house!

"Dave was an Orient player himself in the 50s and I also respect him for his dedication to football and what he went on to achieve after he left Orient. But he was never my cup of tea.

"He gave me a free transfer in the summer of '65, although I knew it was coming. He called me in and said: 'I'm sorry, Tel, we've got to let you go, but I'm sure you'll get a club all right'. That's all he said."

In the summer of '65, McDonald was joined through the exit gates by Stan Charlton, although it needn't have ended that way for the loyal and long-serving skipper. He revealed: "After I quit playing at Orient in 1965, I was offered the job of Reserve team manager by Harry Zussman. But Dave Sexton had taken over the first team by then and he and I just couldn't get on.

"My first falling out with him came when he put a big graph up on the wall and told us how we could earn extra money in the form of bonus incentives. He said: 'Every goal you score, you earn a pound. For every assist, you get 10 shillings. And every clean sheet the goalkeeper keeps, we'll have a whip-round for him.'

"When I asked him where I came into the equation, being a right-back who hardly ever got forward and made only rare goal assists, it was clear that there was no place for me to earn any extra money under his proposed reward scheme.

"I thought I was making a fair comment – I thought any such incentives should be team-based, and not for individuals. The wing-halves might have picked up the odd 10s here and there for making a goal or two, but we didn't score many goals from the back in those days," continues Stan, who wasn't kidding. He managed just two in 408 games!

"And as far as having a whip-round for the keeper was concerned, " he continued, "I could see a scenario where I might head the ball off the line a couple of times, thus saving two certain goals, and yet still have to cough up half-a-crown for the keeper if our defence kept a clean sheet!

"But, with that, Dave took his chart down off the wall and from that day on, he didn't like me too well."

Dave Sexton's dismal record in his 11 months at Brisbane Road – only seven wins and 10 draws in 37 matches – suggests he dispensed with the senior players he fell out with too soon. Good, old Les Gore – him again! – was asked to salvage the wreckage of Sexton's abysmal 1964-65 but, try as he did, the O's sunk to Division Three in May 1966 – as Sexton took a step back from management and headed for a new coaching role at Fulham.

I WON'T FORGET YOU
Jim Reeves, 1964

At 77, Stan Charlton is a Leyton Orient living legend who is still remembered as fondly now as he was the day he left the club.

Terry McDonald sums up his former skipper's stature when he says: "Stan should have become Leyton Orient's next manager."

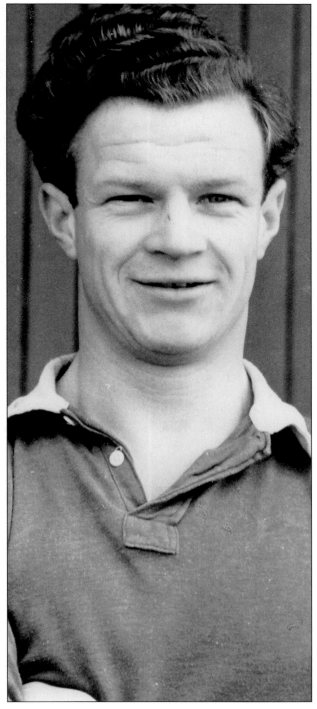

Stan Charlton in his younger days at the Orient.

THE MEN WHO MADE DREAMS COME TRUE!

The Leyton Orient team that clinched promotion from Division Two in the final game against Bury and the one that represented the club in its first-ever top flight league match, against Arsenal.

Back row: Malcolm Lucas, Sid Bishop, Bill Robertson, Cyril Lea and Eddie Lewis.

Front: Norman Deeley, Derek Gibbs, Stan Charlton, Dave Dunmore, Malcolm Graham and Terry McDonald.

GOALKEEPERS

FRANK GEORGE
Goalkeeper 1956-62
Born: Stepney, East London, November 20, 1933
Appearances: 119 League & 20 Cup

FEARLESS **Frank George played most of the first 26 games of 1961-62 –
until the end of January when injury put him out of the side. He lost his
place to former Chelsea keeper Bill Robertson and missed out on the
promotion celebrations.**

Frank, who signed from non-league Carshalton Athletic in 1956 and made his
debut against Fulham the following year, said: "I think I suffered a back injury at
Derby. I was known as being a bit of a mad goalkeeper who wasn't afraid to go out
and meet the ball and throw myself at opponents' feet. And that's how it happened.

"I took one or two bad kicks in my career – not only at Orient, but from my earlier
days with Carshalton in the Athenian League and right up until my last days at
Worcester City.

"My worst injury was a very bad cut over the top of my left eye which happened
during my time at Watford. I can't remember who did it but, to my mind, the person
concerned deliberately nutted me in the head as I went out to meet the ball. It split
my eye right open and I needed a lot of stitches. The scars are still evident now."

Frank also suffered a broken rib in O's 1-1 League Cup draw at Newcastle in
September 1962, although injuries once cost him more than just a place between the
sticks.

Sadly, Frank lost most of his career cuttings when a rat chewed through his
scrapbooks in the garage at his home in Ramsgate. But he managed to retrieve one
report from a newspaper which reported how a foot injury, sustained in the last few
weeks of the promotion campaign, prevented the keeper from joining the end-of-
season promotion party in Majorca.

"There's a picture of me and the report says that while the other players went to
Majorca, I stayed behind and took my wife Iris, son Timothy and 17-month-old
daughter Pauline on a fortnight's holiday to Butlins in Clacton. Much as I love my
family, I was gutted to miss out on the club tour but these things happen!"

Goalkeepers weren't as tall in those days as they are today. Frank stood at 5ft-
11ins. They weren't as fit either.

"I once hurt my rib playing for Orient Reserves at Brighton," recalls Frank. "After
half-time, I thought that although I wasn't fit enough to continue in goal, I'd be OK
to play out on field, so I went on the right-wing.

"I'll tell you what, in the first two or three minutes I was so puffed out, I told them
I was 'all right' and asked to go back in goal! I couldn't get back in quick enough!"

Stepney-born Frank, his cockney accent still in tact, has had to regard injuries as
an occupational hazzard – since his childhood.

He continued: "I broke my ankle at the age of about 12 or 13, playing football with
my mate, but because I still wanted to play the game with the other boys in the street

Fearless Frank . . . Frankie George doing what he always did best, bravely snatching the ball from the feet of an onrushing opponent. This time he denied Fulham's Graham Leggatt in the home match in February 1963.

and over the local park, I went in goal. That's how goalkeeping started for me . . . all because of a broken ankle that stopped me playing out on field."

"I brought the full-back, Alan Eagles, to Orient. He'd played with me at Carshalton, so I approached Les Gore about the possibility of Alan being offered a trial. At first, Les was concerned that I might be wasting his time.

"But Alan played out of his skin for Orient reserves against the first team in a practice match and they signed him straight after that. I can't remember the left-winger's name that day (Joe Elwood does!), but Alan hit him so hard that one ferocious challenge lifted him over the low wall that surrounded the pitch!"

"Alan was a smashing bloke, who finished up working in the west country as a harbourmaster. Sadly, he died at quite a young age. We were pretty close – we'd go to his house and he'd come to ours."

Asked to assess his own strengths and weaknesses, Frank says: "My big strength was bravery. I considered myself to be a fair keeper without being brilliant, although there were times when I did play brilliantly.

"I wasn't a puncher. If I left my line it was with the intention of catching the ball. And if I happened to drop it, it was usually in the vicinity where I could drop on the ball quickly. Whereas if you went to punch the ball and misconnected, you would be left in no man's land."

Frank watches today's football on television and no-one who has followed the game since his playing days will disagree with his comment: "Goalkepers are over-protected now. I used to wear light, white gloves if conditions were wet. With them on, I could really feel the ball properly, whereas the padded things they all wear today . . well, I wonder about them."

Alec Stock was the Orient manager who brought George to Brisbane Road, when Dave Groombridge was still the established keeper.

"Alec didn't care how you won, as long as you did win," says Frank. "We were playing up north one day and although we got absolutely paralysed, we managed to win 1-0. Afterwards, Alec stood up at the front of our coach and said: 'Professional footballers sing when they win, so . . . sing! He then led us into the chorus of *Onward Christian Soldiers*," laughs Frank, who didn't become first choice until the 1960-61 season under Les Gore.

"When Alec dropped me once, I told him I wanted to see him about it. 'Come in, Frank,' he said in his west country lingo. 'Now what did you want to speak to me about?' I explained that I wanted to know why I'd been dropped from the first team.

"He said: 'Now listen here, Frank, I'm gonna tell you something which is the real truth. I can honestly say that you *are* the best goalkeeper at the Orient.'

"I was flabbergasted by what he'd just said. I told him: 'Well, in that case, *why* have I been dropped?'

"He continued: 'Well, I've got to say this . . . just at this time, you're going through a bad patch . . .but there is no doubt whatsoever that it won't take you long to get out of it.'

"After coming out of his office, I thought: 'I can't believe it.' Alec was a great, great talker.

"But the best manager I ever played for was Bill McGarry, at Watford. He was the most honest of them all – never afraid to speak his mind. He could be ignorant at times but he was still the best I came across."

Frank played seven league and one cup match for Orient in the top flight, including the 5-0 battering at Liverpool, followed a week later by a 4-0 drubbing at home to Wolves. He also played in the final game at Old Trafford.

Terry McDonald said of Frank George: "He was very brave and such a nice bloke – he was part of our card school. But I remember that he didn't appreciate pre-season training too much!"

"I really enjoyed my time at Orient, with a great bunch of lads. I was in love with the club," added Frank.

BILL ROBERTSON
Goalkeeper 1960-62
Born: Glasgow, Scotland, November 13, 1928
Died: June 1973
Appearances: 47 League & 4 Cup

BIG Bill Robertson arrived at the Orient in 1960 – five years after collecting a League championship winners' medal with Chelsea in the Blues' first-ever title-winning team managed by Ted Drake.

The big Scotsman joined Chelsea after the war and made his debut five years later when he came into the side towards the end of the season, an introduction that coincided with four wins that secured safety by the narrowest of margins.

Without his heroics there may never have been a title for the west London club. Robertson started the 1954-55 season as first choice but after 26 matches he was replaced by Charlie Thomson in January. He joined Leyton Orient for £1,000 when Peter Bonetti emerged as the undisputed first choice at Stamford Bridge.

Bill, from Glasgow, was nearly 32-years-old when he made his debut, at home in a 3-1 defeat against Liverpool on September 24, 1960.

And it's the man he replaced, Frank George, who leads the tributes to Bill, who died in June 1973, aged 44.

Frank says: "I used to watch Bill when he played for Chelsea and I thought he was a really good keeper, one of the best I ever saw. He was a bit of a hero of mine.

"Chelsea was my team as a kid and I can remember going with my elder brother, Eddie, to see them play Moscow Dynamo (Nov. 1945). They reckon there were more than 100,000 in the ground at Stamford Bridge that day and I remember being passed over the shoulders of the men to the front of the stand. I supported Chelsea right up until I started playing for Carshalton, initially in the Corinthian League.

"I didn't feel threatened by Bill's arrival at Orient. In fact, when he came to us I was told that he was signed as a stand-in for me. When he took my place in the side, he took his chance.

"You're always disappointed when you're out of the side but at the same time, I also realised

that Bill was playing well and took on board the fact that he was very experienced. I took the attitude that I only hoped I was still playing in the first team, and playing as well as Bill was at that time, when I was his age."

Appreciating Robertson's strengths, Frank continued: "Bill was very good at anticipating where the ball was going to go, either when it was pumped down the middle or from a direct shot. I can't ever remember him getting it wrong when it came to anticipation."

Sid Bishop, who marshaled the defence in front of Robertson, agrees with Frank George. He said: "Bill's positional sense, the way he quickly worked out his angles to be in the right position, was uncanny. He was a big, old boy but he did the job. When he came out for the ball, the rest of us defenders would get out of his way.

"He gained a hell of a lot of experience at Chelsea and there was something about him that gave you a bit of comfort. If Bill didn't know what to do in any given situation, then no-one would.

"If he came for a ball, there weren't many forwards brave enough to challenge him. Today, goalkeepers are so well protected by the rules and referees but back then, guys like Bill had to be brave – and you had to be braver still to try and stop keepers like him! Keepers would come for a ball and if they missed it, the chances are the forward would end up with a fist in the back of his ear.

"The fact that Bill would come and commit himself for crosses was ideal for me, because I was only 5ft 10-and-a-half. I'd definitely be classified in the smaller group of centre-halves, so I had to have good timing, and get up earlier than the man I was marking.

"What could cause me problems was high balls played in from freekicks in the wing areas if we had a keeper who wouldn't come and collect the crosses. But catching crosses wasn't a problem to Bill. To him it was like picking apples and he'd hold the ball tight to his chest.

"Bill Robertson was a lovely, quiet gentleman."

Terry McDonald added: "Although Bill had lost his agility by the time he came to Orient, his positional play was still brilliant. And I can't ever remember him dropping the ball."

Safe as houses, Bill Robertson gathering another cross.

MIKE PINNER

Goalkeeper 1962-64
Born: Boston, Lincolnshire, February 16, 1934
Appearances: 77 League & 6 Cup

AS debuts go, Mike Pinner was plunged in at the deep end when he was called upon to face high-flying Spurs in October 1962. Bill Nicholson's former double winners were in rampant form, pressing on towards their famous European Cup Winners' Cup triumph the following May, and poor Pinner couldn't have asked for a tougher start to his O's career.

Tottenham won a one-sided match, 5-1, but the former England amateur international still looks back on the experience with satisfaction rather than horror.

Mike says: "No, I had a good game against Tottenham. When you've let in five you're entitled to have a good game, aren't you?"

"We were always on the back foot. Don't forget, Spurs were near the top of the division at the time.

"I can remember Bobby Smith playing at centre-forward for them but I can't remember the other first division matches I played in," added Mike, now aged 72 and from Boston in Lincolnshire.

Mike can't recall the circumstances of why he replaced Bill Robertson in goal for that London derby at Brisbane Road.

"I never really met him. If I did – and it would probably have happened before my debut against Spurs – it was just to say 'hello'. I never even saw Bill play," Mike admits.

That was the first of 19 first division appearances he made in 1962-63, although the tally would have been higher but for a number of international call-ups for Mike, who represented Great Britain at football in the Olympic Games.

A solicitor by profession, Mike moved around a number of clubs after leaving Cambridge University. He played for Corinthian Casuals and Pegasus before brief spells with a number of League clubs – Aston Villa (four games in 1954-56), Sheffield Wednesday (seven in 1957-58), QPR (19 in 1959-60), Manchester United (four in 1960), Chelsea (one in 1961) and Swansea Town (one in 1961) – before starting a two-year stint with the O's.

"I moved around because I came across a lot of different clubs while training and preparing to play in the Olympics of 1956. We beat Bulgaria to qualify for the Olympic finals in Melbourne and played several more teams in a mini league. I also played in the 1960 Games in Rome.

"Strangely enough, and few people seemed to realise this, I was preceded at Orient by someone else who played in the Olympics – Stan Charlton, who played in the 1948 Games. That's a lovely trick question for a quiz!"

Mike was hardly the archetypal footballer. He would sit quietly among his Orient team-mates on the train or coach travelling to away games and while the traditional card school was in progress a few feet away, and others were just chatting about nothing or where they were

Mike Pinner leaping against towering Tottenham striker Bobby Smith on his O's debut at Brisbane Road.

planning to go later that night, he would invariably be content to sit alone, in his velvet-collared coat, tackling *The Times* crossword puzzle. Norman Deeley and Phil White were probably scouring the *Sporting Life*.

But Mike insists he didn't feel 'different' from the others in the team, even though, as a part-time professional, he would only be seen around the Orient for twice weekly training and on match-days.

He explained: "I was studying to become a solicitor. I was an articled clerk and working mostly during the day. I came up to the ground to train every Tuesday and Thursday, but I trained with the youngsters – not the first team. We rarely trained on the main pitch and would play on the hard pitches behind the ground (behind the old West Stand). We also ran around the pitch.

"I was very fit, because I also played squash to quite a good standard and would play that on either a Monday or Wednesday. I always felt that squash was the best physical training a goalkeeper could have – apart from actually training with the football, with players firing shots at you.

"I never felt isolated from the first team just because I didn't train with them. It wasn't a problem to me. As long as you mucked in and played well, that's all that mattered."

FULL-BACKS

STAN CHARLTON
Right-back 1952-55 & 1958-64
Born: Exeter, Devon, June 28, 1929
Appearances: 367 League & 41 Cup
Goals: 2 League & 0 Cup

IF ever anybody deserves the title 'Mister Leyton Orient', then it is Stan Charlton. The oldest and most experienced of all the players covered in this book, the former skipper is a living O's legend with 11 seasons combined service – split over two spells – and a massive 408 appearances to his credit.

Only two players – Peter Allen, who played 432 matches between 1965 and '78, and Arthur Wood (373 between 1921-31) – have worn the shirt more times in the league than this much revered genetleman of football who initially joined Orient from Exeter City in 1952, via a spell with Isthmian League Bromley. Stan's father, Stanley Charlton senior, was a former professional footballer himself, having been born in Lancashire. Stan's mother, Isabellla, came from Yorkshire . . . but the O's stalwart was born in Exeter, Devon!

Stan, explained: "My father was playing for Exeter City at the time I was born, but he joined Crystal Palace a couple of weeks later and so my family moved to south London."

Capped three times as an England amateur international, he played in the Helsinki Olympic Games of 1952.

Stan, who stood 5ft 10ins tall, played 151 League games for the O's in his first spell between 1952 and October 1955 before his transfer (with Vic Groves) to Arsenal. He played 99 first division games for the Gunners in three years and then returned to Brisbane Road, rather suddenly, midway through the 1958-59 season.

Stan, now aged 77 and his memory for detail still as sharp as one of his tackles, says: "After Alec Stock agreed the deal to sign me with Arsenal manager George Swindin, he suddenly appeared on my doorstep at our home in Woodford Green on Christmas Eve. I was busy putting up a draught excluder when he told me to be ready to play against Stoke at home on Boxing Day.

"George Wright was Orient's right-back when I returned to the club but I moved across to that side to take over from him when they converted Eddie Lewis from a forward to a left-back."

On his return to East London, Stan gave the club another six years of sterling services. He took over the club captaincy and, of course, was the proudest man in Leyton that momentous day, in April 1962, when he was carried off the pitch, shoulder-high, by delirious supporters after having just guided his team to a place in history and the first division.

As skipper – "I always called heads – we once kicked off at the start of *both* halfs in one game!" he laughs – Charlton had the respect of all his peers and a good relationship with manager Johnny Carey, who would have appreciated his leader's

The covering Stan Charlton can't stop this one going past Frank George.

impeccable behaviour on and off the field.

Talk to Stan's former team-mates today and you won't hear a bad word said about the man who became such a great ambassador for LOFC.

Terry McDonald, at 21, the youngest member of the team that started the promotion season, was one who came under Stan's wing and he has always held him in the highest esteem.

He says: Stan was great. He looked after us and I looked up to him – as I still do. We all respected him as our captain and as a team-mate and you couldn't say a bad word about him. He is just a brilliant bloke.

"He was a very good organiser and when we were playing away, he would make sure we were all back in the hotel on time, although none of us ever got out of line anyway. When Stan said we had to be back by a certain time, we were there. No questions.

"On the pitch, he did his job of breaking up the opposition's play and then he'd give it easy to other players around him. Stan never just thumped the ball away.

"He played practice games as if they were league matches – he didn't know any other way to play.

"But Stan was always fair. He never went over the top of the ball on anyone or deliberately injure another player. If he did happen to kick someone, he'd just pick them up, shake their hand and say: 'Sorry mate.' That was his game," added McDonald.

In fact, in 408 matches, Stan was never even cautioned once by a referee.

He said: "I was never booked during my time with Orient. The only time I ever had my name taken was while playing for Arsenal against Huddersfield, when their centre-foreward Dave Hickson deliberately kicked me on the knee. I kicked out at him as I lay on the ground and we both had our name taken.

"After what I'd done, I felt scared to go back in the dressing room at half-time, because thre Arsenal manager Tom Whittaker was very strict on players' conduct. But he said to me: 'Don't worry, Stan, I would have reacted in exactly the same way if he'd done that to me.'

"Hickson was hard. Jimmy Scouler, of Newcastle, was another who liked to put himself about on the pitch.

"Hickson and I had played against each other in the army – we served together in Egypt and Palestine. I joined the first regiment of the Royal Horse Artillery in 1947 and served until 1950. Hickson was in the Royal Marine Corp."

Hickson was a very aggressive player but who was the best Stan ever faced? He hardly hesitated before saying: "One of the best was Albert Scanlon of Manchester United. I played against him for Arsenal in his last game before he fractured his skull in the Munich air crash. United beat us 5-4 at Highbury that day but it was a great game to have been part of."

Stan will no doubt be remembered by older Orient supporters as the slide-tackle specialist – it was his trademark. He admits: "I used to do a bit of slide-tackling – in fact, I once burnt all the skin off the top of my leg!

"I went to slide-tackle Albert Broadbent, the Sheffield Wednesday winger, in a game at Hillsborough one day and as I landed a few yards beyond the touchline, a female Wednesday fan lent over and hit me over the head with her umbrella! 'You dirty bugger!' she screamed at me.

"Her umbrella actually broke in half – well, my head was the best place she could've hit me! I didn't argue with her then and got on with taking the throw-in.

"But later in the game, when I had to go and collect another ball that had gone out of play near the same woman that had hit me, she did apologise for what she did."

Harry Gregory says: "I never saw another player tackle as much as Stan did. Whether the pitch was soft or bone hard, he wouldn't hesitate to put in a slide tackle. The grazes he had on his legs were terrible, but he'd be back up and putting in another slide-tackle just seconds later if required.

"Today you see players get a little whack and they roll over eight times. But Stan Charlton would never have done that – he would have been too embarrassed to do it.

CHARLES BUCHAN'S
SOCCER GIFT BOOK
The World's Greatest Football Annual
1963-64

Stan earned the honour of being depicted in colour on the front cover of the 1963-64 edition of Charles Buchan's Soccer Annual – heading the ball clear from Manchester United's David Herd.

"Stan was a fierce competitor, but fair too. He'd always go for the ball but he'd go through the ball and sometimes the guy as well. If you're saying that he never, ever had his name taken while he played at Orient, then all I can say is that if he played in today's game, he'd be booked every week!"

"If someone whacked you then, you thought to yourself: 'I'm not going to show him that he's hurt me, I'm gonna get up as quickly as I can and carry on.' The amount of diving and rolling we saw in the last World Cup was unbelievable and it's getting worse with the arrival of so many continentals in the English game.

"When I trained with the first team at Orient, I played up against Sid Bishop and, like Stan Charlton, he was another genuine fair player who wouldn't go over the top of the ball."

Eddie Lewis recalls: "Sometimes we trained and played practice matches on Hackney Marshes, where some fans used to park their cars and watch us. We used to say that if Stan missed a tackle, he'd take out two or three cars instead of the opposing winger!"

Stan did once injure himself during training, as he explained: "I damaged my knee playing head-tennis underneath the main stand. Groups of us played a lot of head-tennis there – we enjoyed it so much, they had a job to get us to stop in the afternoons when they wanted to lock the place up for the night.

"The trick to winning at head-tennis was to try and aim the ball at one of the door handles along the side of the stand, which would cause it to fly off at all angles. There was an art to it."

But if we're going to compare the game today and the one we loved 40 and 50 years ago, as we inevitably will in a book of this nature, then there are other issues to consider. Like rule changes. And referees.

Stan admits: "You could talk to referees in those days. I remember kicking Everton favourite Tommy Eglington up the backside while playing for Arsenal but the Yorkshire referee, Arthur Ellis (who later kept score on the popular TV series, *It's A Knockout*), saw the funny side of it.

"The Everton crowd, some 50,000 of them, were baying for blood, but Arthur just said to me: 'That were reet funny lad, I just wish I'd had a camera with me to capture the moment. Now Stan, just you stand there and look serious while I lecture you!'

"Ellis had no intention of writing my name in his little black book, so he made it look good for the fans. There was no harm done."

Stan could be a cute customer, though, and he had a clever way of dealing with any mild barracking from his own Orient supporters at home games, especially when the ground itself was in need of repair. He laughed when he said: "If the fans got on your back too much, one way to get back at them was to chip the ball up onto the old, corrugated iron roof of the stand. When the ball landed on that, the rust from the roof would fall down on the supporters below!"

Stan played under five different managers at Orient. While he has expressed his contrasting thoughts about Johnny Carey, Les Gore, Benny Fenton and Dave Sexton earlier in the book, the boss he most enjoyed playing for was Alec Stock, the man who twice signed him for the O's and who, like Charlton himself, also left Orient for the marble halls and glamour of Highbury before returning to Leyton.

"I liked Alec the best of the managers I played under at Orient. He would build up his players and make you think and feel you were far better than you really were.

"The training was always the same under him – lots of running."

Charlton provides an insight into Stock's famed man-management skill.

"I was once dropped by Alec for a game at Scunthorpe and he told me to help Les Gore carry the kit-skip – as the 12th man did in those days when there were no substitutes and the player left out of the side had to muck in and help the trainer. But I couldn't believe it, so I tackled Alec about it on the station platform as we were about to board the train.

"He asked me: 'You've never played for the reserves, have you Stanley?

"I replied: 'No'.

"He then said: 'So I didn't want to spoil your record!'

"Alec was a good man-manager who had the ability to take the sting out of a potentially volatile situation. Another time, goalkeeper Dave Groombridge came into the dressing room after training one Friday and discovered that he'd been dropped from the team the next day.

"He was furious and was in and out of the shower in a matter of seconds before storming off to confront the manager in his office. But when he knocked on the door, Alec said: 'Come in . . . Oh, I was going to call you in for a chat. Now what about that bad game you had last week?'

"Dave was dumbfounded and after a few more words from Alec he left his office and hadn't said any of the things he'd intended to say to him. Alec was very good at taking the heat out of a situation.

"Years after I'd left Orient, I invited Alec to appear as our guest speaker at the Dorset Combination League's annual dinner. He told everyone present that night: 'If Arsenal had played Stan Charlton in his best position – at left-back and not right-back – he would have played for England.' It was a lovely thing for him to say about me."

Stan has been up close to some of the very best managers in the game, including a well known and very outspoken Scottish legend on Merseyside.

He added: "I remember once after playing for Orient at Anfield, Liverpool boss

Captain Collosus, Stan Charlton is Mister Leyton Orient.

Sid Bishop, (Unknown), Stan Charlton and Tommy Johnston on a visit to PFA headquarters when players from all over Britain were fighting to get the maximum wage limit lifted.

Bill Shankly came into our dressing room. He said: 'There are only two teams in Liverpool . . . Liverpool and Liverpool Reserves! Yet you've just played us off the park, no worries.'

"The funny thing is, I think we'd just lost 3-0 to them!"

Stan Charlton led by example, although he wasn't necessarily the loudest or most demonstrative player in the Orient team. Eddie Lewis never stopped talking, Cyril Lea (who filled in as vice-captain at times) would fight like a tiger for every ball and go around geeing up his team-mates, and the experienced Sid Bishop was a great organiser in defence. They were perhaps all leaders in their own ways.

Bishop says: "I never had any rucks with Stan, because I could read him like a book when it came to covering for him – and I knew he would do the same for me.

"Stan would get forward but only if it was dead certain that it was on to do so. He wouldn't go forward recklessly, though. He had a bit of pace on him too."

Lewis added: "I got on well with Stan, even though I don't think he liked me at first. I think he warmed to me more after I'd saved a couple of certain goals with goalline clearances. Once I knocked myself on the post while trying to clear the ball and Stan told me afterwards how much he appreciated my efforts.

"I think that some of the guys wanted me to be captain, because I had a big mouth and talked all the time. But Stan being captain didn't bother me, even though he didn't talk as much as I did. Stan was a good lad and he did a good job."

An understatement, surely, by Eddie, for Stan Charlton is a true Leyton Orient great. Quite rightly, he is still given a rousing reception by supporters whenever he returns to see a game or attend an old players' reunion.

When Stan finally left Orient in 1965, he left a fine legacy in left-back Dennis Rofe, who starred at Brisbane Road from 1967 until 1972. "Dennis used to clean my boots when he was a young apprentice – I was his mentor!" smiles Stan.

In fact, Dennis played in the Stan Charlton Benefit match at Brisbane Road in 1970.

It was appropriate that on Stan's most recent return visit, for the club's 125th anniversary celebration dinner in April 2006, the new West Stand had been recently completed and in the foyer area hangs an enlarged, framed photograph of Stan being chaired off the pitch at the end of that Bury game in April '62. They should arguably name the stand after this great club ambassador but at least the picture will serve as a lasting tribute to an Orient collosus.

Great memories of a great, great man. To many of us, Stan Charlton *is* Mister Leyton Orient.

Eddie Lewis possessed skill and versatility in switching from a forward to a full-back.

EDDIE LEWIS
Left-back 1958-64
Born: Manchester, January 3, 1935
Appearances: 143 League & 21 Cup
Goals: 5 League & 4 Cup

THEY tall about a lack of flexibility in the game today, where right-footed players hate being asked to play on the left and vice-versa. "I wasn't playing in my best oposition," is a poor excuse we hear too often from one-dimensional and richly rewarded players who cannot adapt to unfamiliar roles and are reluctant or totally unwilling to compromise themselves for the benefit of the team.

Thankfully for Leyton Orient, Eddie Lewis had much more of an open mind than that and he did what very few players have ever attempted and even less have managed to achieve succesfully.

He switched from his regular position of centre-forward (or inside-forward) and became a quality . . . LEFT-BACK!

He didn't merely switch from right wing to left, or go from midfield to a more advanced striking position.

With great success, Eddie went from being a very decent No.9 at Manchester United and West Ham to the regular No.3 berth for Orient and made the position his own throughout the promotion and first division seasons.

You have to take your hat off to the guy.

Speaking from his home in Johannesburg, South Africa, where he is a household name as a television pundit on the main football network, Eddie recalled the origins of that transitional period in his interesting career. He says: "Bobby Charlton was my understudy at United when I played at centre-forward in my younger days.

"But I actually played a few games for them at left-back in a tournament in Switzerland and quite liked it. My old man wasn't keen on the idea, though. He said I wasn't a full-back and told me to persevere up front instead.

"So I basically refused to play at left-back for United and had an argument with the manager, Matt Busby, about it, which was very naughty of me at the time."

But Eddie soon realised that if he was going to make it in the game at a high level, he needed to change.

After leaving United, where he had an impressive record of nine goals in 20 league games for his local club between 1952 and 1955, in what was a very exciting era at Old Trafford with the Busby Babes on their way, he had a brief 12-game spell with Preston North End before moving to London and another 'happening' club.

"At West Ham I played quite regularly as a forward in their 1957-58 promotion side until they signed Vic Keeble."

With Keeble forming a prolific strike partnership with Johnny Dick and the Hammers destined for Division One, at 23 Eddie moved up the road in East London to join the O's in a £10,000 deal that also saw 28-year-old experienced right-back George Wright follow him in the same direction.

"I felt I was doing OK as a striker playing for Alec Stock," continued Eddie, "but

then he suggested to me that I could do even better at left full-back.

"I did play at left-back for the reserves but after Stock left, Les Gore was promoted from managing the reserves to first team boss . . . and so then I was asked to take over running the reserves. We had an old guy called Alex Hird looking after us but I gave the team-talks."

Eddie is claiming some of the credit for helping to push two promotion-winning favorites towards first team stardom. He explains: "I mentioned to Les that there were two kids playing in the reserves here who should be in the first team. They were Terry McDonald and Ronnie Foster. Anyway, a few weeks later he put them both in the side and by the time Johnny Carey came, those two virtually made our left wing. In fact, they did so well that Newcastle came in with a bid for the pair of them.

"When I first arrived, George Wright played at right-back and Stan Charlton on the opposite flank. But they weren't happy with George there, so Les made me captain of the reserves at left-back and then eventually brought me into the first team to play in the same position. That's when Stan took over George's usual position on the right."

Stock, who had left and returned to Orient after brief spells with Arsenal and then Roma in Italy in the late 50s, finally left for good when he took over at Queens Park Rangers in August 1959. Lewis had only played under Stock for half-a-season but the charismatic manager left an indelible mark on the eager, young pupil.

Eddie recalls: "Alec had a football pitch painted on the floor of the Orient dressing room and when he got us all together during training, he'd use tins of shoe polish to represent 'players'. He'd stand over the 'pitch' and kick the tins of polish around and talk about positions where certain players should be. One player would say 'I don't agree with that' and then, of course, I'd have my say too. Before you knew it, we'd all be arguing a point when Alec would suddenly walk out and leave us standing there. Then, 20 minutes later, he'd come back into the room with a tray full of teas for everyone!

"I liked Alec – he was a good man-manager. He gave me my chance at left-back."

A run of eight games in his newly-adopted defensive role at the end of the 1959-60 season convinced new boss Les Gore that Lewis should keep the No.3 shirt from the start of the following campaign. And though injuries limited his appearances in 1960-61, Eddie missed only one of the 42 league games in the promotion campaign

– a hamstring pull that ruled him out of their win at Brighton.

He played most of the first division games, too, although, as has been well documented earlier, his relationship with Johnny Carey deteriorated and he lost his place to Billy Taylor. Ironically, Taylor, who sadly died young, and Eddie both went on to earn very good reputations as coaches at international level – Taylor with the England set-up and Lewis with the national squad in South Africa.

A very vocal character who thought seriously about the game from an early stage in his football career, Eddie Lewis knew his limitations as a player. The physical attributes of strength and power that made him a competent forward in his younger days were not common among full-backs who needed to be sharp and pacy against the very quickest wingers. But that's where Eddie used his footballing intelligence to make himself a good all round player, with clever positioning and his astute reading of the game.

He admits: "I was a good passer of the ball, although I would be exposed for lack of pace if a ball was knocked 50 yards over my shoulder and I had to chase after it. When I was up front, I liked the ball to be played into my feet – it's what I'd been used to at both Man United and West Ham. But if they wanted to knock balls over my head, that wasn't my game.

"I remember we were doing sprints one day and I was struggling. Ronnie Foster said to me: 'Do you know what, Eddie, if you weren't such a brainy bastard you wouldn't be able to get in the team!'

"In the Second Division, if the opposing inside-forward got the ball and put his head down to make a pass out to his winger, I'd anticipate what was coming next and be ready to get there to intercept it. I'd read the pass and nick it off the winger – it was part of my game.

"But the biggest shock I got was when we went up into the first division. For example, Denis Law would have the ball and he'd look at Johnny Giles on the right wing. But instead of actually playing the ball out wide to Gilesy, Law would look up again before passing the pass on the *inside* of me, for Giles to run on to.

"We found that when playing at the highest level, you could run around against the likes of Arsenal and Man United for 20 minutes and not even get a kick of the ball."

Eddie's team-mates at Brisbane Road recognised his weaknesses but also appreciated his strengths too.

Centre-half Sid Bishop observed: "Eddie wasn't the fastest left-back, but Cyril Lea and myself knew that and so if the opposition's right-winger was a flier, one of us had to be ready to cover for him."

Lea added: "Yes, I'd try and help Eddie a bit on our left side and we got a good relationship going. We became good mates."

Lewis said of his old pal: "Cyril was hard. He used to say to me: 'Eddie, let that winger come past you and I'll kick him over the f****** stand!' Wingers used to shit themselves knowing that Cyril was behind me.

"If we had to stay overnight in a hotel before an away game, I'd usually share a room with Cyril, although I was Best Man at Malcolm and Jenny Lucas' wedding. I got on well with both Cyril and Malcolm," Eddie added who, with Lea, Lucas and

Joe Elwood, made up the group of non(or rare)-drinkers and non-smokers.

Sid Bishop considered Lewis' main assets and said: "Eddie was a lovely kicker and placer of a ball and could find his man with a good pass."

Terry McDonald, who is the first to acknowledge that he enjoyed consistently great service from Eddie on the left flank, paid this tribute: "He worked on improving his control and only gave you the ball if it was on. Eddie was a great passer and he would chip long balls up to Dave (Dunmore) or Ronnie (Foster) or play it short to my feet – whatever was required.

"His ability to pick a long pass was excellent and, defensively, he never got caught out because his knowledge of the game was good, even against very quick wingers like Terry Paine. You knew Painey might cause a problem for Eddie, because he could go inside and out, so we'd get back and help him. I was the first line of defence against the likes of Paine but others, such as Cyril Lea and Sid Bishop, would also cover, so Eddie rarely got exposed in a one-versus-one situation.

"I never saw Eddie get roasted by anyone. And then when he got possession again, he came into his own. Technically, no-one could strike a ball better – Eddie struck a ball like Bobby Moore.

"You have to appreciate and respect how well he did after he switched from being a forward to a left-back. He wasn't just a decent left-back, not a mere stop-gap. He adapted very well but he could also whack a ball in from 35 yards if he had the chance to go forward, so he had different strengths to his game. I've seen how well he could shoot, because in my only first team game for West Ham – a friendly against Spartak Prague – Eddie scored two goals from outside the box in a 3-3 draw."

McDonald is eager to ensure that people who might not have seen Eddie Lewis in his prime for Orient, appreciate just what a good team player he became because of his adaptability and understanding of football.

"His body proportion was all wrong," continued Terry. "He had a big upper body and legs, so he would naturally struggle for speed. But how many players could successfully convert from centre-forward to left-back, if they were a bit overweight

Eddie Lewis and Mal Lucas clear the danger.

and not quick, the way Eddie did? His knowledge of the game and his abillity on the ball got him through and you have to give him great credit for that.

"I'm not surprised that he went into coaching and had a good career in South Africa. He probably learnt a bit from being around people like Malcolm Allison and other senior players who were into new coaching ideas at West Ham in the late 50s, where I think Eddie learned more than he did at Man United.

"We were playing the W-M formation in our day, but if we'd been playing today, you could possibly see Eddie playing up front alongside someone like Dunmore in a 4-4-2 system," McDonald added.

Frank George rated Lewis highly, saying: "He was one of the best. He wasn't very quick but he was a bloody great full-back and not many wingers went past him. If he'd been quicker, I'm sure Eddie would've played for England."

Although he scored only five goals in the blue of Leyton Orient, Eddie did net the occasional screamer – notably, in what turned out to be a vital 2-2 home draw with eventual second division champions Liverpool in March '62. It was a brilliantly executed left-foot shot from a short freekick, although Eddie reveals now: "Cyril Lea annoyed me because he took so long to set up the ball for me to hit. I kept screaming at him to knock it to me, so when he eventually did roll the ball forward for me to whack, I wasn't quite ready!

"I was so mad that when Cyril did finally tap the ball sideways to me, I just wellied it as hard as I could – and it flew into the top corner like a rocket past Jim Furnell.

"Leslie Grade told me afterwards that he could hear Bill Shankly shouting to his players: 'Watch the number three!'. The football writers wrote in the papers the next day about a 'well-worked freekick' but the truth is I was pissed off with Cyril for not playing the ball to me early enough, before the Liverpool wall had been set!"

Eddie has always had plenty to say for himself and still does now that he's a leading TV pundit in S.A. One of the characteristics I like most about Eddie is that while he isn't afraid to criticise others if he feels they deserve it, he is willing to apply the same scrutiny to himself and he accepts that he has undoubtedly upset a few people along the way.

He says: "Even though Stan Charlton was our captain, I still talked all the time on the field anyway. I remember once shouting at Gordon Bolland, to try and get him going. I felt Gordon needed a kick up the backside sometimes to fulfil his potential, but he just told me to shut my mouth!"

Gordon has only good memories of Eddie, though, saying: "He was a terrific guy, very friendly and a good player."

I could listen to Eddie Lewis talking football all day and night. Just as he clearly enjoys reminiscing about his days as Leyton Orient's converted left-back.

He concluded: "I've got to say, I was at Man United from the age of 14 until I was 22 and I loved it there. But the best time of my life was at the Orient, without a shadow of a doubt."

HALF-BACK LINE

MALCOLM LUCAS
Right Wing-half 1958-64
Born: Wrexham, North Wales, October 7, 1938
Appearances: 157 League & 19 Cup
Goals: 6 League & 0 Cup

SID BISHOP
Centre-half 1953-64
Born: Tooting, South London, April 8, 1934
Appearances: 296 League & 27 Cup
Goals: 4 League & 0 Cup

CYRIL LEA
Left Wing-half 1957-64
Moss, North Wales, August 5, 1934
Appearances: 205 League & 23 Cup
Goals: 0 League & 0 Cup

THERE have been numerous great examples of sporting triumvirates. In cricket, the famous West Indies W's of Worrell, Weekes and Wallcott. In the 60s English football had the World Cup winners of Moore, Hurst and Peters at West Ham; Best, Law and Charlton at Man United and, at City, they had Lee, Bell and Summerbee. At Leyton Orient they had the immortal trio of Lucas, Bishop and Lea.

They were top players in their own right at Brisbane Road, playing a combined 727 League and Cup matches between them, but they will forever be intrinsically linked as the most successful half-back (or midfield, to use the modern term) line in O's history.

Malcolm, Sid and Cyril were the cast-iron defensive bedrock on which the promotion team was built and, when the chips were down and the pressure was on, when the forward line started misfiring with the chequered flag in sight, it was their drive, resilience and organisational skill that did so much to haul Johnny Carey's men over the finishing line and into first division folklore.

Bishop, the eldest and by far the most experienced of the three, spent his entire professional playing career – 12 seasons – with the O's, having joined them from Orient's old south London nursery, Chase of Chertsey, in 1953.

He played 15 games, mostly at right-back, in the 1955-56 Third Division South promotion-winning side but, when veteran skipper Stan Aldous, the club's first post-war great, entered the twilight days of his career, Sid made the No.5 shirt his own from the start of the 1957-58 season under manager Alec Stock.

Cyril Lea came to Orient in 1957 from Welsh club side Bradley Rangers, initially as a left-back, but by the end of the 1958-59 campaign he too had established

himself at left-half. Former Orient inside-forward Phil Woosnam proved the catalyst for Lea joining the O's, as Cyril explained: "We were both playing for the Welsh amateur international side against England at Peterborough – Phil was in midfield and I was at left-back. He recommended me to Les Gore and I signed for Orient rather than Aston Villa, who were also interested in me at that time."

The son of Welsh miner Frank Lea, Cyril is the youngest of a family of nine children (three boys and six girls) from the little village of Moss, near Wrexham.

"I was a late starter – I signed pro for Orient at the age of 22. To be honest, I thought I'd missed the boat and would never become a pro footballer, so when I got the chance at Orient I grabbed it with both hands."

It was in 1958, and on Lea's recommendation, that Alec Stock also signed Cyril's fellow Welshman and pint-sized pocket dynamo, Malcolm Lucas. Neither Cyril nor Malcolm much fancied following their forefathers down the mines – they were heading for the top, not the bottom.

Sid Bishop admits: "When they first came to the club we had out doubts about them – they were amateur boys who'd come up from Wales. They worked harder and harder to improve their game and after Cyril got into the team, it wasn't long before Malcom did too, so then I had one playing on either side of me.

"They used to put in extra training and they really did work at it. You could see them improve on their weaknesses and gradually they fell in with me easily enough.

"I used to do my share of ordering about on the field, as you would do being a centre-half, but they responded well to whatever was asked of them. They would be there whenever they were needed.

"Malcolm was the more football-minded of the two but they would both run their

The tenacious terrier, Cyril Lea was the toughest tackler at the club.

legs off.

"We had a good balance and would cover for one another. I like to think they gained confidence from myself, knowing I was around them nearly all of the time."

And, significantly, Bishop added: "We all knew what to expect from one another."

As right-half, Malcolm was the more attacking and forward-thinking of the two little Welshmen, whereas it was Cyril's responsibility to provide defensive cover to Bishop and the two full-backs, Stan Charlton and, particularly, Eddie Lewis, who was playing on the same left side of the pitch.

Lea was a tenacious tackler, undoubtedly the hardest at the club in his time.

Cyril says: "I enjoyed the defensive side of the game and was happy for Malcolm to get forward more than me. I had previously played at both left and right-back – in fact, I was naturally right-footed but could kick with both feet.

"I enjoyed winning the ball more than Malcolm did – and yes, I liked a tackle. I don't know why, but I particularly enjoyed that side of the game. Mal pushed on while I sat a bit deeper and we had a good blend.

"The only chasing I felt I got was from Brian Douglas of Blackburn. He had really quick feet and I couldn't handle him. I finished up in a deep hole trying to mark him – he was a good player.

"Sid was a good, steady, week-in-week-out player, a good athlete who was an excellent jumper from a standing position."

It speaks volumes for Mal Lucas' ability and determination that he finally established himself in the right-half spot after taking over from long-serving favourite Ken Facey, who was also an accomplished player in his own right.

Mal says: "Ken had been there so long and perhaps I didn't perform as well as they expected me to at first, or they didn't wish to experiment with the team too much? I never lost hope that I would break through and I was just so pleased to be playing professional football."

As a youngster in Wales, Cyril Lea had played football with one of Malcolm's elder brothers – there is a four-year age difference between the two former Orient midfield stars – and it must have helped both of them to settle into Leyton life that they had come from small villages just a mile or so apart.

"Cyril and I knew each other through playing for Bradley Rangers and we were good mates. He lived in the next village to me," continues Mal.

"When I was a youth international I was on Bolton's books as a centre-forward. I went from there to Liverpool and converted to midfield, but then I lost interest in football. It was only when I bumped into Cyril at Bradley Rangers, and he started talking about the Orient, that I got my enthusiasm back – although I must admit, I'd never heard of the Orient back then!

"Cyril told me that it was a nice, little club and it would be a way of getting me out of the pits and back into football again.

"I went there as an inside-forward but things didn't go too well for me in a practice match, so I mentioned that I really preferred to play in the middle of the park. I don't think I did particularly well at first and the Orient farmed me out to Harlow Town to gain more experience. I had a couple of games for them before returning to Orient.

"At first, I used to travel down from Wales to play at weekends – I stayed in lodgings with an elderly couple in a house just off Lea Bridge Road. I'd come down on the the train on a Friday night, play the game and then return to Wales the next day. I was a country boy, so I found London unbelievably big. When I'd established myself in the first team, Jenny and I rented a house in Barking."

Talking about the respective roles of the famous O's trio, Lucas continued: "Sid was a rock, a tremendous figure. At that time, I don't think there was a better centre-half than him anywhere else in the league. He was outstanding in our promotion season, so very strong physically and commanding.

"Sid, Cyril and myself never really got on at each other verbally during games and we didn't talk together beforehand about what was required. If anything needed saying, we did it out on the park, we worked it out between us. We were all on the same wavelength. I shouldn't say we played it all off the cuff, but we seemed to know where each other would be at any given time.

"Cyril was a more defensive player than myself, because his qualities in that respect were perhaps better than mine. But I thought I had a little bit more going forward and that's what I wanted to do anyway. Knowing Cyril was behind me, I could get forward and attack more but when Benny Fenton came in as Johnny Carey's replacement, he didn't see it that way. He and I disagreed and I said to him that if that's how he felt, then this is where we part company.

"He just wanted us to play the old system, where you had two full-backs, a centre-half and two wing-halfs who played anywhere they wanted to. But I thought we'd moved on from that to a situation where we had to have more discipline and the class of player we were up against was better and more organised. Fenton didn't seem to want me to get forward like I'd been used to doing under Carey.

"Carey never stopped me attacking, he didn't say I couldn't go over the halfway line. He just gave me the freedom to do whatever I thought was the right thing to do. Having been a centre-forward in my younger days, I suppose that desire to score goals never left me – I still wanted to get into goalscoring positions."

No-one was more dedicated to the game than Cyril Lea, who worked dilligently to improve his own game.

"Malcolm was more laid-back than me and, technically, I felt he was a slightly better player," Cyril admits. "I needed to improve my first touch and my passing, so I used to do extra training on my own. Because I lived in digs near Leyton Town Hall (I met my wife there), I used to go to Millfields park in Lea Bridge Road, by the River Lea, in the evenings and practice alone, by kicking a ball against the shelter wall. I also used to practice my sprinting in the afternoons, after our normal training had finished.

"Les Gore, who was good at putting his arm round you if you ever needed it, would come out and see if I was all right. I was brought up in a tough environment, so I

Mal Lucas earned international recognition while at Brisbane Road.

just got on with it – it wasn't a problem doing extra work. The more I practiced, the easier it became and I felt all the hard work paid off for me.

"I also went to watch a lot of other games when the Orient weren't playing. For example, I'd go and see Jimmy Greaves play at Tottenham, which helped prepare me for when I had to mark him in a game. I went up to Wolverhampton to watch the top Hungarians, including Ferenc Puskas, play for Honved against Wolves in a friendly. It took us five hours to get there and five hours back, all the way up the old A5."

Mal Lucas wishes now that he had applied himself in the same dedicated way Lea did.

With great candour, he says: "Cyril was very dedicated. He would go back in the afternoons to train with the coach, Joe Mallett, a quietly spoken bloke who Cyril got on really well with. That showed how dedicated and determined he was about football.

"I didn't go back to do extra training like he did, but I wish now that I had.

"I didn't think, way back then, that Cyril would obviously go on to enjoy the good career he's had in the game as a coach. I mean, who can say how people's lives are going to turn out? They had a little, young Scottish inside-forward at the Orient called Billy Taylor . . . and he went on to become an England coach. Although he was only a young lad at the time he was with us, you could perhaps see the makings of a coach in him, because he talked football. He had views on the game, even at such a young age, but he died young too."

Cyril is inclined to agree with Malcolm's assessment of himself that he might perhaps have developed into an even better player than he was. Lea says: "Maybe Mal could have stretched himself a little bit more. He had enough pace and was a bit deceptive when running with the ball, and he could score a goal too. But, as I say, he was more laid-back than me."

Cyril Lea never scored for Orient in 228 matches. He was the Claude Makele of his day – very tough, a ball winner who played the game simply, without over-elaboration. He knew his strengths and always played to them.

Flyweight Terry McDonald, who would admit that he didn't possess Lea's strength in the tackle, wonders now if Cyril could have contributed more to the team, in an attacking sense, despite his defensive priorities.

He said: "Cyril was a purely defensive player, although he would give you the ball if you were on for the pass. He played the game simply and would never run more than 10 yards with the ball.

"But if the other team was on the charge, you could bet that he would be there to break up the attack, or hold them up. He didn't get caught out of position and he was, without doubt, the hardest tackler at the club. He never went over the top, though. If the ball was there to be won, he would win it, or want to win it.

"And he was also good at geeing up the players around him. He'd keep you going with a shout of 'come on'. He was a great competitor.

"He had a good attitude and was dedicated to his particular side of the game, which was simply to defend.

"We just never knew how good Cyril would have been if he'd been a more offensive player and got forward. I think he sat back too much at times and if he'd got forward on occasions, it would have helped the team more and broadened his own horizons. All right, so it could be argued that if he'd played more that way we might have been left a bit exposed at the back – but then it would have been up to other players in the team to realise that they had to cover for Cyril.

"Cyril would rarely venture further forward than the centre circle, which probably helped Sid from a defensive point of view. But, for some reason, he didn't want to know the attacking side of the game and I wonder sometimes if he ever regrets that? I'm sure he could have contributed three or four goals a season if he'd got forward more but Malcolm Lucas was the only wing-half who got involved in our attacks and would take the opportunity to do so.

"I find it hard to understand, because if you play football at any level – whether you're a kid in the street or over the park, and no matter what position you play – you *want* to score a goal. It's everybody's dream when they play football. So I can't understand why Cyril didn't get forward occasionally and try to score one himself. Why wouldn't *everybody* want to score a goal?

McDonald offers an interesting view of the individual and collective roles Lea and Lucas played in the Orient midfield and wonders if they could have complemented each other even better than they did.

"Malcolm was a good wing-half. His aggression was good and when he won the ball on the halfway line he'd play it simple. But then he'd see it through, still want to get forward and get in the box on the end of moves.

"Whether Cyril Lea sat back because he could see Malcolm getting forward, I don't know. I can see that that's how Cyril might have looked at it. You can also argue that by Cyril staying deep, it allowed Malcolm to get forward.

"But I think it could also have worked well in reverse – Cyril could have gone forward and Malcolm would've had the intelligence and awareness to have covered for him. Malcolm was fit and a tough tackler too, and nearly as good as Cyril, defensively, anyway."

But McDonald paid tribute to Lea when he added: "You could see how dedicated he was to the game – he was fautless in his dedication. He took physiotherapy courses and went on to enjoy a good career in football after he stopped playing, which didn't surprise me. He did very well for himself."

Fitness is an important aspect of pro football that Sid Bishop always prided himself on. "If I wasn't the fittest player at the club, I was very near to being it," he says. "I could push myself as much as anybody. I had that nice, comfortable feeling within myself that I was in good physical shape. I used to love physical training – I was a PT instructor in the army – and there are a million different exercises you can do to keep fit.

"Les Gore used to take us for PE training and before him it was done by Joe Mallett. Les would get me jumping to head a ball dangling from a piece of rope. I was doing hand-springs, an exercise I picked up in the army, before Les then got the other players doing them – he respected the fact that I knew the business when it came to physical training. I found it quite easy and had to bite my tongue at times if I didn't think we were doing enough, or the right things.

"Everybody loved playing head-tennis. We played it in teams of three – two on the base line and one by the net – and if we weren't playing it under the main stand, we were over on the tennis courts behind the West Stand.

"As a team, I think we could have been even fitter than we were, although we found it hard in the first division because we'd gone up a standard. We needed to be classier with our passes forwards."

Sid faced some of English football's greatest centre-forwards and never let himself down. Each one he came up against presented a new challenge to him and some were harder – in every sense – than others. But Bishop was not a clogger. He did his job and would always try and win the ball fairly. And for a centre-back who stood no taller than 5ft 10ins, he was brilliant in the air. His timing invariably impeccable. Like Stan Charlton, the only other player in this squad who played more games for the O's than him, Sid was never booked in a blue shirt.

Recalling some of the toughest battles he endured, Bishop said: "Tottenham's Bobby Smith once gave me a dig in my ribs, just as he set off on a run, but I caught him with my fist as he tried to get away. We both had a quick dig at each other and after that he never tried it on with me again.

"When I see all the shirt-grabbing that goes on in the penalty box today, it makes me sick. If it had gone on in our day, a few people would have got a good wallop. It's so petty and if anyone had tried that on with me, they would have got a dig in the ribs – even if it meant me being sent off.

"It hardly went on back then. Tommy Johnston would occasionally give somebody a shove but I don't know how many shirts he pulled? I did, though, see him get sent-off for something he did to Doncaster's Charlie Williams, the former comedian who died this year. In fact, in the return game at Doncaster, it was Charlie who was sent-off for fouling Tommy!

"Centre-halfs were allowed to tackle from behind then, so you had to do something pretty bad to get sent-off. But I never went in to deliberately kick people from behind. I'd try to get my leg around the player and win the ball. If I got to it first, then no way would it be a foul.

"The ball-playing centre-half I liked most was Sunderland's Charlie Hurley. He praised me up as the best centre-half in the second division and I repaid the compliment. He was tall but light on his feet – like John Charles. John stood on my foot once and then he said to me: 'Sorry Sid'. He was a giant.

"Charlie Hurley wanted to get the ball down and play and so did I when I could.

"I never fouled a player intentionally and don't recall ever causing a bad injury to another player.

"We were playing Liverpool at home once, it was just before half-time, and Ian St. John ran into my elbow as I climbed high to head a ball. He'd charged into me and I didn't even see him coming. There was blood spurting from his left eye. I apologised to him when we came back out for the second half but he just said: 'Don't worry Sid, it was *my* fault'. I was pleased to hear that, because what happened to him *wasn't* my fault. He was very good about it.

"There was the odd occasion when a forward would clobber me off the ball, behind the ref's back. It happened once and I said to the referee: 'Oi ref, can I hit him?' He

Fitness expert Sid Bishop. He wasn't the tallest centre-back around, but with dedicated practice to improve his jumping and heading ability, he was a class act. Les Gore watches Sid go through his paces at the ground.

just replied: 'Don't let me *see* you do it!'.

"You didn't tell referees their job but you could talk to them. You didn't hear players abuse the officials like they do today. Now, it's all one bloody big act with all the diving that goes on.

"I was never booked as a player with Orient. I saw one of our former players, Len Julians, sent off while playing for Arsenal, after he threw mud at another player. But Len did like a punch-up – he was a good boxer in his time, bless him."

Having been an ever-present in the promotion side, Sid missed only three matches of the following first division campaign, when his understudy, David Clark, had to deputise for him against Fulham (away), Manchester City (away) and Blackpool (home). Sid recalled the incident, during a spiteful home game against Sheffield Wednesday, that ended his long unbroken appearance record.

"I was running out wide, to get in a position to cover Stan in case he got beaten on the wing, when 'Bronco' Layne clobbered me from behind. I went over on my right ankle, fell to the ground and couldn't move. I was in real pain.

"Luckily the ligaments weren't too badly strained. I was always top in physical training at school and kept myself very fit. I became a Physical Training Instructor in the army and I think my background helped my body to cope with what happened that day against Sheffield Wednesday.

"It's a mental thing too – your ability to overcome physical adversity has a lot to do with what's going on in your head.

"I was playing consistently well at that stage, I had so much confidence in myself, and I think the Wednesday players knew that I was the one they had to sort out when we played them that day.

"I wouldn't allow what Layne did to affect me. In fact, in the return game against him at Hillsborough, he never came near me. He went to shake hands with me at the end but as I went to shake, I deliberately missed his hand, pulled my thumb up over my shoulders and said 'meet the boys!'. I just walked away from him. If I'd shaken hands with someone like him, I would have felt that I'd let myself down. I would have regretted it all my life.

"We all know what happened to Layne and a few of the other Sheffield Wednesday players who were involved in the football bribes scandal later on. That summed it all up for me.

"I had a lot of confidence in my ability to be consistent. I think opposing teams knew that if they were to rattle us as a team, then they would have to 'do' me – sort me out."

As well as David 'Bronco' Layne, Sid recalls some particularly physical scraps with another notorious hard man from the north.

"Bury had a nutter called Dave Hickson, who would turn around and start growling and shouting at you. He went on to play for Liverpool and once put six stud marks in Stan Charlton from his groin down to his knee in a match up at Anfield. We had a go at the referee about him – it was diabolical.

"I had a gash where Hickson hit me. He even left a bit of his fair hair in the wound! He was as nutty as a fruitcake."

Sid wasn't one for getting embroiled in verbal slanging matches on the pitch, though. "If they wanted to talk to me they could, but they didn't get a lot out of me," he said. As everyone knows, Brian Clough was always a great talker, even in his young playing days for Middlesbrough and Sunderland.

"Cloughie had plenty of mouth," continued Sid, "and he'd even get on his team-mates' nerves during a match. He never said anything to me during the game but if he didn't get the ball, he'd give his team-mates what for. Cloughie was a good player – he would crack a ball from anywhere."

Like all the other Orient players, Sid relished his visits to Anfield, where the O's had mixed results over the years but also enjoyed some thrilling encounters in front of the famous Kop. Sid recalls: "Their fans applauded us off the pitch after the show we'd put on up there one year. We brought in little Dennis Sorrell who, with Terry McDonald and Ronnie Foster, were playing triangles around Liverpool on that left-hand side – little give-and-go's. It was simple stuff, but very effective, the type of push-and-run play Eddie Baily coached us. Poor John Molyneux, who was playing right-back for them, didn't know what had hit him."

Mind you, Sid remembers another time when the scouse Koppites were not so appreciative of his and Orient's efforts. "We were defending the Kop end and I'd just nicked the ball off Roger Hunt's leg. As the ball ran off the pitch at that end, Hunt appealed for a corner but I knew full well it was our goalkick.

"All of a sudden, I felt a sharp pain across my knee – I'd been hit by a cigarette lighter thrown from the crowd. Instinctively, I picked it up, went to switch on the lighter and when no flame appeared, I threw it back into the crowd and shouted: 'It don't f****** work!' Nowadays, players complain if a tiny one penny coin is throw at them."

Players had a much greater rapport with the fans in Bishop's day.

He recalls: "Eddie Brown was a character. Once, after scoring against Bristol Rovers at Eastville, he ran behind the goal, picked a couple of daffodils from the flower beds they had there and then went and presented them to the referee!

"We had some laughs on and off the field but you hardly see a player smile these days, let alone laugh. I'd smile all week on their money, for God's sake!

"Another lively incident involving fans came years earlier, when I was playing right-back at Shrewsbury when Alec Stock was the manager. I'd sliced down their nippy right winger and the next thing I knew, this crazy woman whacked me with her umbrella! Nothing was said about it, though. It happened to Stan Charlton as well – it wasn't that out of the ordinary."

Harlow-based Sid – who says he played on every Football League ground in his day – remains a fairly frequent visitor to Leyton Orient, although he was very disappointed by the manner of his acrimonious departure from the club he had given such great service. He asked for the finer details of what happened to remain off the record, but his dispute with chairman Harry Zussman had undoubtedly left a lingering sour taste.

"I don't want to speak ill of the dead or cause any controversy at the club now after all these years," says Sid, who claims that Zussman denied him the chance to buy his club-owned property – 33 Durham Avenue, Woodford (the same house Tommy Johnston rented previously) – from them, because he had already said that he intended to retire as a player in May 1964.

"In the end, after the dispute, the club held on to my registration so that I couldn't move elsewhere. At that point I just retired from professional football," he added, still barely able to disguise his disgust at the treatment he received at the end of a great career with the O's.

Sid Bishop says he received loyalty bonuses of £270 and £600 respectively after five and 10-years with the club. But surely this one-club man, who wore the O's colours with pride from the days when he captained their junior team in 1951 until he decided to quit pro football in 1964, deserved something substantially more for his 323 appearances and 12 seasons in the first team . . .

There was talk, during Bishop's most consistently dominant period, that he could be called up to the England squad. Unfortunately, it never quite happened for him but both Cyril Lea and Malcolm Lucas were capped for Wales at senior level.

Mal earned all four caps of his caps as an Orient player – against Northern Ireland (April 11, 1962 at Cardiff), Mexico (May 22, 1962 in Mexico City), England (October 12, 1963 at Cardiff) and Scotland (November 20, 1963 at Glasgow).

Orient fans always felt a great sense of injustice on behalf of Cyril, who had to wait until he had left O's to join Ipswich Town in 1964 before finally picking up his two full Welsh caps, although he says now that he was never personally disappointed.

He says: "It didn't bother me not getting a cap for Wales at that time in my career. I was happy at the Orient and as long as we were doing all right, that was the main thing. Playing for Wales didn't really cross my mind."

To underline his selfless approach to the game, Cyril had difficulty recalling how many full caps he has actually won. For the record, he played twice for the full national team, against Northern Ireland in Belfast (March 17, 1965) and Italy in Florence (May 1, 1965).

Cyril Lea enjoyed a fine career as a player and, later, as a coach at Ipswich and a string of other League clubs. Just like Malcolm Lucas and Sid Bishop, he looks back on his playing time at LOFC with great effection.

He said: "I've got no complaints whatsoever about Orient as a club, other than the frustration we felt that we could survive in the first division. It was sad, because we might have gone on from there . . .

"But they were the best days of my life."

FORWARDS

DAVE DUNMORE

Centre-forward 1961-65
Born: Whitehaven, Cumberland, February 2, 1934
Appearances: 147 League & 21 Cup
Goals: 54 League & 4 Cup

ONE of only nine Orient players to have ever scored **20 or more league goals in a season**, Dave Dunmore was the outstanding star of this era, the talented centre-forward blossomed at Brisbane Road after not quite fulfilling his potential in the top flight with Tottenham and West Ham.

Big Dave struck 22 goals in the promotion campaign, followed by 11 in Division One and was just the man Orient had been looking for to replace the legendary Tommy Johnston, who was in the last few months of his own glorious reign when him and 'DD' formed their strike partnership in March 1960.

It was a great signing by manager Les Gore, who effectively swapped the young bustling forward Alan Sealey for Dunmore.

In fact, it was a good deal all round – Dunmore fired O's towards the first division while 'Sammy' went on to net both goals for the Hammers in their 1965 European Cup Winners' Cup final victory against TSV Munich 1860 at Wembley.

But few should have doubted Dunmore's ability to shine at the highest level.

In his year of first division football under the management of Ted Fenton at West Ham, he scored 18 times in 38 appearances alongside Scottish

Reporting back for pre-seasonn training – you can tell because the pitch looks in perfect condition!
Norman Deeley, Derek Gibbs, Dave Dunmore, Terry McDonald and Malcolm Graham.

international Johnny Dick, including a league hat-trick against Arsenal and another in a prestige friendly against top Brazilian side Fluminese. During his most prolific spell, he netted 10 goals in seven matches, which included his brilliant performance against the Gunners in November 1960.

Also on the scoresheet for the Irons that day was playmaker Phil Woosnam, who Dave rates as the best player he played with in a claret-and-blue shirt.

West Ham had signed Dunmore in March 1960 in another swap deal – valued at £10,000 and this time involving Johnny Smith – with London rivals Tottenham, where he had made 97 senior appearances and scored 34 goals in his six seasons at White Hart Lane.

Surrounded by so many great players, one or two left over from the 1951 Spurs championship side and a number who went on to form the double-winning team of 1960-61, it was no disgrace that Dunmore didn't play in the white shirt more often. However, someone who knew that he had even more to offer was Eddie Baily.

Dunmore, who cost £10,500 from York City (25 goals from 48 starts) in 1954, had made his Tottenham debut against Arsenal at Highbury . . . alongside Baily in the Spurs team that day. Six years later they were reunited when Dave joined the O's team coached by his former team-mate.

Dunmore hadn't yet paved the way to O's promotion when the shrewd talent-spotter Baily said: "Dave's still good enough for first division football. I knew when he came here from West Ham he could be really useful to Orient.

"Dave suffered at Tottenham – he was kept back too long in the reserves. Like so many players at Tottenham, they were as good as many other first division players – but not good enough for Spurs' first team. Now Dave can really show himself and in the second division he must shine."

And shine like a beacon he certainly did.

Looking back now, Dave – who lives in York, where his pro career began in 1951 – says he didn't feel disappointed, or believe that he had a point to prove to anyone, when he left behind his previous first division experiences with Spurs and West Ham for a lesser grade of football with their London neighbours to the east.

"Leaving West Ham was something they wanted. It was a last minute thing, so it was a case of 'let's do it.' Why hang about somewhere where you're perhaps not wanted? It was a matter of saying yes or no to Orient on the day – the last day of the transfer deadline, I think – so I had no thoughts of waiting around to see if another top club would come in for me.

"Yeah, of course I was a bit disappointed that they let me go. I'd been part of a good side with some really good stars in the making coming up through the ranks, like Bobby Moore, Geoff Hurst and Martin Peters, to mention just three.

"You've got to play your football wherever you are, that's what it's all about. I knew I was joining a good set of lads at Orient, because I'd played against quite a few of them in reserve team games."

Talking of Baily, Dave said: "I played in the same Tottenham side as Eddie, Alf Ramsey, Harry Clarke, Ted Ditchburn and all them.

"Eddie was all right as the coach at Orient. If we hadn't done enough for him on the pitch, he used to have a go at us but he was a good laugh.

"He wanted me to get stuck in and give defenders a bit more stick than I did.

"I wasn't the hardest of players," Dave admits, "and I wouldn't kick anybody up in the air on purpose, unless they had given me one first.

"I suppose that's why Bobby Smith got on a bit more than me – he had that much more fight and natural aggression in him."

For a player so revered by many older fans at Orient, you won't meet a more self-effacing man than Dave Dunmore. When I called him up to interview him for this book, the reluctant hero said: "There's not much to know about me!"

When I informed Dave of some of the comments his former team-mates had already made about him for *The Untold Story* . . . about him being a great technician, who was both strong on the ground and in the air, with a sublime touch for a big man, who could control the ball quickly and leave bamboozled defenders around him in a spin . . . he just added: "Occasionally I did that, but maybe not enough!"

But Terry McDonald, whose main job it was to supply Dunmore with quality crosses from the left wing, said: "We were fortunate that when Tommy Johnston left, we already had Dave ready to take over where Tommy had left off. Dave suited our style, he was an Orient type of player, with great ball skills and good in the air.

"Alan Sealey obviously had talent, otherwise West Ham wouldn't have picked him up, but for Orient to sign a player like Dave, who scored goals and had such good ball skills . . . well, you have to say he was a great spot by Les Gore."

"Dave is a genuine, nice bloke, really easy-going, who has never shown any animosity towards anyone.

Dave Dunmore – a classy goalscoring legend at Orient.

"He was a bit of a magician as well and would show us a few tricks he'd learned. He'd toss a small coin in the air, catch it on his foot and then flick it from there straight into his top pocket. An out-and-out nice guy, you couldn't say a bad word about him.

"I thought he looked a bit like Robert Mitcham!

"As a player, he was a footballing centre-forward. Dave wasn't one to throw himself into dangerous situations and liked to score nice goals. Dave wasn't in Tommy Johnston's class when it came to heading a ball, although he must have got a few goals with his head, but he could whack 'em in from outside the box. He had great touch and was very good in small-sided training games. That's why he was also so good at golf.

"He was also brilliant at head-tennis, which we'd play for hours after training finished on a Friday afternoon. We'd play under the main stand until about one or two o'clock, when Les Gore would have a job to get us in for a shower because he was waiting to close the ground. As well as Dave and myself, the regular head-tennis group included Stan Charlton, Ronnie Foster, Eddie Lewis, Phil White and Dennis Sorrell."

Dave talks about the service he received from both flanks in his first few seasons at Brisbane Road: "The wingers used to pinpoint their crosses to me. I used to make runs down the right wing more than I did the left. Terry would get to the byeline and pull crosses back for me, whereas Phil White was a bit over-the-top by then, I suppose, and he didn't seem to get over the halfway line as much as Terry did. Phil tended to cross balls from deeper poistions, or he'd slip the ball into the channel for me to run on to.

"Terry was a good player, clever on the ball and he had enough pace to get past people. And he was a good passer of the ball. I wouldn't have swapped him – he was an ace man."

Malcolm Lucas says: "You talk about target men, well . . . Dave *was* the man. When you hit a ball to him, he gave you enough time to get up there alongside him. But with his tremendous strength and skill, Dave could also do the business on his own if necessary. Dave was outstanding in our promotion season and when he was at his peak, there was nobody to touch him."

Harry Gregory, who made his O's debut alongside Dunmore, benefited from the great man's presence in the same forward line at a time when he was still learning the game. He says: "Dave was so good, there was talk of him possibly playing for England.

"I played against the great John Charles and Dave was in that bracket. When you played with him, he just oozed talent and was brilliant to play with.

"Because he was big and tall, opposing defences would try to mark him tightly, which gave the rest of us more room to play around him. He was absolutely brilliant.

"Dave could play but he could also knock people about too – he took no prisoners."

Dunmore enjoyed many highspots in the blue shirt and his brilliant performance at Liverpool, in October 1961, would have to be right up there among them. Dave scored twice in a thrilling 3-3 draw at Anfield – Ronnie Foster scored Orient's other goal. The No.9's first was a spectacular, long-range strike that is still remembered in awe by those O's fans fortunate enough to have been among the 36,612 crowd.

"I nutmegged Ron Yeats and scored from about 35 yards out," says Dave but, perhaps surprisingly, it was his second goal on Merseyside that afternoon that gave him most pleasure. In fact, he rates it the most satisfying goal he has ever scored.

"The ball was crossed to the edge of the penalty area and I managed to get up above Yeats and head it into the net – even though one of the Liverpool defenders tried to punch it off the line.

"My long-range goal was good but it was something special to leap above Yeatsy like that and score with such a powerful header.

"It always felt good no matter how they went in. But I felt just as good if I laid a pass on for someone else to score."

After scoring a brace in three previous games in the promotion season, Dave scored his first league hat-trick for the O's in their 3-1 victory at Swansea Town at the end of December '61, just four days after having scored the only goal when the teams met at Brisbane Road. He was in the middle of a golden period that produced seven goals in five games.

Dave said: "Noel Dwyer, who I used to play with at West Ham, was in goal for Swansea that day and afterwards he came up to me and said in his Irish accent: 'You lucky swine!'

There was definitely no hint of luck anywhere to be seen for the O's on the night Burnley came to Leyton for the mouth-watering FA Cup fourth round replay in February '62 – a tie that is covered in depth earlier in the book. Dave recalls: "How I didn't score four goals against them that night, I'll never know. I hit the bar and post and their keeper, Adam Blacklaw, saved everything we threw at him. That was probably my best game – I couldn't have played any better than I did that night."

Perhaps there was no finer example of Dave's integrity than a strange incident that happened during the home game against his former club, West Ham, in September 1962. Dunmore, who is pictured on the front cover celebrating his goal in the 2-0 home win, reveals: "I had a shot from a corner and volleyed it into the net, but I knew the ball had gone outside the post before going through the netting and landing in the back of the net. Bobby Moore had been standing on the inside of that near post and had watched the ball fizz past him by a matter of inches.

"The Orient crowd thought it was a goal, but it wasn't. The referee asked me whether it was in fact a goal or not, and I told him 'no.'

"I don't know if any fans remember it, but after that happened, the ref tied a handkerchief to that part of the net where the ball had gone through."

A white-hot London derby, with vital Premiership points at stake . . . how many players today would show the same honesty as Dunmore did in the same situation? No, I couldn't think of any either!

Orient were regular visitors to Holland for end-of-season tour matches, and Terry McDonald recalls another time when Dave had dialogue with an official. He says: "We played a game that was refereed by a well known Dutch official named Leo Horn, who was top class. Dave had a bit of a go at Leo after he'd failed to award us a freekick, when Leo quickly turned round and said to him: 'Dave, I'm having a better game than *you!*' Players knew they could talk to Leo Horn, who was one of the top referees in world football at the time."

Dunmore admits he isn't over-impressed with what he sees of football today. "The amount of players diving and feigning injury is diabolical. They roll around on the ground three or four times and then the next minute they're up and running. They're cheats, aren't they? All right, you want to try and get a breakthrough for your team, but that's wrong. And it looks crap as well.

"In our day, you got a bit of pulling and pushing between players but if anybody pulled your shirt, you just belted them on the arm and knocked it away."

And Dave did take his share of bad knocks, of course.

"There were two of three hard men around," he recalls. "Dave Ewing at Manchester City was a big, tough Scotsman who'd kick you up in the air and think nothing of it. They used to climb up the back of your legs to get over you.

"My worst injury was a torn cartilage, which I did while turning sharply at Swansea. It kept me out for six weeks.

"Charlie Hurley was a classic centre-half. He wouldn't chop you down, but he'd tackle from behind and go for the ball. I was in the same army team as Charlie at Aldershot. We had five or six internationals, including Duncan Edwards, while Bobby Charlton came in at more or less the same time as when I left. Gerry Ward, who I played with at Orient, was also in the same army unit side as me."

After leaving Orient in the summer of 1965, Dave returned to York City, the club who gave him his first break in League football after he'd impressed them while playing for York Boys and Cliftonville Minors.

As far as Dave's last spell in the first division was concerned, it was most appropriate that he left the top stage on a high, by scoring in Orient's 3-1 defeat by Manchester United.

"Old Trafford was the only place where I managed to score for all three of the first division clubs that I played for," he added.

Dave Dunmore is far too modest a gentleman to give us a frank assessment of his value to that Orient team, so let's allow Gordon Bolland, who played alongside DD in the top flight, to provide this glowing tribute to a great Orient player:

"There are no two ways about it, apart from being strong, good in the air and a goalscorer, he was a very, very skilful player. If he was still playing at his peak, Dave would do very well in the Premiership today – he was *that* good."

ORIENT HOT SHOTS

Dave Dunmore is 12th in the LOFC all-time scorers' list. He is, of course, the only one listed here to have played in the highest division of the Football League.

	FL	FAC	LC	Total Goals
Tommy Johnston	121	2	0	123
Ken Facey	74	5	0	79
Ted Crawford	67	6	0	73
Kevin Godfrey	63	5	4	72
Mickey Bullock	65	1	3	69
Richard McFadden	66	2	0	68
Steve Castle	56	6	5	67
Billy Rees	58	8	0	66
Reg Tricker	60	3	0	63
Carl Griffiths	51	6	3	60
Peter Kitchen	49	9	2	60
Dave Dunmore	**54**	**2**	**2**	**58**

ORIENT LEAGUE GOALS IN A SEASON

Dave is one of only nine Orient players to have scored 20 or more league goals in a season since the club entered the Football League in 1905-06.

Season	Scorer	Total Goals
1957-58	Tommy Johnston	35
1956-57	Tommy Johnston	27
1959-60	Tommy Johnston	25
1948-49	Frank Neary	25
1935-36	Ted Crawford	23
1955-56	Ronnie Heckman	23
1961-62	**Dave Dunmore**	**22**
1954-55	Ken Facey	22
1977-78	Peter Kitchen	21
1913-14	Richard McFadden	21
1931-32	Charlie Fletcher	20

FIRST DIVISION TOP SCORERS 1962-63

The top 20 First Division goalscorers from O's only season in the top flight:

Jimmy Greaves (Spurs) 37, Joe Baker (Arsenal) 29, David Layne (Sheff Wed) 29, Ray Crawford (Ipswich T) 25, Roger Hunt (Liverpool) 24, Roy Vernon (Everton) 24, Denis Law (Man Utd) 23, Fred Pickering (Blackburn R) 23, Alex Harley (Man City) 23, Ray Charnley (Blackpool) 22, Ken Leek (Birmingham C) 22, Alex Young (Everton) 22, Ken Keyworth (Leicester C) 21, Cliff Jones (Spurs) 20, David Herd (Man Utd) 19, Andy Lockhead (Burnley) 19, Alan Hinton (Wolves) 19, Ian St. John (Liverpool) 19, Geoff Strong (Arsenal) 18, Derek Pace (Sheff Utd) 18.

RONNIE FOSTER

Inside-forward (left or right) 1959-62
Born: Islington, North London, November 22, 1938
Appearances: 72 League & 13 Cup
Goals: 17 League 7 Cup

ALTHOUGH Arsenal fan Ronnie Foster never made a league appearance at Highbury, where he grew up watching football as a boy, the former Islington Schoolboys captain did have the pleasure of once scoring on the hallowed Highbury turf.

It was in March 1960, when the first division Gunners and Orient met in a friendly watched by a crowd of 18,000.

A young O's side – average age 22 – tore Arsenal to pieces, with Terry McDonald setting up goals for Ronnie and Phil White in an impressive 2-0 win. It could have been three but centre-forward Tony Biggs – getting a rare chance as deputy for Tommy Johnston – had what looked a perfectly good headed goal ruled out.

Foster, who was outstanding throughout, also struck an upright on what was a proud day for the lad who lived just around the corner from Arsenal Stadium.

"Orient gave Arsenal a beating and a football lesson," wrote Harry Miller of *The Express*.

One of the most creative and talented ball players seen in an O's shirt, Ronnie once dreamed of playing for the Gunners but he fell in love with the Orient instead. Recalling the build up to him joining the club, Ron says: "Alec Stock came round to my parents' house in St Thomas' Road, just around the corner from the Arsenal ground, to sign me in January 1957. I'd skippered Islington Schoolboys from the age of 11 until I was 15. I'd had trials with Fulham and Charlton before ending up at the Orient. I was an Arsenal fan and watched them all the time – I saw Stan (Charlton) play for the Gunners."

Before National Service was abolished, the forces had proved a fertile breeding ground for future professional footballers.

"I was called up into the army in January 1958. I was stationed at Aldershot, which is where I met my favourite winger, Terry McDonald. He was the business for me. I thought he was a super player when I played with him for the army's football team and then the next thing I knew he'd been given a free transfer by West Ham.

"I told Les Gore about Terry and he signed him. That was beautiful, because Terry was always out there on the left wing – you knew where he was. We had an absolutely smashing understanding. We loved playing football together – and drinking together!"

Some of Ron's memories of his playing days are hazy but he can still recite his army number: "23441848 . . . SAR!" It's funny the things you *never* forget!

Ronnie made his O's first team debut a week before his mate, McDonald, in a 5-1 defeat at Cardiff City on October 10 1959, replacing former England international Eddie Baily in the No.10 shirt.

"What a player to take over from," says Ron. "I'd seen Eddie in action myself when I watched Tottenham play as a boy. He was a great player in the Tottenham push-

Cultured Ronnie Foster played a very big part in Orient's promotion drive before being hit by injuries.

and-run side and I think it was Eddie who really helped me get into the Orient first team, because he liked the way I played the game. I think he pushed Les Gore to pick me."

Baily took youngsters Foster, McDonald and the third member of that left-sided triumvirate, Dennis Sorrell, under his coaching wing and would spend time in the afternoons, after the normal team training session had ended, imparting his great knowledge of the game to these impressionable youngsters.

"Terry and I both liked to dribble with the ball and take people on, and Eddie wanted to help us. Push-and-run had come in and me and Terry played that way too," continued Ron.

"Terry, Dennis and me had a great understanding on that left side. It was nice for your dad and me to know that Dennis was behind us – we'd leave him to do all the tackling! The three of us were always confident of each other when we played together."

One vintage performance the young trio produced came against Liverpool at Anfield in November 1959, when the O's were very unlucky to go down 4-3 in an epic Merseyside clash.

"We always loved playing at Liverpool. The crowd appreciated the football we played and I'd never been to an away game and been clapped off the pitch by the home supporters like they did to us up there that day."

Not that Ronnie and his team-mates were down for long after unfortunately losing by the odd goal in seven. For Ron celebrated his 21st birthday the next day. "When we got back to London after the game at Liverpool, all of the boys and their wives came to our house – my mum and dad were living at Wood Green by then – for a knees-up that night."

Ron loved Liverpool as much as the world would soon come to love the Beatles. He scored on his next visit to Anfield – a 2-1 FA Cup third round defeat – and was on target there again in a classic 3-3 draw during the promotion campaign.

Recalling his strike in the six-goal thriller, he said: "I scored at the Kop end – I think I was about 15 yards out and caught the ball on the half-volley with my left foot. I was naturally right-footed but . . . bosh, get in! . . . no-one was gonna save that!"

Although he was fairly tall, Ronnie admits: "I wasn't very musclely and I pulled the hamstring muscle in the back of my leg a couple of times. I also broke my arm when I landed badly during a game."

Injury meant Ronnie played in only three of the last 11 matches and missed the promotion party, but his contribution to the team's success should not be underestimated. In 33 appearances he contributed 10 priceless goals.

This impressive ratio included five in the first nine games when Ronnie again showed his versatility by playing at inside-right in the No.8 shirt, while the much more one-footed Malcolm Graham wore 10.

A significant factor is that Foster's goals usually led to vital Orient victories on the long and sometimes rocky road to the top sphere. After netting in the opening home defeat by Southampton, goals by Foster and McDonald gave Orient their first away league win of the campaign in the return clash with the Saints, while further 'Fozzie' goals at Walsall (5-1) and in 3-0 autumn home wins over Huddersfield Town and Stoke City set Orient on their way.

But his most decisive goal-scoring contributions came at Middlesbrough, where he netted twice in the 3-2 pre-Christmas victory, and at Brighton on April 7, as the promotion bid began to falter. Given that the team failed to win any of its next three matches, the importance of his winner in the 1-0 victory at the Goldstone Ground – his 17th and, as it turned out, last goal for the club – cannot be underplayed in the context of winning promotion.

It proved to be Ron's last ever goal for the club at first team level. Injury ruled him out of the Bury finale and apart from returning in October for a brief four-match spell in the first division, he never played for the O's again after November 1962.

Derek Gibbs and Malcolm Graham had also retained the inside-forward berths from the start of the first division campaign while Ron was still recovering from a serious thigh injury. When he failed to regain his place, he sought regular first team football elsewhere and after 72 appearances for the O's in just over three years, he eventually made a shock move to Grimsby Town.

Even Ron himself was surprised to find himself heading to Cleethorpes!

He explained: "I couldn't see my situation at Orient improving, so I decided to ask for a move and was really hoping that Ron Greenwood, the West Ham manager, would come in for me.

"Ron had previously picked me twice for the FA team that he managed, so he must have seen something in me, but it was Grimsby who signed me! These things happen."

Terry McDonald was very disappointed to see him leave Brisbane Road, saying:

"Ronnie was my best mate when I joined the club, having met in the army, and as long as he was at Orient we were together. He just liked playing football the way the game should be played – he didn't like the hustle and bustle stuff but he was still a brave inside-forward.

"He had good touch, was two-footed, had vision and we worked well together on the left, playing pass-and-move. He never got caught in possession and would also get in the box to score his few goals.

"When things started to go wrong for the team in the first division, I could see him getting disillusioned and was disappointed when he left. For me, the football at Orient wasn't the same after Ron went to Grimsby."

Ronnie added: "My best playing days were spent at the Orient – I loved it there. All I ever wanted to be was a professional footballer."

MALCOLM GRAHAM

Inside-left 1960-63
Born: Crigglestone,Yorkshire, January 26, 1934
Appearances: 75 League & 9 Cup
Goals: 29 League & 5 Cup

IF the fickle hand of fate had dealt the cards differently, Malcolm Graham would not have become a Leyton Orient goalscoring hero and the O's might never have made it to the highest division of English football.

Just months before his final day double against Bury, Graham had been dropped by manager Johnny Carey and his future at Brisbane Road looked bleak, if not quite non-existent.

In fact, the club was happy to let the Yorkshireman inside-forward leave!

Malcolm, who was signed from Bristol City at the start of the previous campaign, reveals the extraordinary story: "In my second season at Orient, they wanted to sell me to Swindon. Their manager, Bert Head, told me to bring my wife down with me on the train and he'd pay all our expenses. But I didn't want to go.

"Anyway, when we met Bert for talks, I asked him for £500 to sign on . . . and he nearly choked! He said the club couldn't afford it – but if they had, I probably would have gone there.

"Funnily enough, I'm a bit of a horseracing man and I was down at Goodwood for a meeting last year when I had a chat with the ex-jockey Willie Carson, who is now the chairman at Swindon Town. I was telling him the story about how I nearly joined his club years ago and he was really intrigued by it.

"Orient weren't pressing me to go but the previous season, when we'd been struggling near the bottom of the league, chairman Harry Zussman called all the players together and told us the club was struggling financially. That's when he gave us the incentive of the holiday to Jersey.

Who said he didn't have a right foot! Malcolm Graham going for goal with his right peg.

"But, in the finish, I was very pleased that I didn't leave Orient at that time. I came back into the side and went on a good scoring run."

In fact, Graham's strike in the 3-0 home win against Walsall on January 13 sparked a spell of seven goals in 13 appearances, culminating in that emotional finale when he wrote his name into Orient folklore.

Orient signed Malcolm from Bristol City before the start of the 1960-61 season. He'd joined them from his local club, Barnsley, where he began his pro career in 1954, having started out with Hall Green.

"I'd had a year at Bristol City who were managed by Peter Docherty. He'd been a marvellous player and he was a lovely fella, but good ex-players don't always make good managers, do they? It was a hard time for the club."

Although Malcolm enjoyed playing alongside the legendary former England centre-forward John Atyeo, he said that a north-south divide in the dressing room didn't help him and several other new players to settle at Ashton Gate.

Malcolm says it was during his short spell with Bristol City that he honed his lethal left-foot that brought him the vast majority of his goals.

"John Atyeo had me firing long-range shots with only my socks on – no boots! My knee was buggered because of a cartilage injury I'd suffered earlier in my career, but I used to hit 'em from outside the box in those days. I think that's when I learned to strike the ball much harder.

"I wasn't as good with my right foot," he readily admits, "but I scored a few goals with my right, mind you. To be honest, there are not too many two-footed players about, especially these days.

"In my first spell with Barnsley, I once scored four goals in one match against Charlton – three of them with my right foot. They couldn't believe it and our local paper made a big thing of it.

"I used to score the hard ones and miss the easy ones. The problem is, you don't realise your potential until it's too late – and that doesn't just apply to footballers."

Malcolm recalls that his closest friends in the O's squad during his three seasons at Brisbane Road were Cyril Lea and Billy Taylor.

Lea rated Malcolm quite highly but he observed: "If he'd put a bit more effort into his game, he could have become a really top player. For me, it seemed that he accepted things a bit too easily and I always felt he could have done even better from the game."

Terry McDonald says that while he didn't really get to know Malcolm well as a person during their time together at the Orient, he recognised his qualities as a player who had an impressive scoring record for the O's.

Terry says: "Malcolm was strong, quick and although he wouldn't get too involved in our passing, build-up game, he was always around the edge of the box, looking to make an opening.

"He had a good left foot, he was brave and he got his strikes on goal. He scored a good ratio of goals and he was always a likely goalscorer.

"The inside-forwards we had in those days – like Malcolm, Ronnie Foster and

Malcolm putting his lethal left-foot to work.

Gordon Bolland – scored only around 10 or 12 goals a season, but you have to think back and remember all the work they had to do. They weren't just standing around up front waiting for the ball – they had to be up and down like the wing-halfs . . . and on very heavy pitches too."

Graham recalls a six-week period, soon after his move to Brisbane Road, when he shared digs in Leyton with team-mate Malcolm Lucas. They lodged with an older couple just off Lea Bridge Road. Graham laughed out loud when he recalled: "The couple we stayed with, who were both Orient supporters and lovely people, had gone on holiday, leaving me and Malcolm to look afer ourselves. One night we both made an apple pie for tea!"

Another amusing tale Malcolm recalled was a time when he used to catch the bus from his rented home in Buckhurst Hill – where he and his wife Margaret moved – to training in the mornings. It wasn't easy being a Yorkshireman among Cockneys!

"I had no car when I first came down to London," Malcolm explains, "so I caught the bus from where we lived and I had to get off at Whipps Cross roundabout and change to another one. I asked the bus conductor for 'a threepenny'.

"He said to me: 'You wot, guv, I caahnt understand yer?'

I said to him again: 'I want a threepenny'.

"So he repeated himself: 'Soreee, I caahnt understand yer, mate'

"I'll never forget that day – it was a bit embarrassing trying to make myself understood at times because of my accent!

"I think I bought an Austin Mini – a little beauty – in my second season at Orient."

Although Malcolm and his family have long since left Essex and returned to familiar surroundings in South Yorkshire, his affection for his relatively short time at the O's remains undiminished by the passing years and his own health problems.

He says: "I still tell everybody I speak to about Leyton Orient that it was the best club in the world. They really looked after us players that well and what we did to get promoted at such a small club was a very marvellous feat."

There was genuine feeling in Malcolm's voice when he added: "I've loved talking here about all the old times and my memories, which are coming back to me more and more as we speak."

For certain, the memory of his two famous goals that clinched promotion, followed by the triumphant ride from the pitch to the players' tunnel, while being mobbed by thousands of O's fans who had just seen their dreams come true, will live with him forever.

"I'm not bothered about my other former clubs," he concludes, "but it was absolutely marvellous at Orient and I'd go back there tomorrow."

Thank God Swindon Town couldn't afford him!

GORDON BOLLAND

Inside-forward (right and left) 1962-64
Born: Boston, Lincolnshire, August 12, 1943
Appearances: 63 League & 10 Cup
Goals: 19 League & 3 Cup

THERE is a lot Gordon Bolland doesn't like about modern football, Chelsea and the way the richest club in the Premiership is run today – and he's certainly not alone in that. We'll come to his thoughts about the dubious policies of his first pro club later in the book, but let's start here where it all began for him back at Stamford Bridge.

Gordon was signed by Orient for £9,000 in March 1962. He had been one of a bunch of exciting, very promising young Chelsea prospects who would go on to make their mark in the game at one club or another.

"I was at Chelsea for four or five years and we won the FA Youth Cup two years on the trot. We had Peter Bonetti in goal, Alan Harris, Terry Venables, Barry Bridges, Bobby Tambling, Bertie Murray . . . and Ronnie Harris came in to be part of the second youth cup-winning side."

Unlike today, and most notably at Chelski, top flight teams would automatically promote reserve players, and sometimes even very good youth team hopefuls, to cover for injured first-teamers. Gordon made his debut for the Blues (or 'Pensioners' as they were then known) against reigning first division champions Burnley at Stamford Bridge – as a replacement for a goal machine called Jimmy Greaves!

"Out of that Chelsea youth side, about nine of us eventually went on to make first team appearances for Chelsea. At least back then we had that opportunuty, but it wouldn't happen today.

"I'd left my home town of Boston as a raw 15-year-old and made my first appearance for Chelsea on trial – in the semi-final of a floodlight youth cup-tie against West Ham at The Bridge. I had a phone call from my manager at Boston United telling me to get down there for a trial with Chelsea Juniors. My immediate reaction was: 'How do I get to London?' In the end, he took me there himself.

"In the West Ham side there was Bobby Moore, Jack Burkett, Eddie Bovington, Geoff Hurst, Ronnie Boyce – they had a hell of a youth side. Again, as at Chelsea, these good youngsters had come up the ranks through the youth policy.

"I wanted to stay at Chelsea and finish what I'd started but I wasn't as good as what they wanted me to be. I'll admit, it was a big wrench to leave.

"When I arrived at Chelsea I was still only a young lad and a bit green. Tommy Docherty visited me at my digs in Fulham and said that he's had Johnny Carey on the phone. Tommy said that he'd accepted Orient's offer and he added: 'Put it this way, Gordon, there's not a lot of future here for you, so I'd advise you to take it on.'

"Having put it that way, Tommy Doc made it pretty clear that I really didn't have a lot of options."

Chelsea were actually fighting to avoid relegation from the top flight when Gordon joined second division O's and, in fact, the two teams swapped places at the end of that season. It's difficult today to get your head around the fact that Orient were promoted to the top league at the expense of Chelsea, given the massive financial gulf that exists between the respective clubs today. (Don't know about you, but I'd wouldn't swap Martin Ling for that arrogant Mourinho anyway!)

"Yeah, that was funny, and it was even stranger when Orient went down in 1963 and Chelsea passed us again, this time on the way back up," recalls Gordon.

With Ronnie Foster struggling with injury and Malcolm Graham temporarily out of favour, Gordon was brought in for his O's debut in the 1-1 home draw with Sunderland on March 3, 1962, when fellow new signing Norman Deeley scored for Orient against their promotion rivals. Three starts at inside-left, another three at centre-forward (in place of the injured Dave Dunmore) and a couple of outings at inside-right underlined Gordon's value and versatility in attacking areas.

That Gordon, a lean and slender six-footer, failed to score in his eight appearances at the tail end of that season didn't fluster the unflappable Johnny Carey. As Gordon said: "He brought me in to freshen things up and said that as well as hopefully helping the team to achieve promotion, he also saw me as part of the club's long-term future.

"One thing that was obvious to me, though, as soon as I arrived, was that I was joining a very close-knit team. There were some good players there, although not great ones, and they obviously all worked hard for their success. I'm not suggesting that the players there weren't good enough to go up – they were – but the team spirit in that side counted for a lot.

"But they relied on the promotion team too much and, apart from signing Malcolm Musgrove, Orient didn't really add to the squad once they were in the first division.

"It was an exciting season, but obviously disappointing. Tottenham put five past us but that was virtually their double-winning side (from 1960-61)."

Gordon scored three goals in 24 first division games, including one in the famous 3-0 home win over eventual champions Everton, and, at just 19-years-of age, he admits it was difficult to fully appreciate at the time just what a big experience this period was in his career.

"You look back now and I think I was just a young kid coming into a good side. I didn't fully appreciate the importance of it or take it all in at the time. I was fortunate to play against so many good players, including the likes of Bobby Moore. A lot of former players will agree with me that these experiences just seemed to go over your head and pass you by too quickly.

"When we went down at the end of what was a disastrous season, I can look back now and see that it was a great experience and learning curve for me."

Terry McDonald recognised the young Bolland's qualities. He said: "Gordon was the same sort of player as Ronnie Foster. He liked to play neat football and was a good touch player. He was a nice bloke too."

Off the pitch, Gordon formed good friendships in particular with Harry Gregory ("a special guy"), reserve team centre-half Dave Clark and other youngsters similar to his age. "My wife Angela and I were good friends with Harry and Carol. I still have a photo of me and Harry opening a fete on the Isle of Dogs!" laughs Gordon.

No-one excelled better when O's returned to Division Two than Bolland, a fine header of a ball who established himself as first choice in the forward line and top scored with 16 goals in 33 league games, before that tremendous run of form ended abruptly with his big-money transfer to Norwich City in March 1964.

Gordon left the club on a personal high, scoring in the home 2-2 draw against Scunthorpe United before making what was an irresistable £32,000 move to second division Norwich City, who had been showing interest in him for a number of weeks. O's manager Benny Fenton said he wouldn't have allowed the 21-year-old Bolland to leave had it not been for the club's financial plight.

Fenton immediately snapped up Ted Phillips – a 29-year-old who had one of the hardest shots in football – from Ipswich Town at a cost of £7,000, which meant the O's showed a very handy profit of around £25,000 on the transfer deadline deals.

Fenton said at the time: "This was purely a question of economics. Gordon was the last player we wanted to lose but, frankly, we needed the money."

Sadly, it was by no means the first, nor the last time, O's fans would hear those dreaded words from their cash-strapped manager and/or chairman.

"I wasn't looking to leave Orient at that time," explains Gordon. "My idea was to be part of the side to hopefully take us back up to the first division. The move to Norwich came completely out of the blue to me.

"I had two good years at Orient before they then made a decent bit of money out of me – 32-and-a-half grand, or whatever they got for me, was looked upon as considerable in those days – and I moved on to enjoy more happy experiences at other clubs," he added.

Although Ted Phillips didn't quite match Bolland's brilliant strike ratio in his 10 appearances at the end of the 1963-64 season, his four goals did help O's to finish

1961-62 was a great season for the club – and not only at first team level. Here's the Reserve squad that won the Combination Midweek League, many of who also had first team outings. Back row: Joe Elwood, Billy Taylor, Albert Cochran, Alan Russell, Roy Deeks. Middle row: Ronnie Foster, Phil White, Gordon Bolland, George Waites, Ron Newman and Roger Wedge. Front: Harry Gregory, Terry Price and David Clark.

six points off the bottom. And an even better return of 13 goals in 26 appearances by the former Ipswich hot-shot the following season proved he was a good signing. Norwich boss Ron Ashman was delighted with his capture of Gordon Bolland, too.

Gordon was gone from Leyton Orient after two excellent years but certainly not forgotten as far as Benny Fenton was concerned. Manager and player were reunited five years later, when Fenton signed him for Millwall.

HARRY GREGORY

Inside-right or centre-forward 1962-66
Born: Hackney, East London, October 24, 1943
Appearances: 79 League & 8 Cup
Goals: 12 League & 3 Cup

IT couldn't have been easy for a raw 19-year-old making his debut at first division level for a team that was already by then submerged in a relegation battle doomed to fail.

But Harry Gregory had already proved himself a prolific hot-shot for the O's reserve and youth teams and was itching to make his first team bow by the time Ipswich Town visited Brisbane Road on November 10, 1962.

Only the fog that had descended over Bury, and which caused the original League Cup tie to be postponed, had prevented Johnny Carey from giving Harry his senior start . . . a year earlier!

Harry Gregory (far right) and Mike Hollow lead the way during a pre-season training exercise at Ashton Playing Fields, Woodford Bridge. Joe Elwood and David Webb are the next two behind them, followed by Terry Price and Jimmy Scott, then David Clark and Eddie Lewis.

"It was a big disappointment to me at the time," Harry admits. "We were up in Manchester when the game was called off. I'd felt very nervous before the game but the senior players were absolutely brilliant to me.

"As the youngest in the squad, I felt a bit shy but the other players all made me feel welcome and I didn't feel isolated in any way. I felt at home in their company."

After his dream Gigg Lane debut disappeared in the Lancashire smog, Harry just kept banging in the goals at Mid-week Combination League level, where he came up against a decent standard of opponents on a regular basis. With Orient struggling to find the net in Division One, his patience deserved to be rewarded.

Recalling his debut goal against Ipswich, Harry – or Gordon Harold Gregory, to give him his full name – said: "Ronnie Foster had possession, I made a run inside and he slotted a perfect ball through to me. I took the ball with my right foot and scored with my left. I felt absolutely brilliant when it hit the net.

"I missed another good chance, which would have been the equaliser, and Dave Dunmore missed a penalty. We should have either drawn or won that game.

"When the pitches got a bit wet in those days, they were dreadful. I must have tired near the end of the game but with no substitutes allowed then, I had to stay on for the full 90 minutes."

Harry played in the 5-1 hammering by Liverpool at Anfield the following Saturday and recalls: "That game was televised but all you could see of me on the TV footage is kicking off after Liverpool had scored each time! They had Ian St. John, Roger Hunt, Ian Callaghan and the centre-half I played against was Ron Yeats . . . all good players. I didn't get a touch really and the noise of the crowd hit you as soon as you walked on to the field.

"We'd stayed in a hotel overnight and that was the first time I saw Bill Shankly. He was there talking to about 20 reporters. He was holding court and I realised then what a great character he was."

Harry played in another dismal defeat a week later, 4-0 at home to Wolves, a League Cup drubbing at Blackpool, followed by another defeat by Arsenal at Highbury. He didn't get another chance until April, when he came in on the right-wing in place of Norman Deeley for the home game against Bolton in April. Given his inexperience, Harry understood that as the quest for points became increasingly desperate, he would make way for more senior and experienced players.

He made six appearances in the first division and says: "I accepted that I wouldn't play more often, because in those days teams tended to use older, more experienced players. Teenagers had to wait longer for a regular chance, so I had no complaints.

"The first team more or less picked itself every week but I did well for the reserves that season. We lost 2-0 in the reserves' play-off final to Spurs, who had Bobby Smith playing for them, and I've still got the little gold medal we received for finishing runners-up in the Combination League championship."

Harry's main rival for the inside-right berth was Gordon Bolland, who became a good friend.

"Gordon lived near me and my wife Carol in Buckhurst Hill and I knew him from having played against him in youth matches when he was at Chelsea. Carol and I were good friends with Gordon and his wife Angela – our children were also the same ages. Gordon and me played together again for a while at Charlton and he's a smashing bloke."

Harry is a throwback to the days when local kids with obvious football talent dreamed of playing for their nearest professional club when they grew up. For this likeable Cockney, who went on to star up front for Charlton in the late 60s, he really did live the dream.

"I was born in Hackney Hospital and grew up near the Marshes, in flats on the Kings Mead Estate. I was one of 10 children and attended Daubney Road School and then went on to Lea Marsh at Hackney Wick," says Harry, still clearly very proud of his East End roots.

"It was only a couple of miles from our home to the Orient's ground and you could walk there. In fact I did just that sometimes.

"When I was a kid, me and a friend used to bunk into the ground – over the wall behind the West Stand, through the toilets and into the ground! – to see the traditional pre-season Reds v Blues practice match.

"As a young fan, I used to admire Tommy Johnston, and I can also remember watching the likes of Eddie Baily, Les Blizzard and Phil White."

Harry played in the same Hackney Schoolboys team as Chelsea-bound brothers Alan and Ron Harris, as well as Rodney Marsh, who went on to sign for Fulham. His big turning point was netting a hat-trick for Hackney against Tottenham schoolboys at Leyton Stadium in a shield final and following it with two more in the victorious 4-2 replay win. "Our reward for winning that final was a trip up to the West End to see the Flanaghan & Allen Show," Harry recalled.

He signed for Orient as a 15-year-old apprentice straight from school and didn't mind cleaning the senior pro's boots and sweeping the terraces.

"I came under the wing of Jack Tonner, the groundsman who had played for the club when they were known as Clapton Orient. He was a Scottish guy, hard but fair, and a smashing bloke.

"I was the first, and only, apprentice the club had at the time. It was a new thing in football then and I think I went down in the *Guinness Book of Records* as Orient's first-ever apprentice player.

"When I first joined the O's, we used to train on Tuesdays and Thursdays at the Leyton cricket ground, where Essex still played some of their matches. Eddie Heath, a tall dark-haired guy who lived with his mother in Leyton, was in charge of us and I owed a lot to him as our youth team manager.

"When Orient had first approached me about signing, Eddie came round my mum and dad's house and explained what it was all about. He enticed me to go there and I considered it a great honour. My brothers were Tottenham supporters, and they would take me to White Hart Lane to stand against the crash barriers and watch the famous push-and-run side, but I was really an Orient fan as a kid.

"Eddie had a scooter and after meeting up with him at the Orient ground, he would give me a lift up the road to the nearby cricket ground along the High Road."

Harry remembers taking on extra work, away from the club, in the close season to top up his meagre football earnings. "Some of the senior players used to help put down new terracing at the ground in the summer but I worked at the City of London cemetery at Manor Park – as did Terry McDonald and Ronnie Foster – keeping the graves tidy and cutting the surrounding grass. It made me appreciate what being a footballer meant.

"Ronnie was only slight but he had a good football brain. It was the same with Terry, who was quick over 10 yards. He'd go past people on either the outside or inside before putting in a good cross. He scored a few himself too."

McDonald said of Harry: "He was the fittest player at the club and he had good ball control. He was a proper footballer and you could see his potential from a young age."

Dave Dunmore added: "Harry had a lot of ability and could really gallop – he'd run forever!"

Among Harry's team-mates and best friends in the Orient youth and reserve teams was David Webb, who went on to play in the top flight for Southampton and Chelsea, famously scoring the Blues' winner in the 1970 FA Cup final replay against Leeds United at Old Trafford.

"Webby was brilliant," enthused Harry. "When we both got into the first team, he used to pick up a young lad at Hackney who suffered with polio. Before every home game, Webby would go to the kid's house, pick him up, take him to the match and then run him back home afterwards.

"And just before my dad died, Webby came with me to see him in the hospital. Those examples were typical of his caring nature and I was so pleased for him that he went on to have a good career in football."

Harry also appreciated the help and encouragement he received in his Orient days from a well-known local O's supporter, businessman Alfie Cohen.

"He owned his own warehouse that sold women's clothing through catalogues. Alfie was Orient through and through and later, when the club hit very hard times and they held a collection, he used to walk around the pitch holding a large white sheet to catch the money that was thrown to him by supporters. He couldn't do enough to help the club.

"He used to look after me and Carol. We'd visit his warehouse on a Friday after I'd finished training and he looked after us both with clothes. Alfie was an Orient season ticket holder and he had a few quid."

Harry Gregory, who now lives near Chelmsford, reflects on his four years at Leyton Orient with warmth and affection, as perhaps you would expect from someone who earned the right to play for the local team he supported as a boy.

He concludes: "Orient was a small club but they treated you very well and made you feel relaxed. I was glad I started my career there and I think every youngster should have that kind of grounding when they first come into the game.

"The same applies to managers – it would do them good to begin their careers at a small club that doesn't have much money and where they have to learn to wheel and deal in the transfer market, instead of being given millions to spend."

Harry Gregory with two other youngsters from 1965, Colin Shaw and Dave Metchick.

JOE ELWOOD

Inside-left or Outside-left 1958-66
Born: Belfast, Northern Ireland
Appearances: 101 (+ 2 sub) League & 8 Cup
Goals: 25 League & 4 Cup

LOOK at Joe Elwood's goals-per-games ratio and you have to ask why the former Irish Under-23 star didn't start in the first team more regularly in his eight, loyal years with the club that had signed him from Glenavon in 1958.

The record books reveal that he hit the net in roughly every third game he played for the O's, so why was he regarded by many as a bit-part player, when his scoring performances surely demanded more time on the pitch? He lost his place on the left wing to Terry McDonald at the end of 1959, but Elwood proved himself in the inside-left position too. In fact, he believes this was his best position.

As far as the promotion season is concerned, Joe made only 10 league appearances, seven at inside-left when brought in at the expense of Malcolm Graham. He scored two goals – in home wins over Newcastle United and Brighton.

In the first division campaign, he had to wait patiently until the 26th game of the season, the visit of Manchester City towards the end of February, before getting his chance to prove himself on the big stage. And he wasted no time at all by scoring 14 minutes into the 1-1 draw against the side that ultimately went down with the O's at the end of the season. "Twenty-six games . . . Goodness, was it *that* long!" he asked. Joe made 10 further appearances in the top flight without scoring

Admitting his disappointment, he says: "I think Johnny Carey should have had me

Joe Elwood and the Leyton Orient beauty queen.

in the team. He dropped me because I missed chances – but I made my own chances. I was quite annoyed that he didn't play me as often as I thought he should have done."

The lack of chances in the top flight were even harder to take because Joe had declined an offer to join Bristol City – against whom he had a fine scoring record, including four in one game in November 1958 – the previous summer.

He reveals: "Carey actually came to me and asked if I wanted to go to Bristol City. I turned the chance down because Orient had just been promoted and I wanted to stay and play in the first division for them. But now I regret not moving. I made a mistake not going there.

"Today, teams have great, big squads. But in those days, if you weren't actually in the first team, you didn't feel included. Even when we won promotion, they had a team photograph taken but those like myself, who had played only about a dozen games or so, weren't included in the pictures. So you didn't really feel part of the celebrations.

"I thank Leyton Orient for giving me my chance in professional football but if you're not in that first team, you're not going to be very happy."

He played 23 more games spread over the next three seasons, under three different managers (Gore, Fenton and Sexton), to take his final League and Cup tally to 109 (+ 2 sub) and 30 goals.

Joe Elwood had an impressive scoring record and was unlucky not to have featured in the first team more often.

"I was happier playing inside-left, where I had more chances to get in on goal and more or less have a free run up front, although I kicked with both feet."

Terry McDonald said: "An out-and-out working winger, Joe had good control, he was a touch player, but he was also brave for his size. He had a little bit more aggression than I did.

"Off the field, he usually kept himself to himself and would tend to mix with Cyril Lea and Mal Lucas. Although Joe was a non-drinker, he was a popular bloke and enjoyable company with his funny one-liners."

Joe Elwood's name will forever crop up in pub quizzes among O's fans who ask: 'Who was the club's first substitute?'

PHIL WHITE

Outside-right 1953-64
Born: Fulham, West London, December 29, 1930
Appearances: 217 League & 16 Cup
Goals: 28 League & 0 Cup

WINGERS are virtually extinct in the modern game, but that tricky torturer of floundering left-backs, Phil White, was a master of the art at Orient in the late 50s and he played an important role in helping Orient to promotion in '62 before injury struck him an untimely blow.

A prominent member of the 1955-56 Third Division South-winning side, Phil's pinpoint crosses from the right to centre-forward Tommy Johnston became the focal point of most O's attacks . . . and the lethal combination produced innumerable goals.

A loyal one-club man who turned down offers from other bigger clubs, notably Liverpool, Phil played in all of the first 30 league games of the 1961-62 season before a bad knee injury ruled him out from March onwards.

With Norman Deeley signed to replace him on the right wing, he didn't play any part of the first division campaign, while an attempted comeback in 1963-64 lasted just five matches before he was forced to retire from the game.

The club awarded him a thoroughly deserved testimonial on April 21, 1964, when an Ex-Leyton Orient XI – including his old mate Johnston, who was so indebted to Phil for the sterling service he provided – played against the O's team of that day. It was a fitting reward for 10 years of some of the most memorable wing artistry ever seen by O's supporters.

Sadly, Phil died in the year 2000 but memories of him are still fresh in the mind of those former team-mates who admired his sublime skill, enjoyed his dressing room banter, laughed with him and shared his cigarettes and horeseracing tips!

Terry McDonald, who was one of Phil's best friends in his latter years with the club, says without hesitation: "He was the best crosser of the ball I've ever seen – he was superb at it. I can never, ever remember Phil putting a cross behind the goal. Tommy Johnston loved him – they were good mates – and Tommy will tell you just how many goals Phil made for him.

"I used to watch Phil play for Orient even before I signed for them and I always admired his control and his dribbling ability, which was superb.

"Whitey always wanted the ball to his feet, so that he could go on a dribble. He had good change of pace and body movement – he would drop his shoulder to beat his man. If the pass was played inside the full-back and he knew he couldn't get past his man, he wouldn't bother to chase the lost ball – he'd just stop and gesture to his team-mate who had wasted the ball that he wanted it played to his feet!"

Frank George said: "Phil was so frightened of getting kicked but I think that fear in him made him an even better player. He wanted to keep out of the way of full-backs, so he used to skin 'em. He was a real character."

"I remember Whitey slaughtering Noel Cantwell once," continued McDonald, "but then there were a couple of left-backs that he just couldn't beat. Jack Brownsword

One of the best dribblers and crossers in the game, Phil White kept the crowd and his team-mates entertained and Tommy Johnston among the goals.

of Scunthorpe was one. Ray Wilson was another.

"We were playing against Huddersfield once and at half-time, Les Gore had a go at Phil. He wanted to know why he hadn't gone past their left-back. Les kept on at him and in the end Whitey turned round and said: 'Les, that lad will play for England one day.' It was Ray Wilson.

"Whitey was a good player but he was a non-contact player who didn't want to know about 50/50 challenges. He just wouldn't have it. He just wanted to play football the right way. If he couldn't beat the full-back, he'd pass it it back to Stan Charlton and then want it back from him again."

Malcolm Lucas, who usually played just inside Phil, said: "Whitey was a little bit like Stanley Matthews – his pace was over 10 yards. His crossing of the ball was something else. He could drop the ball on a sixpence. And speaking as a right-half, he always made himself available for a pass."

Popular Phil often amused his team-mates, even when he didn't intend to.

Stan Charlton says: "I helped Phil organise his testimonial and I told him that a wealthy Orient fan, who owned a clothing factory, had given us some expensive ladies dresses to raffle or auction and raise money for Phil's fund. But when I told Phil, he just said: 'What's the use of them – they won't fit me!' He was always making the other players laugh with his quips and comments.

"There was also the time when an old Orient supporter, who'd been a bit of a critic of Phil, had died and his family arranged for the bloke's ashes to be spread over the pitch. One day Phil was in full flight down the wing when he suddenly stumbled and lost the ball.

"He came off the pitch afterwards and said: 'I knew that bastard didn't like me!'."

Gordon Bolland added: "I'd only been at Orient a day or so when we were training on the pitch at Brisbane Road. Terry McDonald and Phil White were good mates and Phil was performing his ball skills in front of us all during a practice match when I put my foot on the ball and dragged it away from him.

"I don't think Phil was too impressed by my cheek and I can still see it now . . . your old man looking at Phil and almost falling over laughing at him. It's just one of those things that stick in my mind. I suppose Phil and the other senior players looked upon me as a young upstart."

McDonald recalls: "Another funny story I heard about Phil happened before I came to the Orient, when they were playing at Brentford one day. Apparently, Ken Facey took a throw-in but the ball intended for Phil was neither at head-height or aimed lower towards his feet – it was waist-high. Phil told me that he didn't know whether to lift his foot up or lower his head, so he did the latter and the Brentford defender Ken Coote went 'bosh!' and kicked Phil in the jaw.

"Afterwards, a few of the players went to see him in hospital, where he was laying there with his jaw broken and wired up. All of a sudden, Phil's mum walked in and said to Les Gore: 'That's it, Les, he's not playing anymore!' Phil was about 25-years-old at the time!

"Whitey knew that he needed a cartilage operation in our promotion year, because he'd been playing with the injury for some time."

NORMAN DEELEY

Outside-right
Born: Wednesbury, West Midlands, November 30, 1933
Appearances: 73 League & 13 Cup
Goals: 9 League & 4 Cup

NORMAN DEELEY remains one of the biggest names to have ever been signed by Leyton Orient. Capped twice for England at full international level, the clever right-winger won the first division championship with Wolverhampton Wanderers in 1958 and 1959 and played for them in two consecutive European cup competitions.

Deeley's 10-years and 206 senior games (66 goals) at Molineux, between 1951 and his departure to Orient in February 1961, coincided with the club's greatest domination of the post-war period. Apart from winning those league title medals in 1958 and 1959, the diminutive 5ft 4ins Deeley was a key member of the side that finished runners-up to Burnley in 1960, only missing out on a hat-trick of championships by a single point.

He played against the Barcelona side that defeated Wolves in the quarter-final of the European Cup in 1960 and in the losing team again a year later, when Glasgow Rangers ended Wolves' interest in the European Cup Winners' Cup at the semi-final stage.

Wolves, managed by Stan Cullis and captained by England's Billy Wright, qualified for the ECWC after beating Blackburn Rovers in a thrilling 1960 FA Cup final. That day belonged to Deeley who scored twice in Wolves' emphatic 3-0 victory.

Having fallen out of favour with Cullis as Wolves started to decline in the early 60s, Deeley took the chance to leave and join the O's when Johnny Carey went in for him in February 1962. With regular right-winger Phil White troubled by a cartilage problem, Carey bought Deeley to help the final promotion push that looked like being derailed.

Norman scored on his debut in a 2-1 defeat at Plymouth on February 17 but netted – "direct from a corner," he recalls – on his home debut, a 1-1 draw with promotion rivals Sunderland. His only other goal in his 14 appearances at the end of that season came in a 2-1 win at Charlton.

Deeley's wealth of experience in top class football would hopefully prove a big asset to the team but, with his 29th birthday approaching, he admits he had become a fading force by then. His 36 games for the O's in Division One produced five goals, including one in the brilliant 3-0 home win against Everton.

Fellow winger Terry McDonald said of Deeley: "His control was still brilliant and his passing was also very good. But he'd probably lost a bit of pace. He played it easy and his knowledge of the game was good.

"He was approaching his 30s when Orient signed him, but he'd been a top player for Wolves and, when I think about it, Orient did well to get him."

Mal Lucas commented: "Norman didn't have the skill of Whitey but he had more running power than him."

Norman looks back now on his time at Brisbane Road with a tinge of disappointment and the feeling that he failed to do himself justice.

"I was just glad to get away from Wolves at the time," he admits. "I don't know why, because Wolves were such a good club. But Cullis had started to lose it, he was doing his nut as results went against us and I ended up in the reserves.

"I missed Wolves after I left them and couldn't settle easily at Orient. It was hard for me, having left my local club and the team I'd grown up with.

"We rented a house in Hillside Avenue, Woodford, but my wife, Dorothy, and our kids found it hard down there.

"But I got on with most of the players – Terry, Whitey and Bishop in particular. Whitey was very deep person – he wouldn't divulge a lot – but we got on well. We both used to love a bet.

"Ronnie Foster, who lived near me, used to pick me up on the way to training each morning. He was always late!" laughed Norman, now retired and living back in his native Black Country.

Although he is another who has criticised Carey's laid-back management style earlier in this book, Deeley admitted: "I wasn't happy with the form I produced either. I thought I could have done more for the club."

How the Orient could have done with Deeley in his prime, as one of the most feared wingers in the British game. Norman is the only member of the O's promotion and first division squad to have won a full England cap.

On May 13, 1959, he played on the right-wing against Brazil in front of (according to the FA Yearbook) 160,000 fans inside the Maracana Stadium in Rio de Janeiro. Joined in the team by three Wolves team-mates, Billy Wright, Ron Flowers and Peter Broadbent, Deeley came up against renowned left-back Nilton Santos but he "did OK" in England's 2-0 defeat.

He kept his place for the next match – his only other cap – and although Walter Winterbottom's team were beaten 4-1 by Peru in Lima, at least Norm had the satisfaction of crossing the ball from which a young Jimmy Greaves scored on his international debut.

Great experiences (Pele wore the No.10 for Brazil) that no-one can take away from Deeley, although he was disappointed earlier this year when he was remembered in a negative way by current Wigan Athletic chairman and benefactor, Dave Whelan.

Although Deeley's two goals in the final at Wembley won the FA Cup for Wolves in 1960, the match is also remembered in Blackburn circles for the broken leg that their full-back, Whelan, suffered in an accidental collision with the man he was marking on the day.

That incident, in which his broken left shin clashed with Deeley's right shin, came flooding back to Whelan early in 2006 when he was asked to comment on a bad tackle by Chelsea's Michael Essien on Liverpool's Didi Hamann. He compared it to the challenge Deeley made on him – even though his Wembley leg break had been a complete accident. Whelan was stretchered off, his top flight career effectively ended at 23, but, in fact, the referee on the day didn't even award Rovers a freekick.

Norman Deeley brought a wealth of experience to Orient's right-wing after Phil White was sidelined. He was the only player at Orient in this era to have won full England international caps.

When Whelan's inappropriate and imflamatory comments appeared in the press, Wolves supporters were up in arms that the reputation of one of their club legends had been besmirched in this way by the outspoken Whelan, the multi-millionaire owner of the JJB Sports chain.

"I couldn't understand why Dave Whelan came out and said what he did," sighed Norman. "What happened between us was a complete accident and after the game I even went into the Blackburn dressing room to check that he was all right. I spoke to Ronnie Clayton, as Dave had gone off to hospital.

"The following week, my parents happened to be on holiday at Rhyl when they bumped into Dave's mum and dad. His parents told mine that Dave had told them after the game that I was in no way to blame for his injury. I heard his shin crack when it hit mine but he knew as well as I did that it was a complete freak so why he brought it up again 45 years later, I don't know.

"Still, maybe it did him a favour, eh? Look what he went on to do after giving up football!"

Norman Deeley was released by Benny Fenton in May 1964, as part of a mammoth clear-out that also included Bobby Mason, Eddie Lewis and reserve team keeper Reg Davies, who had been signed on a free transfer from Millwall the previous summer.

Reserves Phil White, Alan Russell and Peter Vaspar were also released as Fenton was forced to prune the cash-strapped club to just 16 professionals and replace them with young amateurs, including 22-year-old Enfield full-back Jeff Harris (who made 14 appearances before moving on to Romford a year later). Fenton had previously snapped up Jimmy McGeorge (who would make 17 first team starts) from Spennymore and Tony Harding from Barnet.

TERRY McDONALD
Outside-left or Outside-right 1959-65
Born: Stepney, East London, November 12, 1939
Appearances: 152 League & 19 Cup
Goals: 23 League & 4 Cup

SIR Alf Ramsey wasn't often turned down by players in his illustrious management career, but the man who created English football history by winning the World Cup in 1966 failed in his efforts to sign O's winger Terry McDonald!

The East London-born McDonald was doing his National Service in the army's medical corp (RAMC) at Aldershot, and had just heard the disappointing news that he'd been released by his first club West Ham United, when Ipswich Town boss Ramsey tried to lure him to Portman Road.

Explaining his decision to choose Leyton Orient instead of the fastest-emerging team in the country, Terry says: "I still had to complete the last couple of months of my National Service when I joined Orient after being given a free by West Ham. I'd seen a lot of the Orient from watching them play every other week, so I knew the players by name, but I got to know more about the club from speaking to Ronnie Foster, who was in the same army regiment as me.

"I was still weighing up what to do next in football when Alf Ramsey rang me from Ipswich, who were an up and coming side then, although they soon went on to win the second and first division titles (consecutively, in 1961 and '62). The major called me in and said Ramsey was on the phone wanting to talk to me.

"I spoke to Alf, who spoke with a posh accent even then, but as Orient were my second team, and knowing the type of football they liked to play, and then going by what Ronnie had told me, I chose the O's instead.

"It had been very difficult for me to get into the West Ham first team at that time. They effectively had four pro teams, which meant at least four left-wingers in front of me vying for one spot. They were Malcolm Musgrove, Ken Tucker, Doug Wragg and Harry Hooper."

McDonald had come to Hammers' boss Ted Fenton's attention by starring for West Ham Schoolboys, alongide prolific George Fenn and wing-half Clive Lewis. In fact, he scored a hat-trick on his first-ever appearance at Upton Park, against Dagenham Schoolboys.

Although he continued to score regularly and was very successful at youth and reserve level, starring in the Hammers' team beaten by Manchester United in the 1957 FA Youth Cup final, McDonald made only one first team appearance for his boyhood favourites – in a home floodlight friendly against Spartak Prague in October 1958.

"I'm sure Ronnie Foster must have spoken to Les Gore about signing me for Orient," Terry continued, "because the next thing I knew, Les got in touch with me. He wanted his team to play good football and the likes of Ken Facey typified that style. I also knew I had a much better chance of getting in their first team, so joining the O's was really an easy choice to make.

Terry McDonald showing his balance on the ball and (below) in his West Ham Youth team days. Terry is in the middle of the front row – and how many of you spotted Bobby Moore (standing far left) and John Lyall (far right)?

"Joe Elwood was in the first team then but I think he got injured. I was brought in for my debut and scored direct from a corner against Hull City.

"I considered myself fortunate to have played with Tommy Johnston, Phil White and Ronnie Foster. The football they played suited me – Ronnie was a pass-and-move player with great control, there was no kick-and-rush, so it was quite easy to blend into the side."

McDonald played a major part in the O's promotion campaign. Apart from creating chances and goals for Dave Dunmore and the inside-forwards with his darting runs, dribbling ability and consistently accurate crosses from the left, he weighed in with half-a-dozen useful goals himself. Match-winning strikes at Southampton and Bury, plus one in the 2-0 victory at Scunthorpe, proved invaluable in the final analysis.

In the first division, it's fair to say that, like most of his team-mates, the diminutive and frail left-winger found it much tougher against more physically imposing and more accomplished opposition. That said, he enjoyed one of his best performances in the No.11 shirt when he gave a brilliant display in the thrilling 3-0 home win over Everton, no doubt buoyed by his famous winner against Manchester United just four days earlier.

That last-minute winner to defeat United stemmed from a ball from Eddie Lewis, who said: "Every time I got the ball I used to give it to Terry. I'll never forget Johnny Bond of West Ham, who used to come and watch a few of our home games, once saying to me: 'Can't you f****** pass the ball anywhere else?'

"I said to Bondy: 'Listen, every time I get the ball, Terry McDonald wants it. If Terry received a thousand passes per game, I must have given him 999 of them.

"He always used to run away from me and shout for the ball. But when the full-back marking him went with him, Terry would check back so that he could receive the ball from me to his feet. But if the full-back came back with him, Terry would go again and I'd stick the ball past the defender and in front of your dad for him to run onto.

"He used to prefer the ball to his feet, though, and we had a very good understanding on the left side."

Malcolm Lucas said: "Eddie's distribution of the ball was tremendous but whenever he was in trouble, Terry was always there to help him. He was like an antelope down that left wing – his work-rate was tremendous."

Cyril Lea added: "Terry was a good player, he had a lot of ability. We'd give him the ball because we knew he could take the full-back on."

McDonald said elsewhere how disappointed he was when Ronie Foster left Orient for Grimsby and he was sorry, too, so see the departure of another good mate, Dennis Sorrell, to Chelsea in March 1962.

McDonald and Sorrell have remained in fairly regular contact over the years, meeting up as recently as the 2006 LOFC Supporters' Club dinner, and Terry says: "Dennis deserved to play a lot more often than he did and only got in the side when Cyril Lea was out through injury.

"Dennis was a good player – very strong in the tackle, but he could play a bit too. If he looked at you while he had possession off the ball, you knew he would give it to you."

McDonald's 20-game spell in the first division spotlight ended halfway through that season after another defeat at Arsenal. Johnny Carey, who Terry admits he never got on with, dropped the young winger and turned to experience when he signed Malcolm Musgrove, another capture from West Ham. McDonald has nothing but respect for Musgrove but had to wait until relegation, and Carey's departure, before reclaiming his first team place.

Lucas added: "They were different types of player. Terry did a lot of work in behind Eddie Lewis, whereas 'Muzzie' was one of those wingers who just attacked. But whether that helped the left-back is another story . . ."

Mal admits that he has lost touch with most of his Orient team-mates, although he enjoyed meeting up with Terry when they were both invited to attend the supporters' club's end-of-season bash at the Prince Regent Hotel, Woodford, in 2005. "It's funny, " he said, "I was never close to Terry when we played together but we got on like a house on fire that night.

Joe Elwood, who effectively lost his first team place to McDonald at the end of 1959 and never enjoyed another regular long run in the side, added: "There were cliqués of players at the Orient at that time, and Carey had his favourites, but your dad was straight down the middle – he'd talk to everyone."

While his goal against Manchester United will forever be the highspot of his six years at Brisbane Road, McDonald loves to reflect on many happy days, like classic games at Liverpool. The roar of the Kop evokes special memories for all the O's players who were lucky enough to experience it.

Looking back on the 3-3 draw at Anfield in the season in which both teams were promoted, Terry says: "The Liverpool fans clapped us off the pitch even though their team hadn't won. You wouldn't see home fans do that today.

"In the supporters' club bar afterwards, they said how much they appreciated the football we played. Playing in front of a large crowd and The Kop inspired us. We played the same type of football as Liverpool – and we matched them all the way."

McDonald never asked to leave Orient and he revealed another time when he turned down an approach from a well known club.

"Les Gore called me in once to ask how I felt about a move to Newcastle. I told him to forget it – it was a non-starter. I know my wife, Jean, wouldn't have wanted to move all the way up there.

"Les also spoke to me about interest from Alf Ramsey, who had watched me play for Orient while he was managing the England under-23 side, but it turned out that I was already over the age limit anyway. Alf must have fancied me a bit as a player, I suppose, because that enquiry came three seasons or so on from when he first tried to sign me for Ipswich."

McDonald just laughs at the thought that, had he accepted Ramsey's offer to join Ipswich at the start of the 60s, he might have been in contention for a senior England call-up (to add to his one England Youth cap gained against Hungary in 1956) after Ramsey took over as senior England manager in 1964 . . .

MALCOLM MUSGROVE
Outside-left 1963-65
Born: Newcastle-upon-Tyne, Tyne & Wear, July 8, 1933
Appearances: 83 League & 8 Cup
Goals: 14 League & 4 Cup

EVEN before Malcolm Musgrove arrived at Brisbane Road in the freezing cold winter of 1962-63, the Orient were already in dire straits as far as their first division future was concerned.

But no-one did more than this very direct, goalscoring left-winger to try and lift O's out of the mire.

An £11,000 signing from West Ham United, Malcolm had perhaps never quite received the respect he deserved from Hammers' fans for scoring 84 goals in his 10 years at Upton Park.

If he wasn't quite sure what he had let himself in for when he made the short hop from E13 to E10 around Christmas '63, he surely did before long! After scoring on his debut, a 2-2 draw at home to Birmingham City, 'Muzzie' found the net again four days later on his away bow at Leicester . . . where his new team were already five down before his late strike!

He also found the net on his next two appearances, against Hull City in the FA Cup, but after the thaw finally came, and he scored again in the 1-1 draw at Ipswich, still there was nothing the experienced Geordie could do to save Orient from their inevitable fate.

Terry McDonald, who lost his place to the man who had previously kept him out of the West Ham first team, said of Malcolm: "I knew Muzzie from West Ham and once he arrived I knew that my first team days were numbered, especially as I'd gradually fallen out with Carey.

"Muzzie was a diamond, a nice bloke, and I had no problem with him.

"Malcolm was a brave forward, he got his shots in and his goalscoring record is better than mine. I can't remember what his crossing was like but he could score goals.

"He wasn't a skilful dribbler, he was a very direct winger. He was two-footed, so you couldn't knock him – and I wouldn't – but he was a totally different type of winger to me."

In the aftermath of relegation, Musgrove's experience and goals proved an important factor in keeping O's clear of the relegation zone in Benny Fenton's first season, when his 11 strikes in an ever-present 1963-64 league campaign was bettered only by 16-goal Gordon Bolland.

The Orient youngsters would continue to appreciate Muzzie's influence even more when, in 1965, he began his impressive coaching career at Brisbane Road under manager Dave Sexton, who had been a team-mate of Malcolm's at West Ham.

NOT FORGETTING...

A few words from Terry McDonald about the other players who featured briefly in the two seasons we've covered . . .

DEREK GIBBS (right-half or inside-right)
"Derek was a busy sort of midfielder-cum-inside forward who was not noted for his touch. But he was strong and aggressive – a workhorse.

"It should be remembered that without the two goals he scored in our last away game, at Luton, the final match in our promotion season against Bury would have been meaningless.

"Derek will also be remembered as the man who scored the club's first-ever goal in the top flight, at home to Arsenal."

BOBBY MASON (outside-right or inside-right)
Norman Deeley played with Bobby in the successful Wolves team of the late 50s and he said: "He was a good lad and I may have mentioned Bobby's name to Eddie Baily before the Orient signed him from Chelmsford City."

"Bobby played in every round of our FA Cup run in 1960 but he was left out of the Wolves side for the final against Blackburn. Stan Cullis decided to bring in the raw youngster, Barry Stobart, instead."

Terry McDonald said: "During my latter days at Orient, Bobby used to pick me up every morning in his car on the Eastern Avenue at Chadwell Heath and give me a lift to training. He lived at Chelmsford at the time.

"He was a lovely bloke. As a footballer, he could dribble but he didn't score."

"To be fair, he came into the side at a very difficult time, when we were already struggling badly in the first division."

BILLY TAYLOR (left-back or inside-forward)

"Tommy Johnston recommended Billy to the Orient and he came in at left-back for a few games to cover when Eddie Lewis was injured.

"I don't think he had Eddie's vision but he was a good, little footballer.

"And, of course, he went on to enjoy a very good career as a coach."

GEORGE WAITES (outside-right)

"In our army team at Aldershot, George played outside-right, I was outside-left and Ronnie Foster was inside-left.

"George had more ball skills and dribbling ability than anybody could wish for and he had also great control. But, a bit like Dougie Wragg at West Ham, he just didn't deliver often enough. You'd get caught offside three times waiting for George to cross the ball! He'd threaten to cross it, then come back and beat the same full-back again.

"He once slaughtered Ron Ashman who was playing at full-back for Norwich against Orient . . . and when Ron became Norwich's manager, he signed George. When they played at Orient near the end of that season, Ashman asked Les Gore if he wanted George back!'

"Georgie Waites was Dennis Sorrell's mate from Stepney."

DAVID CLARK (centre-half)

"A promising, young footballing centre-half, Dave was unfortunate to come into the side when we were on the skids.

"He was a nice bloke and it was a great shame when he suffered his bad injury. I played in the reserve game when he broke his leg – and I don't know what happened to him after that . . ."

AFTER THEY LEFT THE O'S

FRANK GEORGE

Frank left Orient in 1964 and joined Watford, where he played 10 league games in a couple of years. He signed for non-league Worcester City but the injury jinx struck again when he broke his collarbone in only his third match for the club, in a Southern League game at Romford.

"I'm a lover of jellied eels," says Frank, "and my brother Eddie, who followed me all over the place, was there watching at Romford that day. He took me to hospital but before he did, I insisted on him taking me for my traditional post-match bowl of jellied eels. I love 'em . . . I've got some in my fridge now for later tonight!

"After every home game at Orient, we nearly always finished up joining Eddie for a drink and jellied eels at the Green Man pub in Leytonstone," says Frank, who lived nearby with his family at 14 Steele Avenue. "Most cockney pubs used to have a jellied eels stall outside but you don't see them as much these days.

"It's not just jellied eels – I also enjoy mussels and cockles . . . and now you can buy oysters too – but they weren't around in our day!"

"Eddie died young, at the age of 38. He had some trouble with his lungs."

After his playing days ended, Frank became self-employed and worked for his friend, Harry, who owned a print finishing firm. "I delivered in my van all over London and must have worked for him for all of 20 years until I had a very bad accident."

In the late 80s, Frank spent 11 weeks in St. Thomas' Hospital after his van was in collision with another vehicle while on his way to Newbury, Berkshire.

"I was badly injured, including a busted hip which has never mended properly. It can be very painful at times. I have to use a walking stick all the time now and my right shoe had to be built up because one leg is shorter than the other. But I don't wish to be all doom and gloom and I suppose I'm lucky to still be here. Life goes on."

Frank and his wife Iris have lived in Ramsgate, Kent for the past 14 years and they have two children, Tim (42) and Pauline (38). Iris gave birth to Pauline in Forest Gate Hospital while her dad was playing in O's 6-2 FA Cup demolition of Gillingham on January 7, 1961. They have six grandchildren – Samantha (24), Danny (22), Terry (15), Josh (14), Georgia (7) and Adam (4).

The Georges appreciate the fresh sea air on the north Kent coast, where they like to relax in the bay and enjoy a drink and a bit to eat. Frank says: "We live just a short distance from the seaside . . . and a nice jellied eel stall!"

BILL ROBERTSON

Big Bill left the O's in 1963 and ended his playing days at Southern League Dover. He retired to run a pub in Epsom, Surrey, but died aged 44 in June 1973.

Terry McDonald recalls: "When Bill opened his pub, a few of us – Stan Charlton, Dave Dunmore, Ronnie Foster and Norman Deeley – went down there to celebrate with him."

MIKE PINNER

After 77 matches with the O's, Mike left in 1964 for a "fun" couple of seasons in Ireland with Distillery.

"As my work as a solicitor got busier, it was getting harder to combine the two, so I gave up playing. It was always in my mind to qualify as a solicitor. I'd often received requests to play football professionally, right from my younger days, but that wasn't possible because I was studying law at Cambridge University."

Mike played for the Cambridge University football team, which happened to be coached for a while by Eddie Baily.

"I could earn £25-per week at Orient. Football wasn't a very well paid job back then, so there was never a doubt about me continuing my studies and going on to become a solicitor."

He spent the last five years employed as a partner in a firm of solicitors called Marshall Hatchick, who have branches in London and Woodbridge, Suffolk.

"I was a property lawyer but retired last Christmas (2005). I now keep fit by playing a lot of tennis and doing the gardening."

Mike returned to Orient in March 2006 to attend the 125th anniversary celebration dinner, when he met up with several former team-mates. "Orient was the friendliest club I ever played for and it still seems that way from what I saw at the dinner that night," he added.

Mike has four sons – Jason, Julian, Mark and Hugh – who are all living and working overseas.

STAN CHARLTON

The skipper took over as player-manager at Weymouth in July 1965. "But I played only 18 games of my first season there before injuring my knee in the last minute of a cup-tie against Bideford Town. That's when I had my first cartilage operation," recalls Stan.

Even so, Stan – as manager – guided The Terras to a second consecutive Southern League championship. He remained Weymouth boss for seven years, until he was replaced by Graham Williams in May 1972, despite winning the Southern League Cup that season.

Stan later served the Dorset club as both secretary and groundsman, as well as helping out behind the scenes.

"I had two knee operations and, having continued to play local league football until I was 58, I became arthritic and was in a lot of pain. My ankle also gave me trouble.

"I had a knee replacement fitted. The PFA paid £6,000 for one operation and I had the other one done on the NHS.

"I broke two ribs playing in goal for Weymouth Labour Club in a Dorset Division Four game – at the age of 58. But, having drunk a few Tennents Export lagers in the bar after the game, I didn't realise the damage I'd done and, in fact, rode home on my bicycle! But I was still hurting a bit the next day, so my partner Dorothy drove me to hospital, where they confirmed I'd broken two ribs."

It wasn't Stan's first experience as a stand-in goalie, however. In October 1963,

Stan Charlton and Malcolm Graham with the boots that fired the O's to the top in 1962. This was taken in the dressing room after the Bury game. The picture below shows the same two receiving their awards from the LOFC Supporters' Club at the Star Man Dinner at Woodford Bridge in 2000.

keeper Reg Davies hurt a finger playing for the O's at home against Portsmouth. Stan had scored a rare goal to make it 2-2 but Pompey had romped into a 6-3 lead when he had to take over from Davies between the sticks.

"I'd scored to make it 2-2, I kept a clean sheet as goalkeeper . . . and we still lost the game 6-3!"

When the marriage to his first wife, Shirley, ended after 33 years, Stan met Dorothy when she took him in as a lodger and they have been together since 1986.

"I still keep fit by cycling down to the seafront here at Weymouth and play the occasional round of golf on the nine-hole course. I do a bit of gardening as well.

He still follows the fortunes of Weymouth who, as a fully professional club, won the Nationwide Conference (South) in May 2006. "I'm also a life-president at Weymouth FC," said Stan who had just seen them play at Tamworth when we last spoke.

Stan has two sons, Gary and Kevin, and a daughter Karen, who all live fairly near to him and Dorothy in Ferndale. Stan has 11 grandchildren – Lee (20), Hannah (19), Ben (18), Tom (18), Josh (15), Callum (13), Ryan (12), Alfie (10), Tara (10), Finlay (8) and Ollie (2).

EDDIE LEWIS

"After I left Orient, I went to Southern League Folkestone Town for two years when Wilf Amory was manager there. In the second year, we had a hell of a cup run and played against Gillingham, who were top of the Third Division at the time. I was playing inside-forward but I never got a kick – I was finding the pace too much – so I dropped further and further back and ended up playing sweeper. But Tony Biggs scored and we beat them 1-0.

"Folkestone was the only club who paid me a signing-on fee – five hundred pounds. I never made a penny when I went from Man United to Preston, from there on to West Ham, or when I left the Hammers to join Orient. I was so naive.

"I played centre-back/sweeper for Ford Motor Company and passed my coaching prelim badge. My first managerial job was for Clapton, at the Spotted Dog ground, Forest Gate in the late 70s, and we had a spell when we were top of the Isthmian League, out-performing top amateur teams like Enfield and Hendon.

"I achieved my full badge in November 1969. I'd been working for Jack Turner, the former Welfare Officer at West Ham who later became an agent for Bobby Moore. He had an insurance agency with the Royal London and I started working for him. I ran my own 'book' and in the winter I'd go out every morning dressed in trilby hat, raincoat and over-shoes – it nearly always seemed to be raining – to do my rounds at places like Millwall and Canning Town. I was making something like 200 calls some days and I did ever so well at it."

Eddie's life, and career, changed when he emigrated to South Africa.

"Bobby Moore came out to coach in Johannesburg with Terry Venables, Geoff Hurst and Bill McGarry when one of the local teams out here, who had just been promoted to the first division, needed a new coach. Bobby and I had been good friends from our time at West Ham and it was him who recommended me to them.

Eddie Lewis pictured recently with his partner Stephanie in South Africa.

I didn't come here to South Africa with the intention of becoming a football coach but that's how I got started.

"I was the first white coach they'd ever had at Kaizer Chiefs, the team who beat Manchester United on their tour earlier this year (2006). We won the league when I was there. I also coached a team called Moroko Swallows in the late 80s."

Eddie also has a wealth of coaching experience at international level.

"I was manager of the South Africa national team in 1979 but we were due to play Rhodesia just as they declared UDI, so the game was aborted.

"I went with the South African team to the 1998 World Cup finals in France as a technical advisor, having taken Burkina Faso to the CAF Cup the previous January. Two years later I went to Ghana and Nigeria with the South African squad. I was the only white person coaching a team of black players.

"Molefi Olifant, president of the South African FA, demanded to know why we lost 2-0 to Ghana and I was cheesed off by his rudeness. I wrote a letter complaining about him . . . and never got any more work from them.

"We had players like Mark Fish, Lucas Radebe and Benni McCarthy, who have all played in the English Premiership.

"I've had offers to become a consultant to clubs but it's just been talk.

"I was coaching at Witwatersrand in Johannesburg, one of the leading universities in the country, in 1974 and one of my players at Wits (pronounced Vits) was a 16-year-old goalkeeper called Gary Bailey, who actually went out with my daughter Julie before he joined Manchester United. Richard Gough was also there with me before he went on to much bigger things with Dundee United, Spurs, Rangers and also became captain of Scotland.

"Another of the youngsters I coached at Wits was Dimas Teixeira, who left us to go and play in Portugal for Benfica and joined Juventus in *Serie A* in the late 90s. When Juve met Real Madrid in the 1998 European Cup final, his brother sent me two tickets and I went to Amsterdam to watch the final. Although he was born in Jo'burg, Dimas was capped 44 times for Portugal and played for them in both the Euro 96 and 2000 tournaments.

"I had a reputation for bringing on young players, I liked to put my faith in them."

These days, Eddie enjoys a reputation as one of the most forthright football pundits on South African national television.

Explaining his last career move, he says: "I was doing work on the World Cup for SABC, with Bruce Grobbelaar, before a new show called *Supersport* started here five years ago. Gary Bailey worked for them and he asked me to join him as a studio pundit. Terry Paine is also on the panel and we often joke about the time we played against each other when Orient faced Southampton.

"The TV work has gone really well for me. I've been getting around 20 assignments a month and have earned more money in the past five years than all the others years put together.

"I've got a reputation for being very outspoken. Some people within the TV organisation think I'm too negative but I say to them: 'Listen, I'm a coach'. Me and Paine are the only two ex-coaches working for them – the rest are ex-players with no coaching experience – so I like to call a spade a spade when commenting on games we cover from the English Premiership, international matches and major tournaments like the World Cup and European Championship."

Eddie hopes to be expressing his honest opinions when his adopted country stages its biggest soccer fest of all – the 2010 World Cup finals. But he does have some concerns: "Crime in South Africa is getting out of hand, and they're going to have to do something about that with the World Cup coming here next. But it is God's own country and the climate is fantastic, it's so healthy. I love it here."

Eddie revealed the health problems he has endured in recent years and his personal loss. "About three years ago my knee kept swelling all the time and I was told I needed a complete knee replacement.

"About 18 months ago, I had a colonoscopy and they found two tumours in my colon. As it happened, they cut them out and when I went back to the hospital in March of this year for another check-up, they thankfully said that the cancer had all cleared.

"In February of this year my knee started playing me up again but when I saw the specialist, he said the real problem was with my hip, so it meant having a hip replacement instead. After all the treatment I've had for my knee, hip and the surgery to my colon, I think there's more of me to be found somewhere in that hospital than there is stood here talking to you now!

"My mother, Hetty, used to say to me how lucky I was to still be alive. My mates – Eddie Coleman, David Pegg and Duncan Edwards – were all killed in the Munich tragedy in '58. If I'd been a better player, I would probably have been sitting with them on that plane. So the fact that I wasn't as good as any of them probably saved my life.

"However, My wife, Shirley, was diagnosed with cancer in 1990 and died three weeks later. I'd lost my mother, who came out here to live near us, only about a month before Shirley passed away. In fact, it was because Shirley became ill herself that she couldn't attend my mum's funeral.

"It was a real double whammy but, apart from that, life's been good to me. I'm doing well here. I've got a new car, I'm living with my youngest daughter Suzanne in a nice cottage at the moment but my lady friend, Stephanie, and I have put our names down for a retirement home that we hope to move into soon. Steph's got a flat just around the corner from me. We're very happy together and she's a great woman. She even runs her own gardening business even though, like me, she's now in her seventies."

As well as daughters Suzanne and Julie, Eddie also has five grandchildren – Fallon, Keagan, Devlin (who are Julie's children) plus Suzanne's two, Chaid, and Kyllah.

It's four years since Eddie last returned to England. He says: "I attended the annual Christmas dinner of the Association of Former Manchester United Players in 2002 but I'm hoping to visit England again next summer (2007).

BILLY TAYLOR

After 23 league (+ 4 Cup and O goals) for the O's Bill spent five years with Nottingham Forest (10 games + 10 sub and 0 goals) under his former boss Johnny Carey between 1963 and 1968. His last league club as a player was Lincoln City, where he made 74 league appearances (+ 4 sub) and scored seven times.

He retired from professional football in May 1971 and went on to become the Fulham reserve coach, where he was employed by another former Orient chief, Alec Stock. Bill worked his way up to first team coach and was a key member of Stock's until the arrival of Bobby Campbell in 1976. In his time at Craven Cottage, Bill coached Fulham to the 1975 FA Cup final, where they lost 2-0 to West Ham.

During October 1974 he was on the coaching staff for the England national squad and in May 76, after leaving Fulham, he was appointed as Manchester City's assistant manager, working with manager Tony Book.

He left City to become coach at Oldham Athletic in July 1979 under Jimmy Frizzell.

A couple of years later he suffered a viral infection that attacked his nervous system and although he recovered, he fell ill again on November 18, 1981. He went into a coma and passed away in Oldham 12 days later.

At the time of his death Bill was still coaching with both Oldham and England.

MALCOLM LUCAS

The wing-half had five enjoyable years at second division Norwich City between 1964 and '69, making 108 (plus three sub) appearances and scoring eight goals.

After his pro career ended at Torquay United in 1973 (where he played under

Sid Bishop at home in Harlow this year with Belle, his pet Border Collie.
Inset: Sid in his peak playing days, with his late wife Vera and their prize Poodle collection!

former Orient team-mate Malcolm Musgrove, who managed at Plainmoor), Mal returned to East Anglia.

He played at non-league level for Lowestoft Town and Gorleston. After hanging up his boots, he then managed Gorleston to the Eastern Counties championship.

"I always said that after winning the league, I'd finish with football," says Mal, who ended up in the leisure business. He worked for a friend at Brent Leisure Services, touring the Norfolk pubs to collect the fruit machine takings.

He retired two years ago and lives with his wife, Jenny, on the outskirts of Norwich. Their two daughters – Paula (42) and Sally (40) – both live nearby.

Mal says: "I'm doing as little as possible! I used to play a lot of golf but I had trouble with my wrists and it meant taking too many painkillers. Now I go down to the local gym to try and keep a bit fit. I also like to do a bit of coarse fishing on the nearby lakes and the Norfolk Broads."

SID BISHOP

After 13 years with the Orient, Sid hung up his boots at the age of 30 but remained in football before going into the pub trade, as many ex-players did in those days.

"Firstly, I went to Southern League Hastings United as player-manager but the wrong type of people were running the club and I wasn't at all happy there," he recalls.

"I quickly moved on to Guildford City, where I stayed for 18 months. We won the Southern League Cup, and I took on the manager's job, but I didn't feel I was getting anywhere in life.

"I wanted to get myself a pub and I did when I moved into The Greyhound – at Lea Park, on a council estate a little bit inland from Portsmouth. I was a licensee for Brickwoods Brewery.

"We were only there a year when my wife, Vera, had to go into hospital for a hysterectomy. She had an operation to remove a cyst from her ovary. But they later found another cyst and had to operate on her again. I was furious with the surgeon and doctors that they hadn't noticed the second cyst when they did the first op.

"With Vera back in hospital, and having to run a pub and look after our two kids, I found it very stressful. I'd had enough, so I told the brewery we were quitting the place.

"We lived with my brother, Clive, in Tooting for a while and I scratched around for different jobs. The way I look at it, if you're prepared to use your hands, you won't starve. I was a milkman in the Epsom area for about three months before we moved back to Vera's mum's flat in Hackney, and I got another milk round there. I ended up chasing some little urchin, who'd nicked stuff off the float, around a block of flats. It was a nightmare.

"I did one or two other odd jobs but my main job after football was managing The Phoenix pub for John Doyle, at Harlow. I ran it for him for three years in the early 70s before I began to suffer anxiety attacks – a sort of mini breakdown. Everything had got on top of me and I felt horrible. Physically, I was all OK but, mentally, I didn't want to work in the pub anymore. I just used to sod around in the garden.

"I went from one little job to another – working for big companies like Cossers, the radio electronic people, and then BOC, where I worked in the stores. It was easy but boring – I had to keep money coming in.

"Vera was the head barmaid at the local pub and we got through it."

Sid was devastated when Vera sadly passed away a few years ago, although he remains in close contact with his son Warren (45) and daughter Denise (44), who have given him four grandchildren – Joe (18), George (14), Mollie (12) and Elle (8).

The O's legend lives at home in Harlow, Essex with Belle, his pet Border Collie, who keeps him looking as slim and fit as in his playing days.

CYRIL LEA

Of all the former Leyton Orient players featured in this book, Cyril went on to achieve the most in football after retiring as a player.

Cyril spent hs pro career with just two clubs – and he joined Ipswich Town in 1964 to begin four years as a player under manager Bill McGarry.

"Bill was a good manager – I idolised him," says Cyril. "He was tough, a real winner, and he worked us hard, but he'd stand by his players. Portman Road was a much bigger pitch than Orient's and I found it much harder to give the same amount of cover there as I'd done at Brisbane Road.

"When I reached 34, I had the choice of either carrying on playing under Bill at Ipswich or going on the coaching side. He actually promised me a job when I signed for him – and he kept true to his word. In 1967 he re-signed me as a player but also took me on the coaching staff," explained Cyril, who made 107 league appearances for the Suffolk club.

"I played the odd game after that but my fitness levels dropped and soon I was looking after the reserves – Sammy Chung was Bill's first team coach at the time.

"When Bill left to go to Wolves in 1967, he asked me to go with him, but I said I'd only join him there if I could go as first team coach. I felt I needed to push on, but he already had Sammy working under him, so I stayed at Ipswich.

"I took over the team as caretaker manager for around six matches. I believed in what Bill had been doing, so I didn't change it much. Then the chairman of Ipswich Town, Patrick Cobbold, asked me if I was interested in taking the manager's job full-time. I'd only just started on the coaching side and felt I was still too young to go into management, so I declined his offer.

"Dave Sexton, who was working with the England set-up at the time, rang me and said: 'I'm glad you've turned down the Ipswich job . . . I've just recommended Bobby Robson to them'.

"Bobby came and, on the chairman's recommendation, he kept me on as his coach. We had 10 successful years together, winning promotion to the first division (1967-68) and the FA Cup (beating Arsenal, 1-0, in 1978).

"I didn't think Bobby was a great coach, and not as good as Bill McGarry, but his man-management was excellent. Bill had sorted the club out and I think Bobby was a bit lucky in that I'd kept the continuity going before he arrived and he changed very little when he came. We had a lot of very talented, young players coming

Cyril Lea, Terry McDonald and Joe Elwood pictured at a reunion in 2004.

through and they stood us in good stead.

"Bobby and I had one or two up-and-downers and after 10 years together he wanted to make a few staff changes. I had my own ideas and I think he sensed it, so I left (August 1979).

"I went with Alan Durban to Stoke City, where I learned a lot from him. Alan was a good manager, an excellent technician and one of the best defensive coaches I've ever come across. He kept Stoke in the top flight with a very average team.

"Prior to that, while I was still at Ipswich, I'd worked as part-time coach for the senior Wales international side, under manager Mike Smith, who was also in charge at Northampton. I spent about 11 years coaching the national side.

"Then, in 1980, Mike asked me to follow him to Hull City as his assistant – they were struggling at the bottom of the third division. He offered me a five-year contract and doubled my money. Well, I had a family of four and I felt it was the right time to do it.

"But where I went wrong was in going from the top division to the bottom of the third, where it was much harder working with lesser quality players who couldn't take things on board as well as the ones I'd been used to working with before. It was a struggle and just when we thought we were turning it around, they sacked us after two-and-a-half years."

A highly respected coach, Cyril did become a manager in his own right at Colchester United, having initially gone to Layer Road in 1983 as assistant to his former Ipswich team-mate, Alan Hunter, who soon quit management. With former Arsenal and Manchester United full-back Stewart Houston as his No.2, Cyril did well for the Essex club but admits. "It's hard managing a small club – you get your legs cut off from under you. It all comes down to money.

"Unbeknown to me, the chairman sold out to an Ipswich-based entrepreneur, but

I was let down and Stewart and me got the push. It was unfair. We had a decent team, including Perry Groves (who went on to Arsenal) and Alex Chamberlain."

Cyril's next port of call was Leicester City, where another former Ipswich favourite, Bryan Hamilton, appointed him Youth Development Officer in 1986. And he was on the move again in 1989, when yet another ex-Ipswich star, Brian Talbot, asked him to join him at West Bromwich Albion and run the youth operation at The Hawthorns. "But neither of those jobs lasted longer than a year," says the nomadic Cyril . . . "because both Brians got the sack.

"I got on well with Bobby Gould, who got me a five-year contract after he replaced Talbot at West Brom, but then he too got the sack, so that was the end of me there.

"I finished up back working with Brian Talbot when he went to Rushden & Diamonds, where I was his youth coach and chief scout from 1997. We had five or six good years together. I also went with him to Oldham but he couldn't settle there, so I found myself back at Rushden, this time with Alan Hunter's cousin, Barry Hunter.

"But the owner, Dr Marten's manufacturer Max Griggs, pulled out, the club had to cut staff and I was one of those to lose my job. I wasn't out of work for more than a few days, though, when Terry Westley, who had coached at Luton and Charlton, went to Derby County as Academy Director. He asked me to join him there last year (2005) in a scouting role and although Terry has since moved on to Birmingham City, I've stayed there on a part-time basis. I watch two or three games a week for Derby, which suits me fine.

"I've been lucky to have been able to stay in football all my working life. I got into it at 22 and I haven't been out of it since. I've been a player, coach, assistant manager, first team manager and now a scout. I couldn't have asked for any more," added Cyril, who lives with his family near Lutterworth, Leicestershire.

Cyril and his wife Val have four children – Charlotte (40), Isabel (39), Daniel (37) and Amelia (35), and seven grandchildren (including two sets of twins) – Rowan (10), Morgan (9), Noah (7), Ellen (7), Ewan (6), Louis (3), Hope (1) and Esme (1).

DAVE DUNMORE

"I wasn't really surprised that no first division clubs came in and tried to sign me after we were relegated at Orient – I was getting on by then, you know," says Dave.

"Lincoln and York were the only offers I received. Lincoln were offering slightly better terms but, as I came from York, I decided to come back here to play."

After a season with York City (61 league games + 2 sub and 13 goals), Dave dropped into northern non-league circles with Wellington Town and then Bridlington Trinity. "They transferred me to Scarborough for the princely sum of one hundred quid! I only played about half-a-season for each of those clubs.

"I also played briefly for Sligo Rovers in Ireland. I used to fly over on a Saturday, play on Sunday and come back on the Monday. Ken Turner, who I'd played with at York, became the manager at Sligo and he got me over there, but it didn't last long."

Worcester City and Harrogate Railways were the next stopping off points for Dave before he ended his playing days with the Golden Lion pub team!

Stan Charlton, Terry McDonald, Ronnie Foster and Dave Dunmore at the Orient in 2002.

"I was in my early forties when I finally packed up playing football – and that's when my mate and I decided it was time to take up golf."

When he is not honing his 13-handicap on the courses around his native York, as he does at least three days a week during the summer, Dave still works for the car dealers, Evans Halshaw. "I'm virtually a taxi service for them, working two hours on four mornings a week, and all day on a Friday."

Dave and his wife Barbara have a daughter, Anne (52,) and two sons, Peter (49) and Michael (46), plus five grandchildren – Trudie (26), Christopher (20), Thomas (18), Helen (17) and Rachel (9) – and one great-grandson, Joel (20 months).

RONNIE FOSTER

The cultured inside-forward was one of the most accomplished players to wear the Orient shirt before he left for Grimsby Town in November 1963.

Ron says: "I had a couple of good years at Grimsby (129 apps + 24 goals) before coming back south to play for Reading, Brentford and then at non-league level for Barnet and Dover. I then had a year in Texas playing for Dallas Tornado in the North American Soccer League.

"The Yanks didn't know what soccer was in those days. I went there originally on a two-year contract but, in between, I was also doing the Knowledge back in London around that time. I told the Dallas manager, a Mr. Spurgeon – I can't recall his first name – that my wife Margaret and I were going back to live in England."

The chances are, a few Orient fans reading this may have literally been taken for a ride by Ronnie without even realising it. "After my playing days finished, I drove a London black cab for 30-odd years," he continues.

Ron retired from cabbing in 2005 and he and Margaret continue to live at Earley, near Reading in Berkshire, with their family relatively nearby. Their children are:

Karen (43), Tony (41), Tania (37) and Kelly (36), plus grandchildren Alex (11), Zoe (7), Ethan (7), Lauryn (6), Lucas (5), Cameron (4) and Finlay (2).

"Margaret and I do the shopping together," laughs Ron, "and I play the occasional round of golf. I like a good walk . . . and a couple of beers, too!"

Ron reckons he has now added a couple of stones to his regular playing weight of 10st 7lbs. "I'm fine and it's nice to be reminded of these memories. Give my regards to my favourite winger!"

HARRY GREGORY

Harry's six games for Leyton Orient in the first division turned out to be his only experience of top flight football.

After 79 league matches, he left Brisbane Road in 1966 to join Charlton Athletic (146 league games + 3 sub and 24 goals), where he was a star in their promotion-chasing second division team. He was the Addicks' captain when they narrowly missed out on promotion to the big time in 1968-69, finishing third.

However, Harry did win two Third Division championship medals – firstly with Aston Villa (18 league games + 6 sub and two goals) in 1972 and then, a year later, with Hereford United (71 league games + 2 sub and six goals) in what was their first-ever season in the Football League.

His playing days finished in the non-league backwaters of Essex – with Southern League Chelmsford City, Brentwood and then Maldon Town, where he played under the management of former Spurs centre-half Peter Collins. Harry succeeded Collins as the Maldon boss, combining that task with his main job as a heavy goods vehicle driver for Baxters, the meat distributor.

Harry Gregory in 2006.

It is a measure of Harry's love for the game and his determined character that he played at Maldon despite previously breaking his leg in three places during his spell with Brentwood. "My knees are playing me up now – I've already had key-hole surgery – but Peter Collins was a good friend. He'd been through a similar thing himself and he drove me on to make a comeback," explained Harry.

Harry now works delivering products for Prism Leisure, a software company in Enfield. "I've been with them for 15 years, they've really looked after me, and I'm hoping to retire soon."

Harry and his wife Carol live near Chelmsford, Essex and they have two sons. Gary, who drives a petrol tanker, and Terry, an underpinner, who turned down the chance of a football apprenticeship at Norwich City. The Gregorys have three grandchildren – Abbie (11), Georgia (7) and Reggie (2).

MALCOLM GRAHAM

After three very turbulent seasons with the O's, Malcolm remained in London for another year, playing for a former Orient boss across the opposite side of the capital at Queens Park Rangers (21 league games and seven goals).

"We'd just been demoted at Orient and it seemed like a good time to go. Alec Stock was manager of QPR then and he was a good boss. I liked Alec, who did very well for the players where money was concerned. I bought myself a nice car when I was at QPR, thanks to him."

After just one season in the third division at Loftus Road, the stocky Yorkshireman returned to his native county and Barnsley, where his pro career had begun 10 years earlier. In a further 20 league matches for the Oakwell club, he added five more goals to the 35 (from 109 games) he notched in his first spell. He finished his pro career with a very respectable 84 goals from 239 league games.

Malcolm had then intended to gain his football coaching qualifications.

"I attended coaching courses, including one at Arsenal run by West Ham manager Ron Greenwood," he said. "I'd already passed the theory part of the test in Barnsley. Terry Venables was on the same Highbury course as me.

"I'd had quite a bit of success coaching the Wolverhampton Wanderers junior team that played to a good standard of intermediate football near where I lived. They had a great set-up – better than Barnsley FC's at the time – and we used to play the likes of Leeds United.

"I went on a coaching course at Durham University, to get my full badge, and although I felt I'd done well enough, I finished up failing the exam. There were a lot of schoolteachers there who did pass, though – they were good at the theory side of it and were good at keeping their cool under pressure – and I became very disillusioned with it.

"A week later I took my Wolves team to Middlesbrough and we beat them. The coach who had failed me on the course the previous week happened to be in charge of Middlesbrough's juniors that day. After we'd won the game, he came up to me and advised me to go on another coaching course that was coming up in Cardiff the following week. 'Go there,' he told me, 'and you will *definitely* pass this time'.

"Well, him saying that that just upset me even more, and I fell out with the game for a while after that. Don't get me wrong, I still love football and I've been to watch Leeds and Barnsley quite a bit over the years, but I dropped my ideas of going into coaching after that experience."

After a year back playing for Barnsley, Malcolm quit the Football League in 1964 and continued to play locally at non-league level for Buxton and Alfreton Town. Then began a chain of health problems that have plagued him over the years.

"I quit playing at Alfreton because I needed another operation on my bad knee when it became arthritic – the same knee I'd had the cartilage removed from when I was aged 21 at Barnsley," he explains. "There was a bit of controversy over that first op' – it was said that the surgeon responsible was removing people's cartilage just for the sake of it."

Malcolm's first taste of the 'outside world' after football was at the *Sheffield Star* newspaper, where a friend got him a good job in advertising sales. After two years there, he had just 12 months working in a betting shop before spending 23 years as a salesman for the East Midlands Gas Board, working in Rotherham and Barnsley. "They were very good to me– better than football had been, because I got a pension with them. I stayed there until I had to retire through ill health."

Malcolm underwent heart bypass surgery seven years ago, shortly before his last return south for an Orient reunion, when he was a special guest of the LOFC Supporters' Club at their Star Man Dinner in year 2000. He has had to continue to pay careful attention to his health but his Yorkshire wit has not deserted him during difficult times and he laughed several times while bringing me up to date with his his current daily routine.

"I've had a defibrillator fitted – it's called a pacemaker-plus," he says. "If my heart stops, it 'jump-leads' me back in! I call it a jump-lead . . . and so far it's gone off three times! Ooh, it's like a bomb going off! For a split second, you wonder what's happening . . . you think you're on your way out. Then you realise what it is.

"I got myself an exercise bike and I was using it three times a day for five minutes each time, because it's important that I stretch my heart a bit. Five minutes is enough for what I need. But I've had to stop that now because my knee's buggered again! Now I've been told I've got to do a lot of exercises with my hands instead.

"I walk every day, without a stick, but I don't walk too far. I just take it easy.

"I lost my driving licence for 18 months, after I had a slight stroke, but I've got the licence back now, so at least I can drive again."

Malcolm certainly sounded chirpy when we spoke on the telephone in November 2006. He says: "I've felt better in this last six months than I have for the past 14-years. I put that down to exercising, eating properly and, of course, the tablets!"

Malcolm and Margaret live in Barnsley and they have two daughters – Tracey (46) and Nicola (33) – and three grandsons – Wayne (25), Mark (23) and Tom (13).

GORDON BOLLAND

Norwich City paid in the region of £32,000 for Gordon in March 1963, but it proved money very well spent as he maintained his impressive goals-per-games ratio with 29 in 104 starts (plus one sub) appearance for the second division Canaries until 1967.

He recalls: "After an enjoyable stay at Norwich, I came back to London to play briefly for Charlton (nine league games + 2 sub and two goals).

"I didn't play well for them, though, and that was my most unhappy time in football before Benny Fenton signed me for Millwall in 1968. My wife Angela and I had been living in one of Charlton's club houses at Blackheath but when I got to Millwall, Benny told me I had to buy my own place! It was the best thing that happened to us really, because it pushed us into buying our own house."

After 239 league appearanances (+ 5 sub) and 62 goals for Millwall, a hip injury hastened Gordon's departure from the old Den in 1975 and he was grateful to Lions' boss Gordon Jago for allowing him to join his home-town team, Boston United, on a free transfer.

"We won the league in my first two years at Boston, under Howard Wilkinson, although it was actually the chairman who brought me to the club and looked after me. Howard would rather have used the money the club was paying me to sign two or three other players but in the end he left under a cloud.

"After Howard went, me and another player – Freddie Taylor – took over the running of the side for the rest of that season on a caretaker basis . . . and finished up winning the league again.

"When my hip problem got too bad, I had to pack up playing and was disappointed not to be offered the manager's job at Boston. I then left them and went into a sales job with a local tie company.

"I got back involved at Boston United again, though, and chaired a group that raised funds for the club, which led to me being invited onto the football club's board for a short spell. Having started there as a youth team player before I went to Chelsea in 1961, I'd virtually done everything at Boston United before I left there the last time in the late 90s.

"I rejoined the tie company as a manager and retired about three years ago.

"But then I got fed up sitting around, so now I run a little mini cab service – within a larger firm called Acorn Taxis. I've got a couple of eight-seater mini buses, we have regular contract work through the council and it keeps me out of trouble."

Gordon has continued to follow Boston United's fortunes since they gained Football League status, watching them occasionally, but certain aspects of the modern game have slightly soured his love of football.

He said: "I'm very concerned that clubs aren't doing enough to produce good, young English players. Don't get me wrong, a lot of the foreigners have been good for the game in this country but the long-term future doesn't look good for the English national side. We had a very poor World Cup in the summer but my biggest fear is come the World Cup finals in, say, eight years time, where are the players to be found who will be good enough? Unless the FA does something about it, in 12 years time, England may not even qualify."

Gordon is also highly critical of the club that gave him his first professional contract. He said: "I look at what's happening at Chelsea. The media have been going on about Mourinho being a breath of fresh air, but I don't see it. He's been given all the money in the world to buy the best players available.

"But despite their incredible wealth and all their talent, Chelsea couldn't even fill their stadium for a Champions League game the other night . . . yet Manchester United, with entertaining British players like Giggs and Rooney, fill their stadium with 75,000-plus people every week. I can't see players at Chelsea who can take people on and entertain. They've got Joe Cole, but how often does Mourinho play him? I don't like the way Mourinho sets his Chelsea team up to play. In fact, I don't respect anything Chelsea are doing now."

An avid TalkSPORT radio listener and Sky TV armchair critic, Gordon was also sickened by the unsavoury fiasco surrounding Ashley Cole's protracted transfer to the Blues in August 2006.

"When he can turn round and say that £60-65,000 a week wasn't enough for him at Arsenal, the club who brought him up as a kid and taught him the game, it's outrageous. I think he'll look back in 10 years time and realise what a prat he's been.

"The millions being spent on today's players should be reduced and used instead to reduce admission prices for the supporters who pay their wages. Why don't Chelsea pay Ballack a lesser weekly wage of, say, 25 grand a week, which is still an exceptional sum, and drop their top ticket price from £40 or more to £20?"

Of course, Gordon has just posed a rhetoric question. With the Premiership elite about to become even more awash with Sky's seemingly limitless pot of money, the next TV contract running into billions of pounds, we all know that football at the highest domestic level will just continue to become even further removed from the days when Gordon and his Orient team-mates were just happy to be picking up a maximum £30 or £40 a week. "And we were proud to play for the club too," he points out.

"What gets me is that there is no-one in the media prepared to stand up to anyone playing or working in the Premiership – they are all frightened of upsetting the likes of Mourinho. But the time has surely come when someone has to stand up and be counted, and speak out about all the money that has taken the romance out of football.

"If 40,000 people at Old Trafford and another 40,000 at Stamford Bridge said 'enough's enough, we aren't going anymore until you stop paying out these ridiculously high wages', I tell you what . . . they'd be in the shit, wouldn't they? I know it won't happen, though," he adds with an air of resignation in his voice.

Gordon has undergone two hip replacements – the first 10 years ago, the legacy of the injury that brought about his retirement as a player, and had his second operation early in 2006.

Gordon and his wife Angela live at Boston, Lincolnshire. They have two daughters – Sharon (42) and Debbie (40) – and five grandchildren – Ben (21), Jessica (19), Becky (16), Emma (13) and Ashley (13).

JOE ELWOOD

Irishman Joe was disappointed to be released by Orient at the end of the 1965-66 season, after undergoing back surgery, but he recovered and played football again for Ards, near his native Belfast, in the Irish League.

Returning to London in the 70s, he began working as a PE teacher at Upton House school in Homerton (later to become Homerton House secondary school), where he was employed for 18 years.

Joe subsequently worked in North-East London as an insurance sales agent.

He is now retired and living in Walthamstow, East London with his wife Rhona. They have four children – Christine, Jannette, Denise and Joseph – and four grand-daughters – Sarah (18), Abigail (14), Elizabeth (5) and Harriet (4).

Joe is still an occasional visitor to the Orient and despite his disappointment by the manner of his unfortunate exit from his only English League club, he says: "The people at the club now have been good to me and always look after me well whenever I go back."

PHIL WHITE

As has been covered earlier in the book, this popular former right-winger was forced to retire from football due to a bad knee injury in May 1964.

Phil lived in Fulham with his wife, Ivy (who has also passed away), and their two children, Phil (jnr) and Julie.

After his playing days ended, he worked as manager of a betting shop in South London.

Sadly, Phil died of cancer in year 2000.

NORMAN DEELEY

After leaving Brisbane Road at the end of the 1963-64 season, Norman continued to play a high standard of non-league football – two years at Worcester City (a strong side that included Welsh legend Ivor Allchurch, plus Gerry Hitchens and Peter McParland), a couple of seasons with Bromsgrove Rovers (managed by Gil Merrick), followed by spells with Darlaston and Stourbridge.

Norman's working life outside football saw him employed on the assembly line at the Longbridge car plant in Birmingham, where he worked for 10 years from the early 70s. He then spent a further eight years as a Placement Officer in the Job Centre in Walsall before retiring.

Cyril Lea said: "I once bumped into Norman when he was collecting cash on the turnstiles at Walsall FC."

Many more footballers smoked in Deeley's playing days compared to today's more health-conscious times. Norman, Phil White and Terry McDonald all smoked during their time at Orient and Deeley admits he used to get through between 15 and 20 cigarettes a day back then.

Sid Bishop commented: "The biggest gamblers in the side were Norman Deeley and Phil White – they were also the heaviest smokers. Deeley would take a packet on cross-country runs through the forest, then sneak off to have a quick puff behind the bushes!"

Terry McDonald quit smoking cigarettes many years ago, and now enjoys only a mild cigar if he's drinking socially.

But Norman was forced to give up smoking some years ago for health reasons.

His croaky voice told its own story, as he explained: "I've got emphysema. Basically, my lungs are knackered and I get out of breath after walking just 20 or 25 yards. I have to use a nebuliser four times a day to help with my breathing."

In fact, Norman has suffered a series of serious health problems since he was forced to give up work.

"I had a heart attack 10 years ago," he says, "and then I had a stroke which caused

Ronnie Foster, Dave Dunmore, Dennis Sorrell, Terry McDonald and Clive Lewis (Dad's Best Man and a former West Ham Youth team-mate) on a social visit to Dennis' old pub in the East End in 2002.

me to lose the sight in my right eye. The eye just suddenly closed on me one day – it was like a curtain coming down.

"I don't go out that much now and when I do, I've got friends who usually pick me up and help me to get from one place to another. I like to watch the horseracing on the telly – and yeah, I still have a bet now and again."

Now divorced from Dorothy, Norman lives alone back in the part of the Black Country where he was born 73 years ago, at Wednesbury. His eldest son, Andrew (50) lives in Australia. He also has a daughter, Jayne (48), who lives nearby in Wolverhampton, and another son, Robert (29), who emigrated to New Zealand. Norman also has two grand-daughters, Lyndsey and Olivia.

TERRY McDONALD

In the summer that Orient boss Dave Sexton gave him a free transfer, McDonald joined Division Three Reading, who were then managed by one of Chelsea's championship stars of a decade before, Roy Bentley. His team-mates for the 1965-66 season at Elm Park (way before the Madejski Stadium) included Peter Shreeves, who went on to manage Spurs at the highest level, Denis Allen, the late father of the current MK Dons boss Martin Allen, and future Oxford boss Maurice Evans.

But McDonald had played only 13 matches (2 goals) for the Royals when, on October 23, they visited Bournemouth and he was sent-off. He never played another first team game for the Berkshire club, who were struggling fifth from bottom at the time.

Explaining the rumpus that caused him to be banished to the reserves, he said:

Terry McDonald at his 65th birthday and retirement party – held in the South Stand bar at Leyton Orient in 2005 – with his daughters Lisa and Joanne, and son Tony.

"I stopped the ball in the 'D' by the corner flag, facing the crowd, when their big Northern Ireland international right-back Dick Keith – he used to be with Newcastle – came running over and smashed me from behind." (Keith died following an accident at work in 1967.)

Terry continued: "I fell among the St. John Ambulance staff around the edge of the pitch, spreadeagled on top of the first-aiders, with my arm in the air, fully expecting the referee to award me a freekick.

"But he just waved play-on. I couldn't believe it – it was an outrageous challenge. So I called him a 'f****** w*****!'and was sent off.

"The Reading chairman (A.E. Smith), wanted to see me on the Monday morning. He said: 'You'll never play for our first team again'.

"Nobody got sent off years ago but he just couldn't accept any of his players swearing. The game had to be 'nice', I suppose. It wasn't high or dangerous tackles that you were sent off for then, it was usually for abusing the officials.

"I asked the chairman if he'd actually seen the incident and what he thought. He said: 'I think you were harshly treated', and so I said: 'Well, thank you very much!'.

"Roy Bentley laughed about it and said he felt sorry for me. 'I'm with you,' he told me. But the chairman wasn't happy and had made his mind up. He told me I had to go and play for Jimmy Wheeler, who managed Reading Reserves. Jimmy said to me: 'You'll enjoy it here – where do you want to play!' As it happened, I played for them against Orient Reserves at Brisbane Road."

In the summer of 1966, when England's heroes were running round Wembley with the Jules Rimet trophy, McDonald was on his way to Wimbledon and the hustle and bustle of the Southern League. Although the Dons were a force to be reckoned with, Terry moved on to Folkestone Town the following year and he enjoyed it there, with fellow former O's players Tony Biggs and Alan Russell, until increasing work commitments forced him to confine his football to local Sunday morning teams in Essex.

Since his playing days finished he has worked in and managed a number of betting shops and, at 67, is still working four days a week for Coral in one of their prime City shops. "I ran my own shop for a year in the mid-80s, in Snaresbrook High Street, but it was difficult to make it work, especially after they finished building the nearby crown court and all the labourers disappeared from the area! The new parking restrictions they brought in outside my shop also hit the business, so I closed it and went back to managing for other people."

But Terry has never lost his love for football. For six or seven consecutive summers from the mid-80s he visited the USA to head up coaching schools for kids in Philadelphia and Boston.

In England, he has worked for a number of league clubs either in a part-time coaching or scouting capacity. It was while talent-spotting for his first club, West Ham (whose chief scout was Eddie Baily), that Terry also coached in schools for the Greater London Authority (GLA). "Eddie asked me to take a couple of sessions at Langdon school in Poplar, where he wanted me to have a look at a young kid they had their eye on called Paul Ince. I think Incey was in the under-12 or 13s age group at the time."

Ken Brown, a senior colleague from Terry's West Ham days, called him up after taking over as manager at Norwich City in 1980. "Ken asked me to run a Norwich under-14s team for him in Essex. Michael Gilks, who went on to play for Reading, was the pick of that lot.

"I did a bit of work for Leyton Orient, too, when Bernie Dixon ran the youth side of things there. And when Bernie moved to Chelsea as Youth Development Officer, I went with him, coaching an under-13s group for them at Dagenham Sports Centre. The star player in the side I coached there was the striker Leon Knight, who joined Swansea last season."

It's true to say that, given his extensive coaching skills (he holds the UEFA B Licence), McDonald could easily have held down a long-term coaching role at a League club years ago . . . if only he'd been prepared to be a 'yes man'.

He said: "I've loved going to watch games and certain players but a lot of the time in football it's not what you know, it's *who* you know in this game. And a lot of the time these clubs expect you to give up your evenings and weekends to watch lots and lots of games and yet pay you only expenses. As if you're working for them purely for the fun of it."

Terry was the coach of Leyton Orient's under-15s side in the early 90s, when Jeff Brazier was no more than a regular substitute for the team before he found fame with reality TV celeb Jade Goody!

"I'd like to have become a bit more involved on the coaching side with Orient," said Terry, "but I probably didn't push myself hard enough and I certainly wasn't going to go begging for work.

"When John Sitton was manager at Orient, I think he made some dismissive comment about me, along the lines of me being too old to know anything that could be of much use to him or the club. I got on all right with Tommy Taylor, and like him as a person, but Paul Brush was another who wasn't my cup of tea.

"I remember a silly situation when Brushy was in charge of the youth development at Orient and Tommy had arranged for me to go and see him, with a view to me possibly doing some work for the club. I made my way to Brushy's office at the ground one day, to talk about what he might have in mind for me. At first he asked me to fill out a form explaining my background and what I'd previously done in football . . . and then he asked me to sit there and wait for him while he popped out to get himself something to eat. After having sat there for about half-an-hour, and with still no sign of him returning to his office, I decided I'd waited long enough and so I left. I never spoke to or heard from him again. I think, in a lot of cases, people in his position can feel a bit threatened by having former players from the club around them. There's too much self-preservation going on in football."

Still, Terry remains a regular and keen spectator at both Orient and West Ham, where he has a season ticket alongside myself and three of his grandsons, George (17), Jack (13) and Connor (12). He has another grandson, Oliver (9), who will no doubt be joining us at matches before long, and a grand-daughter Mia (18), who is a talented dancer and whose theatre shows Terry usually attends, along with his daughters (my sisters), Lisa (41), who is a hairdresser, and Joanne (39), a dance teacher.

"I must thank the staff at Orient who always look after me so well and all the supporters who still say nice things about me and our team from the early 60s. They were great days and we'll never forget them.

"I had my retirement party in the South Stand bar two years ago and that's where I watch most home games from – that's the stand, not the bar!"

Terry has not remarried since him and our mum, his childhood sweetheart Jean, were divorced in the early 80s (they continued to remain good friends right up until her sad death from a brain tumour in December 1997). But there have been a string of romantic interludes – and at least one broken engagement – in the intervening years! Meanwhile, he is thankfully fit and happy in his batchelor 'pad' in Leyton and continues to enjoy a very active social life.

Nothing's changed there, then!

MALCOLM MUSGROVE

After he finally put his boots away for the last time in 1966, aged 33, Malcolm became coach at Brisbane Road under fellow ex-Hammer Dave Sexton, and also had a spell as Chairman of the Professional Footballers' Association.

In the early 70s he assisted his former West Ham team-mate Frank O'Farrell at Leicester City (1968-71) and Manchester United (1971-72).

However, Mal chose a much less glamorous United for his first job as boss, at Torquay. He took the Plainmoor post after nearly joining up again with Bob Stokoe at Sunderland and so missed the Wearsiders' shock FA Cup final win over Leeds.

Malcolm held the helm at Torquay from 1973 to 1976 when, between jobs, he met up with his old West Ham boss Ron Greenwood. Ron asked him if he'd like to go over to the States for a week to help select a team franchise in the North American Soccer League for Connecticut Bi-Contennials. When he got there his old West Ham colleague, ex-Orient star Phil Woosnam, persuaded him to join Connecticut on a pre-season tour to Portugal, where they met Benfica and Sporting Lisbon. He helped manager Bobby Thomson, the former Wolves full-back, with training and the whole trip turned into a marvellous adventure.

On his return, 'Muzzie' was offered a coaching post with Chicago Stings who had a really cosmopolitan playing staff including Americans, Scots, a Yugoslav, Germans, two Haitians and a young Dutchman named Dick Advocaat, who went on to lead Holland to the 1994 World Cup finals in the States. The one-week invite turned into a two-year stay in the USA.

When he returned to the UK, he had one of his rare spells out of the game selling insurance. But one day, while selling policies at Exeter City, he was asked by Grecians' manager, ex-Villa star Brian Godfrey, to come back into the game as physiotherapist at St James's Park. Mal spent three happy years with Exeter before being made redundant.

Then he was off on his travels again, accepting a physiotherapist post in oil-rich Qatar in the Gulf. He accompanied the national side to the Asian Games and the Under-16s to the Junior World Cup in China. Returning from the Gulf in 1984, he was lucky enough to land a job under Dave Smith at Plymouth Argyle, as reserve team manager, coach and physio. Then his West Ham buddie Ken Brown took over the reins and Mal had five wonderful years at Home Park.

After a long spell as physio at Shrewsbury Town and a lifetime in football, Mal retired in the late 90s.

Sadly, his health has deteriorated somewhat in the past year with the onset of the early stages of Alzheimers. He wasn't able to talk in person for this book but his son, David Musgrove, has been a great help and he says that Malcolm now recalls very little of his time at Brisbane Road.

David went on to say that his father had opportunities to join either Brighton or Fulham as player-coach but went to the O's because of his friendship with Eddie Lewis (who still keeps in touch on a regular basis) – and also because it meant he did not have to move house.

Malcolm remembers that it was very easy to fit in at the Orient, as the club was a bit like West Ham – a place everyone got on with each other.

Mal is now living in retirement with his wife Jean at Torquay in Devon.

JOHNNY CAREY

The only man to ever manage Orient at the highest level of English football said Nottingham Forest made him an offer he couldn't refuse. He joined them before the 1963-64 season and so nearly brought trophies to the City Ground.

Forest were runners-up to first division champions Manchester United in 1966-67

Malcolm Musgrove pictured in recent years at home in Torquay with his wife Jean and son David.

and were beaten by Spurs in the FA Cup semi-final that same season.

Carey was sacked in December 1968 and returned to Blackburn Rovers the following year in an administration role. He became manager there again in October 1970 but he was dismissed in the summer of 1971.

After doing some scouting to his first club, Manchester United, he left football to work for the Trafford Treasury Department in Sale, Cheshire before retiring.

He died on August 19, 1995, aged 76.

LOYAL O'S SUPPORTERS REMEMBER

WE asked a number of Leyton Orient supporters who followed the O's between 1961 and 1963 to share with us their own special personal memories of those exciting times. Some have had to be edited for space reasons but we believe they illustrate just what the team's achievement in winning promotion to the first division meant to so many people whose lives were touched by the experience of seeing history made.

John Parke, in particular, gave up a lot of his time to offer his opinions on the players he saw play in his youth and, most importantly, why he believes the people who were running LOFC more than four decades ago missed a golden opportunity to secure the club's longer-term future in (or at least close to) the top flight of English football.

Now 61 and based at Newbury Park, Ilford, Essex, John said: "I was eight when I saw my first game at Orient on September 12, 1953 – a 2-2 draw with Millwall. My uncle, Jack Cantor, took me and we stood at the Coronation Gardens end."

Born in Leyton, John lived in Blyth Road. He attended George Mitchell School and then Leyton County High.

"I was 17 in the promotion season and had just started work, in the Stock Exchange in the City, although I soon moved back to Leyton to work for Porter Nicholson, a furniture wholesaler."

John didn't miss a single Orient match, home or away, in either the promotion season or the first division campaign.

"The 3-3 draw at Anfield was undoubtedly Orient's best performance of the '61-62 season – they matched everything Liverpool could throw at them and Dave Dunmore was brilliant. There was no segregation of fans in those days, although I was told by a local policeman not to stand on The Kop, so I stood at the opposite end instead. Anfield is the only ground I went to then where I was advised not to stand in a certain area of a ground for my own safety."

John recalls the struggle O's had to go up.

"I feared that we would throw it away," he continued. "We were very unconvincing towards the end of the season. I'd say in the last seven games, it was the defence that saw them through. They conceded only one goal in six games. Sid Bishop was superb. Even though he wasn't tall, he was very strong and he could hang in the air. And he overcame the fact that he didn't have a left foot. Sid was one of the best players Orient has ever had.

"Towards the end of that season, I thought we missed Phil White's crossing and also Frank George, who I rated a better keeper than Bill Robertson. Frank was more active, braver and would dive at people's feet. He was also a good shot-stopper. Bill had experience but he didn't come off his line very often.

"I still wasn't confident after beating a weakened Luton side at Kenilworth Road in our penultimate match. And our chances looked even slimmer when I was watching a home reserve team game at Orient the next night, and we heard that Sunderland had won at Rotherham.

And so to Bury – D-Day.

"After a haircut in the morning (we were hopeful of going out that night to celebrate), I was over there at about 1.45pm. It was just a great experience. Sunderland's game at Swansea finished just before ours and then all the fans ran on the pitch to mob Stan Charlton and Malcolm Graham.

"Orient kicked towards the Coronation Gardens in the second half, which meant Stan was marooned over the far side of the pitch from the tunnel, by the old West Side, when the final whistle blew. He had no chance of getting off the field before being swallowed up by the crowd. They carried him from that far corner of the ground all the way to the dressing room.

"I had a great view of all the celebrations, because my friends and I always stood on the wall just above the players' tunnel, right in front of the directors' box. I'd stood there since I was a kid.

"There was a crowd of about 25 of us at the last game and after a drink in the Coach & Horses, we all went up town to continue the celebrations. I think we moved on to the Blind Beggar pub at Whitechapel. To be honest, we all felt shattered. It had been a long season and the 42 games were crammed into a short season. There was a lot of travelling involved too. There was a sense of relief at the end that we'd finally won promotion.

"For away games, we'd book on the old Football Special excursion, which cost around 10s-6d. To get to Newcastle for our first away match, we left King's Cross at about half-past 11 the previous night, and didn't get to Newcastle station until about four or five o'clock in the morning.

It was a case of either staying on the train to get more sleep, or find something to do until it was afternoon and time to go to the ground. Sometimes a group of us would go to South Shields in the morning and play football on the beach

"It was the same when we went to Sunderland.

You had to get a specific train that was designated as a 'special'. After the game finished, we'd usually have a beer and then make sure we were on the 11pm train back to London. We'd arrive back in at about 5am the next morning, get ready and then go and play Sunday morning football!

"There was many a time when supporters would see our players on the same train, and they were always approachable. They had a meal in their own separate carriage but you could still get to speak to them. I got to know Malcolm Lucas very well."

Supporters of West Ham and Arsenal would adopt the O's as their second favourite team. "We were always their 'second club' and when West ham and Arsenal were away, as they were every time we were at home, a crowd would come from the other side of Hackney Marshes to see us play.

"Because there was no segregation in those days, you didn't really know who was who inside the ground. Away fans didn't all gather in one area, as they do now – you'd see Orient fans all over the place and so there was no concentrated area of noisy support for the team. At Fulham, it was possible to walk all the way round the ground. There wasn't really any singing anywhere, just the usual noise of a football match, apart from Liverpool where they sang You'll Never Walk Alone.

"I never saw any trouble at matches then. Fans of both teams would mix freely."

John says that the arrival of Johnny Carey took supporters by surprise. "No-one could believe that we could get him from Everton," he says. "Under Carey, the defence was far better and superbly consistent. Dunmore was the big difference although if Tommy Johnston hadn't left because he couldn't get on with Carey, who knows what would have happened. They could have been a good combination up front and the team might have gone up a lot easier than they did."

John admits there was a great buzz of anticipation when the fixture list sent Arsenal to Brisbane Road on the opening day, but it was also tinged with realism. "A lot of us thought that staying up would be impossible," he says with the air of a man who, like all diehard Orient fans, has spent a lifetime expecting little or nothing by way of success for his team.

"It was unrealistic to expect Dunmore to score another 20 goals in the first division, while Robertson was 34-years-old. There wasn't a lot of hope and we were disappointed by the lack of signings. We thought that a forward, a keeper, and possibly a left-back was needed, but Carey bought nothing new and went in with the same team he had from the year before. Saying that, Gordon Bolland was young and Carey seemed to think he would be the answer.

"We thought me might have a chance after those three home wins early on, including a massive result against Everton, and after winning at Fulham there was a feeling of hope that we might survive. But we didn't win another game until May! We didn't have the players. I think it was the same old story of money not being available.

"And when Carey did buy, he got Malcolm Musgrove cheaply and Bobby Mason from Chelmsford for next to nothing, but the team needed more. Billy Taylor was a very good player, with a sharp footballing brain, but he was moved from inside-forward to left-back!

"I wasn't surprised when Carey left. I think he'd lost his way and everyone around the club felt totally demoralised - we finished 16th in our first season back in Division Two. The club was in total disarray."

But Parke believes that Orient should have had the revenue to build a better foundation for success. He says: "Between winning promotion in 1956 and then again in '62, the club sold a lot of players for what was then very good money, so the directors must have done very well out of it. The likes of Woosnam – at £30,000 – and Johnston – £35,000 – were sold for big money . . . and they didn't spend what they got for the likes of them on replacements. The club had never been run properly since the mid-50s when they were getting unbelievable crowds of between 20,000 and 30,000. And yet the most they paid out in that time was £8,000 to Newport County for Johnston.

"When you think that Liverpool went up at the same time as Orient in '62, and they went on while Orient just went further and further down, it shows how badly the club was run."

John Parke has continued to support his beloved O's through thin and thin, although he believes the club's board at the time the club reached the top flight missed a golden chance to cement Orient's future among the elite.

Of course, it would have been impossible over the years to have competed consistently with the likes of Arsenal, Spurs, West Ham and Chelsea. But Parke says: "Orient could have become a Charlton or a Fulham – holding their own in the top flight, or perhaps going down and coming back up again. Had the board invested in the team in 1962, we might have gone down one division sooner or later, but not three divisions, as was the case in the years that followed. The board had a big chance but they didn't take it.

"They didn't make the investment – and it's the same this year. Every club that goes up has to get in three or four good players to survive in a higher division. The only time they did it was immediately after winning Third Division South – but that was 50 years ago! Since then, we've always sold our best players. In Third Division South, they were playing teams like Coventry, Ipswich, Norwich and Southampton – they've all moved on. Even Millwall got to the top flight. But Orient have not done it again since 1962."

From Roy Ludlow, Winsley, near Bradford-on-Avon, Wiltshire

It was fascinating for me to read of your forthcoming book in today's *Sunday Times* and I shall certainly order a copy. I am 61 now – only a litlle younger than your father, I guess! – and so was just 17 when the Orient won promotion to the old first division. I am a life-long Orient supporter despite the fact that I have lived in the West Country for many years. I watch them whenever I can in this part of the world.

I grew up in Leyton, near the Baker's Arms, and, as far as I recall, did not miss a single home match in the promotion season. My favourite place was just to the side of the goal at the 'Windsor Road end', and it was just from there that I watched every match that season.

The Orient had two great games v Liverpool in the promotion season – 3-3 at Anfield, then 2-2 at Leyton. After the Leyton match I remember that the Liverpool manager (Bill Shankly) said: "All season I've been saying that the Orient will go up with us. Now I've changed my mind; we shall go up with the Orient!"

Certainly the Orient played the finest football I have ever seen them play that season.

During the following season in the first division, your father was the star player, waltzing past the best defenders in the country at will – and he was only 9st. 4lbs. All supporters lived in fear of him being transferred for a huge fee – the O's were always short of cash, of course!

One final memory, if I may. Sid was badly injured that season, v Sheff Wed (just mention Bronco Layne to him!). This was rare, as he was a tough bloke. Shortly afterwards he was crossing my street (Belmont Park Road) and, thrilled to bits, I asked: "Fit, Sid?"

His reply stays in my mind: "Don't know yet, cock". A good East End reply!

Pete Bush, Cockermouth, Cumbria

Being drawn at Burnley in the FA Cup and travelling to Lancashire with hundreds of O's fans on a football excursion from Euston. As we arrived a dense fog descended over the town from the surrounding hills and the match was postponed. We congregated outside the main entrance at Turf Moor until the official announcement was made, and then a wag in the crowd shouted: "Bob Lord (outspoken Burnley chairman and Football League official) opened his mouth and the fog came out!" The tie was eventually played mid-week and Ronnie Foster scored to earn a 1-1 draw. I can remember the grainy black-and-white pictures on late-night pre-*Match of the Day* BBC.

C.J. Horsnell, Woodford Green, Essex

I started supporting the O's about halfway through their only season in the top flight of English football, when I was 14-years-old. The first time I saw the O's was in a home draw with Fulham.

During the 1962-63 season I saw all of the home League and FA Cup games from the Fulham match until the end of the season. I also saw the O's play away at Spurs and West Ham. Three games are particularly memorable for me during that brief period of time – against Leicester in the FA Cup; the home win over Liverpool and the last match of the season at Brisbane Road, which I believe was against Burnley.

I seem to remember that there was a crowd of 25,000 at Brisbane Road for the FA Cup match v Leicester. Owing to a clash of colours – both Orient and City played in royal blue at that time – *both* clubs changed their shirts, with the O's turning out in red while the visitors wore white.

The last home match of the season was also an evening kick-off and it was a sad (in the old-fashioned sense) evening and a sad night. We had all known for months that Orient were not going to survive in Division One and perhaps that made it worse. A plaintive heart-felt chant of "Orient, Orient" went round and round the ground. I have never heard a chant like it before or since at a football stadium.

I write now, of course, with the knowledge of hindsight but it really did seem at the time that the O's were not coming back to the top. Nevertheless, Leyton Orient won promotion last season (2005-06), and it seems the finances are in order thanks to Mr Hearn, so who knows what the future holds . . .

Despite losing many games during the 1962-63 season it seemed to me that every player who wore an Orient shirt gave his best on the field. The forwards could not score enough goals so the pressure fell on the defence and yet the defence often played well. My favourite players of that historic era were right-back and captain Stan Charlton (of sliding-tackle fame), reliable and strong-in-the-air centre-half Sid Bishop and big Eddie Lewis at left-back.

Barry Brown, Billericay, Essex

The summer of 1962 saw the Orient add a North Wing to the main stand, in preparation for the new season, and I, along with my friends ,would often cycle over to see how the improvements to the ground were taking shape during school holidays. The first game in the first division was against the Arsenal and unfortunately the O's were beaten 2-1. It looked like it would be an uphill struggle that season, but there were some good performances, namely beating West Ham at home early on and Fulham away. I also remember a certain Terry McDonald having a blinder against Don Howe who was then playing for WBA.

Probable highlights of that hard season in the top flight were the beating of Manchester United, (Denis Law doing the twist over the ball, and that man McDonald getting the winning goal), and beating the league champions, Everton, 3-0 at home. I also remember the beating of Liverpool 2-1 – Sid Bishop getting a rare goal with his feet.

I recall Malcolm Musgrove being signed from West Ham that season to strengthen the team and scoring with his first kick against Birmingham, to force a draw.

John D. Munday, Caythorpe, Nottingham

I can remember your 'old man' giving Don Howe a good run for his money when we played West Brom mid-week, prior to us embarking on our best run of the season. For me, however, all was not well. Can you believe that I was ill during September and missed the matches against West Ham, Manchester Utd and Everton at home? On the night of the Everton match BBC *Sportsview* (if I remember correctly) did a feature on Everton which they finished by announcing that 'Everton are currently losing 3-0 at Leyton Orient' – just the boost I needed! If my memory serves me correctly, after that game Orient were the highest placed London team in the League!

I reported back fighting fit for the Sheffield Wednesday game, which was a match of significance for it was the first time that I (and probably many others) encountered crowd trouble. Apart from some well publicised problems on the pitch and at the end of the game, a crowd of Sheffield 'yobs' were intent on making trouble at the Coronation Gardens end. Not that we knew it at the time but it was a sign of things to come and the plague of football in the 70s.

I can remember coming away from the home game against Spurs, having lost 5-1, and some bright spark claiming a moral victory because we had stopped Jimmy Greaves from scoring!

Against Wolves at home, and in obvious desperation, Johnny Carey made numerous changes and it became clear that we were already in a dire situation. My own football career, however, was peaking and as much as I hate to say it, I began to miss a number of Orient games as my team stood perched on top of the Dalston and District League. (We eventually won the League and I collected one of the only two football medals in my mediocre career. Some weeks we played on the East Marsh and with the wind in the right direction, I could hear the crowd cheer the occasional home goal.)

Although the home game against Liverpool looks good on paper, I can remember feeling that the season was over for us and relegation beckoned. The attendance was now down to around 8,000 (now considered a bumper crowd).

I still have some programmes, a partially completed scrap book (I must have lost interest), the *Charles Buchan's Football Annual 1963*, which featured a picture of the Orient v Manchester Utd match on the cover, but, most of all, loads of memories . . . Lucas, Bishop and Lea – on their day, as good as any half-back line.

Watching Orient play at Highbury and White Hart Lane and not disgracing themselves. I can still picture Bobby Mason dribbling past what seemed the whole Spurs defence!

And for 35 years I've bored hundreds of people with the fact that we beat the League champions and FA Cup winners for both the current season and the following season!

P.S. And but for the Asian flu, I would have seen the 'old man's' winner against Manchester Utd!

David Block (via email)

I have some wonderful memories . . . I remember as if it were yesterday, the last-minute winner against Manchester United by the magnificent Terry. The massacre of Everton (I think their biggest defeat of the season?) had been a mid-week *hors d'oeuvre*.

I have it in my head that the defeat against WBA was extremely unlucky and included two own-goals and a goal from a free-kick taken much nearer to the Orient goal than it should have been.

I also remember Terry McDonald endeavouring all match to get past Jimmy Armfield (against Blackpool) and not having much success.

In the promotion season the highlights were, of course, the final match (with the Swansea v Sunderland game on the radio and Stokoe's pre-match comments about Sunderland deserving promotion more than the Orient) and the Cup defeat by Burnley, a game dominated by the Orient and I think preceded by Arthur Askey kicking a ball on the pitch.

I am sure it was against Burnley in Division One that the habit of booing every opposition player – and cheering every Orient player when he touched the ball – started.

Tony Hogg, Romford, Essex

My friend, Geoff Thompson, and I watched the majority of home games in the two seasons covered by your book, even though we were 14-year-old West Ham fans at the time (a lot of Hammers supporters did also cheer on the O's when our boys were playing away).

I recall us travelling back on the tube from Leyton to Stratford, after the home 2-2 draw against Shefield United, and speaking to two Sheffield Utd players on the train. We approached Doc Pace and Gerry Summers and had a bit of friendly banter with them about the 'dodgy' penalty the visitors had been awarded that day.

Can you imagine two Premiership stars being seen on the Central Line after a game today!

Roy Clifford, London E15

My main memory is the last game of 1961-62, v Bury, that I watched as a 12 year-old with my dad, who had supported the O's since their Clapton Orient days. He often referred to Orient as the 'Ornaments'.

I remember that many O's supporters had radios on the terraces, as Swansea Town v Sunderland was live on BBC. An almighty ROAR erupted when Swansea equalised near the end and this lifted the Orient players. The noise of the shouting and the rattles all around until the final whistle was unbelievable. At the end Stan Charlton was carried, shoulder-high, like a God, with other players lost among the hordes of supporters on the pitch. Malcolm Graham was my hero that day.

Another game I remember was Scunthorpe at home that we expected Orient to win (we lost 0-1). Sunderland, I believe, were just behind the O's in the league. The day started badly as we got to Brisbane Road slightly late (you had to get in an hour before the game to get a place by the wall on the East Terrace). I had my blue Leyton Orient flag and it got burnt by a cigarette (I still have this flag – burn hole as well!) after we lost.

On our train journey home to Stanford-Le-Hope we were very dejected and thought Orient had blown it. I'm just glad the team of 1961-62 had other ideas.

I think most Orient supporters, and everyone else, expected us to get relegated from Division One but, just for a short time in September 1962, we started to believe the impossible may happen and the O's would hold their own. Alas, it was not to be.

My dad's favourite player in that era was Sid Bishop, while mine was Dave Dunmore. I was at the Leyton Orient v Manchester United game that we won 1-0 with a late goal. Please, author, remind me who scored . . .

Tony Willis, Clayhall, Ilford, Essex

1962-63 was a dream come true for Orient fans, in the first division at last, but there had been no additions to the squad. The strength of the team came from the half-back line of Lucas, Bishop and Lea who had all played in every game of the promotion season. I remember thinking, 'same old Orient, don't spend anything and trust to luck'.

They didn't start too well, but they didn't get hammered either, and I will never forget the three home wins on the trot in September – West Ham, 2-0 (very satisfying!), Manchester United with a last-minute goal from Terry McDonald (top right-hand corner past Gaskell at the Coronation Gardens end, if I recall) and then 3-0 against Everton, who ended up as champions that season.

A few weeks later I went to Fulham to see the O's get their first away win (2-0). Although they hadn't set the first division alight, they had beaten some very respectable names. I then went to Aston Villa, away, where the O's only lost 1-0. Following that game it was Spurs at home, Greaves, Allen and all the rest. I recall that Spurs went one up before Norman Deeley equalised – and that seemed to inflame the Spurs who then scored another four, one of which was a volley from Les Allen from the edge of the area. He returned a punch-out by Mike Pinner (typical amateur keeper!). It seemed to hit the back of the net before Pinner hit the deck.

From then on up until Christmas I can't recall much that was particularly encouraging happening, culminating in a 5-1 defeat at Leicester in a snow storm on Boxing Day. This was the start of the big freeze-up of winter 1963 – the O's didn't play another league game until the middle of February.

After that there were only two more wins, one of which was against, of all teams, Liverpool who had gone up with the O's and have been there ever since – not doing too badly either! It was exciting at first but the long mid-season break certainly didn't help, together with the lack of class players added to the squad. I think the only two who came in were Bobby Mason, who had been a good player for Wolves but was recruited from the Southern League, and Malcolm Musgrove who, although he packed a kick like a mule, was certainly not in his pomp!

One other player that I remember from those days was Billy Taylor, who I think went to Nottingham Forest and was eventually involved in the England coaching set-up, even though he was a Scot.

All in all the season ended as a great disappointment, with lots of 'what might have beens' and 'if onlys'.

Tony Clement (West Ham fan)

I'll set the scene . . . July '62 and this young 14-year-old boy attends Brisbane Road with his dad for a trial for Leyton Orient. I had a trial at Ilford (they played in the Isthmian League in those days) and later, through various events, finished being 'part' of Dagenham & Redbridge before starting again in the Spartan League (I think). Anyway, a man at Ilford suggested I'd have a good chance of getting in at Orient. I arrive, along with about 30 other 14-year-olds, with my boots in a brown paper carrier bag. Could I be the brown-haired version of Bobby Moore waiting to burst on the scene? (Funny the things you think at 14, isn't it!)

We're all standing in the centre circle at Brisbane Road when the Great Man, Stan Charlton, walks out to meet us, bright red socks down over his ankles and a pair of shorts covering his knees. In that split second this potential, new star becomes a nervous wreck. Approx 75 minutes later, after having ran over every blade of grass, covered by tons of sand, we're standing back in the centre circle. The Great' Man is standing there and he says something along the lines of: 'Thank you all for turning up but we can only have a few of you. When I call your name you can leave, thank you'.

As I say there were about 30 of us there – and who's the first name he calls out? You've guessed it – me! My whole world ended. Do I laugh or cry? I think I did both. In all my football playing days I never got sent off but, you know, they're right when they say it's a long walk back to the tunnel. My dad, bless him, didn't have to say anything.

I'll never forget that day but the O's are still my second team. It may have been the O's greatest years, and it was good to experience them, but I have some slightly different memories of 1962.

Ron Hudson, Chingford E4

I'm buying this on behalf of my late father, Ronald Hudson, and late uncle, Arthur Hudson, who would have loved this book. It was their greatest time as O's supporters, spanning some 60 years.

Bill Hadgkiss

I'm now 57, and my Dad (himself a lifelong Orient supporter from the Clapton Orient days) first started to take me to the O's when I was five. We used to be first through the turnstile on the North Terrace and stood behind the goal, against the wall, with me standing on a wooden box that Dad had made me, so I could see.

I was 13 when the O's were in the first division, and we then had a regular spot right at the top of the old West Stand, where there was a large concrete block that I stood on. It gave the best view at Brisbane Road, over everybody's head.

My lasting memory of that season was a magical five days in Orient's history when, in Septmber, we beat Man Utd, 1-0, on a Saturday, with a late goal from your Dad, and on the following Wednesday beat Everton by no less than 3-0!

I lost my Dad in 1983 but my son is a loyal O's supporter and we still get to home matches despite now living in Sussex.

All the very best with the book, Tony, and I look forward to reading it and bringing back fond memories of those magical years.

Colin Matthews

My most vivid memory of the period 1961-63 is not one of the matches of the promotion season, which towards the end, when we started to lose and draw, seemed too full of anxiety for me to be able to believe in the possibility that we might actually go up; but the first match of the Division One season.

Not that I remember much about the match itself (which, as everyone should know, we lost 2-1 to Arsenal). It was the fact that we were playing Arsenal at all, and before a crowd of over 26,000, that was so exhilarating.

I can remember walking along Leyton High Road towards Brisbane Road, past the County Cricket Ground (where, if I remember rightly, Essex were playing that day), as part of a moving wall of fans, and the crush on the North Terrace where I often stood (no home and away segregation at that time) was astonishing. It seems hard to believe that I just turned up with my father without buying a ticket in advance; but the same had been true of the last match of the season, where the crowd was 'only' 21,600. I wasn't there, at the end of October, to watch us beaten 5-1 by Tottenham, to the biggest home crowd of all, nearly 31,000. I'm ashamed of myself now that I became a fairweather fan, and, like many others, couldn't face the long decline of the rest of the season.

But that first match was special.

Dick Richards, Hornchurch, Essex

My recollection of Saturday April 28, 1962 is as follows:

Noon, turn on the radio for best ever football preview programme (can't remember title), just a little mention about O's chances of first division football next season.

Lunch, which consisted of steak & kidney pudding, mash and peas with gravy. Now the excitement for this 14-year-old started to build, as I began to contemplate the most important match in O's history.

Set out from my home at 68 Mayfield Close, Dalston, E8 at five-to-one, walk down Forest Road to Queensbridge Road to get on the lower deck of bus number 236, passing Queensbridge Road School, which I had attended as an infant and secondary school pupil. Past London Fields, Victoria Park, along past Hackney Wick stadium and Lesney's 'Matchbox toy' factory, then past Eton Manor playing fields, just over the bridge to Temple Mills bus stop. I always alighted there as it was the nearest to the West Stand, where I was about to witness the greatest day in not only my own brief history, but also that of my team, LOFC.

Reaching Leyton Stadium at approximately half-past-one, the queue stretched along the back of the West Stand and appeared to go all around the other sides of the ground. This match was not all-ticket, just first-come-first-served, except for the main stand, which in those days always seemed to be 'sold out'.

As I joined the queue, anticipation was at a very high level among O's fans and upon passing through the turnstile opposite the then bowling green/tennis courts, I entered the West Stand at a quarter-past-two. Already assembled was a very large number of excited O's fans who had already covered at least half of the terraces behind the goals and the West Stand was also filling rapidly. Bearing in mind that apart from the main stand, only standing accommodation was available.

As both teams entered the arena the whole place seemed to erupt in a cauldron of noise, which was measured by some local boffin as '112 decibels'.

I am sure the match itself has been covered in great detail but just to say the two most memorable episodes, apart from two Malcolm Graham goals, were as follows:

Midway through the second half, from my West Stand vantage point, I could see Harry Zussman and his daughter, Delia, suddenly jump to their feet and almost simultaneously the whole of the main stand was in pandemonium. Yes, Swansea had equalised against Sunderland!

The roar spread immediately to behind both goals and then to the West Stand. The noise was unbelievable – it was registered by the aforementioned boffin at '118 decibels, which, in those days, was said to be bordering upon danger level for a sudden sharp sound in the human ear!

The second was the euphoria of the fans at the end of the match . . . yes, I was swept on to the pitch by what seemed to be a wave of never-ending supporters clamouring to get to the O's captain, Stan Charlton, who was soon engulfed by the delighted O's faithful and carried, shoulder-high, off the pitch. Eventually the players returned to the dressing room but still the rapture of the fans was at fever pitch, the pinnacle of which was reached when Johnny Carey appeared in the directors' box.

I was in heaven, the O's had done it! All 11 in blue shirts were heroes!

SUBSCRIBERS

Adrian Weston	Jacob Collins	Mr L S Drake
Alan Burge	Jeff Fraser	Mr Michael B Gannon
Alan Harvey	John Barrie	Mr P Lewis
Alan Knight	John Philbey	Mr P Nash
Alan Nicholls	John Regan	Mr P O'Toole
Anthony Michael Carter	Justin Lindy	Mr Paul Fox
Arthur Lewis Pearse	K R G Mortimer	Mr Paul Roberts
Bob Holbrook	Keith & Denise Simpson	Mr R Cullum
Brian Boardley	Keith Byrne	Mr R K Bowers-Brown
Brian Smith	Keith Davis	Mr S Hillman
C J Horsnell	Keith Johnson	Mr Steven C Mitchell
Chris Barnes	Keith Randall	Mr W J Bowers-Brown
Chris Lambert	Keith Treadle	Mrs A Butcher
Clive Cooper	Ken Beech	Mrs D Bird
Clive H Rosen	Kevin Jordan	Mrs R Hudson
Colin Matthews	Len Collins	Natham Collins
D Edwards	Marc Shaffer	Nick Somerfield
D L Knight	Mark Cain	Nigel Barber
Dave Bishop	Mark Dollemore	Paul Howard
David & Shirley Dawkins	Mark Pessell	Peter Brennand
David Burrells	Mark Taylor	Peter Coplestone
David John Collyer	Martin Lawrence	Peter Holland
Dennis Dawkins	Martin P Smith	R J Wolstenholme
Dick & Abigail Richards	Martin Scott	Rene Collins
Don Hanley	Michael & Maureen Sargent	Robert Budd
Doug Marsh	Michael Gray	Roy Clifford
E J Jones	Michael Grayson	Roy Ludlow
Eamon Perris	Michael H Williams	Seaton Lee
Edward Cole	Michael Oliver	Stephen Collins
G A Richards	Mick Meachin	Stephen Fraser
Gary Bullen	Mr Alan Budd	Stephen Jenkins
Gary McCullum	Mr Alan Coatz	Steve Fowell
Gary Stewart	Mr B Bates	Terry Brown
George Kent	Mr D W Gibbs	Terry Hurley
Gerry Warner	Mr David Jones	Tom Saul
Graham Goodall	Mr G A Salmon	Tony Bell
Graham Price	Mr G E Hill	Tony Clement
Ivor Chinman	Mr Holland	Vic & Robert Lindsell
J N Mills	Mr J L Bearryman	

Many thanks to everyone who has bought this book. I hope it has proved enjoyable and brought back many happy memories for you and your friends and family.

I would be delighted to receive any comments from readers with your thoughts on what you've read here, which – with your permission – we might like to publish in the reviews section of our website at www.footballworld.co.uk

You can write to me via email to: tony@footballworld.co.uk

Or send a letter to: Football World, 103 Douglas Road, Hornchurch, Essex, RM11 1AW.

All the best! Tony Mac

1961-62   MATCH-BY-MATCH

FOOTBALL LEAGUE DIVISION TWO

Date		Team	Score	1	2	3	4	5	6	7	8	9	10	11
19/8	A	Newcastle Utd	0	Hollins	Keith	McMichael	Neale	McGrath	Bell	Hughes	Harrower	McGuigan	Allchurch	Tuohy
26,638		Leyton Orient	0	George	Charlton	Lewis	Lucas	Bishop	Lea	White	Foster	Dunmore	Graham	McDonald
21/8	H	Leyton Orient	1	George	Charlton	Lewis	Lucas	Bishop	Lea	White	Foster (1)	Dunmore	Graham	McDonald
12,479		Southampton	3	Godfrey	Davies	Patrick	Clifton	Knapp	Huxford	Paine	O'Brien (1)	Reeves	Mulgrew (2)	Sydenham
26/8	H	Leyton Orient	2	George	Charlton	Lewis	Lucas (1)	Bishop	Lea	White (1)	Foster	Dunmore	Graham	McDonald
9,269		Middlesbrough	0	Appleby	Jones	McNeil	Yeoman	Thompson	Horner	Day	Harris	Livingstone	Peacock	Holliday
30/8	A	Southampton	1	Godfrey	Davies	Patrick	Clifton	Knapp	Huxford	Paine	O'Brien (1)	Reeves	Mulgrew	Sydenham
14,352		Leyton Orient	2	George	Charlton	Lewis	Lucas	Bishop	Lea	White	Foster (1)	Dunmore	Graham	McDonald (1)
2/9	A	Walsall	1	Christie	Palin	Partridge	Hill	McPherson	Dudley	Askey	Hodgkinson	Wilson	Younger (1)	Meek
15,963		Leyton Orient	5	George	Charlton	Lewis	Lucas	Bishop	Lea	White	Foster (1)	Dunmore (1)	Graham (3)	McDonald
9/9	H	Leyton Orient	2	George	Charlton	Lewis	Lucas	Bishop	Lea	White	Foster	Dunmore (1 pen)	Graham	McDonald
12,316		Derby County	0	Oxford	Conwell	Davies	Parry	Young	Hopkinson	Roby	Powell	Thompson	Hutchinson	Swallow (1 OG)
16/9	A	Bristol Rovers	2	Radford	Hills	Frowen	Mabbutt	Pyle	Slocoombe	Petherbridge	Sykes	Bradford	Jones (1)	Hooper (1)
11,824		Leyton Orient	1	George	Charlton	Lewis	Lucas	Bishop	Lea	White	Foster	Dunmore (1 pen)	Graham	McDonald
20/9	H	Leyton Orient	3	George	Charlton	Lewis	Lucas	Bishop	Lea	White	Foster (1)	Dunmore	Graham (1)	McDonald (1)
9,957		Huddersfield Town	0	Fearnley	Parker	Wilson	Saward	Coddington	Dinsdale	McHale	Kerray	Stokes	Massie	O'Grady
23/9	A	Preston North End	3	Kelly	Ross	O'Neill	Wylie	Singleton	Smith	Humes (1)	Biggs (1)	Alston	Sneddon	Thompson (1)
9,956		Leyton Orient	2	George	Charlton	Lewis	Lucas	Bishop	Lea	White	Foster (1)	Dunmore	Graham	McDonald
27/9	A	Huddersfield Town	1	Fearnley	Parker	Wilson	Saward	Atkins	Dinsdale	McHale	Kerray	Stokes	Bettany (1)	O'Grady
16,917		Leyton Orient	1	George	Charlton	Lewis	Lucas	Bishop	Lea	White (1)	Foster	Dunmore	Graham	McDonald
29/9	H	Leyton Orient	1	George	Charlton	Lewis	Lucas	Bishop	Lea	White	Foster	Dunmore (1)	Graham	McDonald
13,398		Plymouth Argyle	2	MacLaren	Robertson	Fulton	J. Williams	Fincham	Newman	Anderson	McAnearney	R. Williams (2)	Jackson	Malloy

Date	V	Team	Score	1	2	3	4	5	6	7	8	9	10	11
7/10	H	Leyton Orient	3	George	Charlton	Lewis	Lucas	Bishop	Lea	White	Foster (1)	Dunmore (1)	Graham (1)	McDonald
10,621		Stoke City	0	O'Neill	Asprey	Allen	Howitt	Andrew	Skeels	Ratcliffe	Mudie	Bullock	Thompson	Adam
14/10	A	Sunderland	2	Wakenham	Irwin	Ashurst	Anderson	Hurley	McNab	Hooper	Herd	Clough (2)	Fogarty	Dillon
36,780		Leyton Orient	1	George	Charlton	Lewis	Lucas	Bishop	Lea	White	Foster	Dunmore (1)	Gibbs	McDonald
21/10	H	Leyton Orient	1	George	Charlton	Lewis	Lucas	Bishop	Lea	White	Foster	Dunmore	Graham (1)	McDonald
10,581		Rotherham United	1	Morritt	Perry (1)	Morgan	Lambert	Lancaster	Cassidy	Wilson	Weston	Houghton	Kirkman	Taylor
28/10	A	Liverpool	3	Slater	White	Byrne	Milne	Yeats	Leishman (1)	Lewis	Hunt (2)	St. John	Melia	A'Court
36,612		Leyton Orient	3	George	Charlton	Lewis	Lucas	Bishop	Lea	White	Foster (1)	Dunmore (2)	Graham	McDonald
4/11	H	Leyton Orient	2	George	Charlton	Lewis	Lucas	Bishop	Lea	White	Foster	Dunmore (2, 1pen)	Graham	McDonald
13,120		Charlton Athletic	1	Duff	Sewell	Hewie	Tocknell	Hinton	Bailey	Lawrie (1)	Matthews	Edwards	Leary	Kinsey
11/11	A	Leeds United	0	Younger	Hair	Bell	Smith	Goodwin	McConnell	Mayers	Bremner	Revie	Peyton	Hawksby
7,967		Leyton Orient	0	George	Charlton	Lewis	Lucas	Bishop	Lea	White	Elwood	Dunmore	Graham	McDonald
18/11	H	Leyton Orient	4	George	Charlton	Lewis	Lucas	Bishop	Lea	White (1)	Foster	Dunmore (1)	Elwood (1)	McDonald
10,395		Brighton & H.A.	1	Baker	McNicholl	Sitford (1 OG)	Bertolini	Jennings	Burtenshaw	Tiddy	Nicholas (1)	Brown	Goodchild	Laverick
24/11	A	Scunthorpe United	0	Jones	Hemsted	Brownsword	Gibson	Neale	Howells	Marriott	Kaye	Thomas	Godfrey	Wilson
11,712		Leyton Orient	2	George	Charlton	Lewis	Lucas	Bishop	Lea	White (1)	Foster	Dunmore	Elwood	McDonald (1)
2/12	H	Leyton Orient	2	George	Charlton	Lewis	Lucas	Bishop	Lea	White	Foster	Dunmore (2)	Elwood	McDonald
12,908		Norwich City	0	Barnsley	McCrohan	Ashman	Scott	Butler	Crowe	Waites	Allcock	Conway	Hill	Punton
16/12	H	Leyton Orient	2	Robertson	Charlton	Lewis	Lucas	Bishop	Lea	White (1)	Foster	Dunmore	Elwood (1)	McDonald
13,761		Newcastle United	0	Hollins	McKinney	McMichael	Wright	McGrath	Bell	Hughes	Allchurch	White	McGuigan	Wilson
23/12	A	Middlesbrough	2	Appleby	Stonehouse	McNeil	Yeoman	Thomson	Neal	Day	Kaye	Peacock	Harris (2 pens)	Halliday
9,955		Leyton Orient	3	George	Charlton	Lewis	Lucas	Bishop	Lea	White	Foster (2)	Dunmore (1)	Elwood	McDonald
26/12	H	Leyton Orient	1	George	Charlton	Lewis	Lucas	Bishop	Lea	White	Foster	Dunmore (1)	Elwood	McDonald
14,550		Swansea Town	0	King	Sanders	Griffiths	P. Davies	Nurse	H. Williams	Jones	R Davies	Webster	Donnelly	G. Williams
30/12	A	Swansea Town	1	Dwyer	Sanders	Griffiths	P. Davies	Nurse	H. Williams	Jones	R. Davies	Reynolds	Donnelly (1)	G. Williams
9,000		Leyton Orient	3	George	Charlton	Lewis	Lucas	Bishop	Lea	White	Foster	Dunmore (3)	Elwood	McDonald

Date	H/A	Team	Score	1	2	3	4	5	6	7	8	9	10	11
13/1	H	Leyton Orient	3	George	Charlton	Lewis	Lucas	Bishop	Lea	White (1)	Foster	Dunmore (1 pen)	Graham (1)	Newman
15,113		Walsall	0	Boswell	Sharples	Guttridge	Hill	McPherson	Dudley	Meek	Hodgkinson	Beaman	Foster	Taylor
20/1	A	Derby County	1	Matthews	Barrowcliffe	Davies	Parry	Moore	Hopkinson	Roby	Havenhand	Curry (1)	Swallow	Palmer
22,136		Leyton Orient	2	George	Charlton	Lewis	Lucas	Bishop	Lea	White	Foster	Dunmore (1 pen)	Graham (1)	Newman
3/2	H	Leyton Orient	2	George	Charlton	Lewis	Lucas	Bishop	Lea	White	Foster	Dunmore	Graham (1)	McDonald (1)
14,737		Bristol Rovers	3	Radford	Bradford	Frowen	Bumpstead	Pyle	Sykes	Jarman (1)	Williams (1)	Mabbutt (1)	Jones	Hooper
9/2	H	Leyton Orient	0	Robertson	Charlton	Lewis	Lucas	Bishop	Lea	White	Foster	Dunmore	Graham	McDonald
18,899		Preston North End	2	Kelly	Cunningham	Ross	Wylie	Singleton	Smith (1)	Wilson	Biggs	Alston	Sparin (1)	Thompson
17/2	A	Plymouth Argyle	2	MacLaren	Robertson	Fulton	J. Williams	Fincham	Newman (1)	Kirby	McAnearney (1)	Carter	Anderson	Maloy
20,531		Leyton Orient	1	Robertson	Charlton	Lewis	Lucas	Bishop	Lea	White	Foster	Dunmore (2)	Graham	Deeley
24/2	A	Stoke City	0	O'Neill	Asprey	Allen	Howitt	Andrew	Skeels	Matthews	Thompson	Nibloe	Viollet	Ratcliffe
21,846		Leyton Orient	1	Robertson	Wright	Lewis	Lucas	Bishop	Lea	Deeley	Taylor	Dunmore (1)	Foster	Elwood
3/3	H	Leyton Orient	1	Robertson	Charlton	Lewis	Lucas	Bishop	Lea	Deeley (1)	Taylor	Dunmore	Bolland	Elwood
19,974		Sunderland	1	Montgomery	Irwin	Ashurst	Anderson	Rooks	McNab	Davison	Herd	O'Neill	McPheat (1)	Overfield
9/3	A	Rotherham United	2	Ironside	Jackson	Morgan	Cassidy	Madden	Waterhouse	Kirkman	Weston (1)	Houghton (1)	Butler	Bambridge
10,697		Leyton Orient	1	Robertson	Charlton	Lewis	Lucas (1)	Bishop	Lea	White	Taylor	Dunmore	Bolland	Deeley
13/3	A	Bury	0	Harker	Gallagher	Eastham	Turner	Stokoe	May	Calder	Beaumont	Hickson	Jackson	Hubbard
9,592		Leyton Orient	1	Robertson	Charlton	Lewis	Lucas	Bishop	Lea	Deeley	Bolland	Dunmore	Graham	McDonald (1)
17/3	H	Leyton Orient	2	Robertson	Charlton	Lewis (1)	Lucas	Bishop	Lea	Deeley	Taylor	Bolland	Graham (1)	McDonald
25,880		Liverpool	2	Furnell	Byrne	Moran	Milne	Yeats	Leishman	Callaghan	Hunt	St. John	Melia	A'Court (2)
24/3	A	Charlton Athletic	1	Duff	Sewell	Ord	Hewie	Hinton	Bail	Lawrie	Matthews	Leary	Edwards	Kinsey (1)
29,298		Leyton Orient	2	Robertson	Charlton	Lewis	Lucas	Bishop	Lea	Deeley (1)	Bolland	Dunmore	Graham (1)	McDonald
31/3	H	Leyton Orient	0	Robertson	Charlton	Lewis	Lucas	Bishop	Lea	Deeley	Taylor	Bolland	Graham	McDonald
13,290		Leeds United	0	Younger	Hair	Mason	Goodwin	Charlton	Smith	Bremner	Collins	Lawson	Peyton	Hawksby
7/4	A	Brighton & H.A.	0	Baker	Carolan	Baxter	Bertolini	Jennings	Burtenshaw	Tiddy	Nicholas	Caven	McNeill	Laverick
12,927		Leyton Orient	1	Robertson	Charlton	Clark	Lucas	Bishop	Lea	Deeley	Foster (1)	Bolland	Graham	McDonald

Date	H/A	Team	Score	1	2	3	4	5	6	7	8	9	10	11
14/4	H	Leyton Orient	0	Robertson	Charlton	Lewis	Lucas	Bishop	Lea	Deeley	Foster	Dunmore	Graham	McDonald
16,867		Scunthorpe United	1	Jones	John	Hemsted	Gibson	Neale	Howells	Marriott	Godfrey	Kaye	McGuigan (1)	Wilson
20/4	H	Leyton Orient	0	Robertson	Charlton	Lewis	Lucas	Bishop	Lea	Deeley	Taylor	Dunmore	Graham	McDonald
21,292		Luton Town	0	Standen	McNally	Bramwell	Morton	Kelly	Pacey	Clarke	Turner	Ashworth	McKechnie	Fleming
21/4	A	Norwich City	0	Kennon	Thurlow	Ashman	Burton	Butler	Mullet	Mannion	Lythgoe	Scott	Hill	Punton
20,454		Leyton Orient	0	Robertson	Charlton	Lewis	Lucas	Bishop	Lea	Deeley	Taylor	Dunmore	Bolland	McDonald
23/4	A	Luton Town	1	Standen	McNally	Bramwell	Morton (1)	Kelly	Pacey	Clarke	Ashworth	Baynham	McKechnie	Fleming
13,681		Leyton Orient	3	Robertson	Charlton	Lewis	Lucas (1)	Bishop	Lea	Deeley	Gibbs (2)	Dunmore	Foster	McDonald
28/4	H	Leyton Orient	2	Robertson	Charlton	Lewis	Lucas	Bishop	Lea	Deeley	Gibbs	Dunmore	Graham (2)	McDonald
21,617		Bury	0	Harker	Gallagher	Eastham	Turner	Stokoe	Atherton	Leech	Beaumont	Calder	Jackson	Bartley

FA CUP 3

Date	H/A	Team	Score	1	2	3	4	5	6	7	8	9	10	11
6/1	A	Brentford	1	Cakebread	Coote	Gitsham	Belcher	Gelson	Higginson	Summers (1)	Brooks	Francis	Edgley	McLeod
19,700		Leyton Orient	1	George	Charlton	Lewis	Lucas	Bishop	Lea	White	Foster (1)	Dunmore	Elwood	McDonald

FA CUP 3 Replay

Date	H/A	Team	Score	1	2	3	4	5	6	7	8	9	10	11
8/1	H	Leyton Orient	2	George	Charlton	Lewis	Lucas	Bishop	Lea	White	Foster (1)	Dunmore	Elwood(1)	McDonald
22,690		Brentford	1	Cakebread	Coote	Gitsham	Belcher	Dargie	Higginson (1)	Rainford	Brooks	Francis	Edgley	McLeod

FA CUP 4

Date	H/A	Team	Score	1	2	3	4	5	6	7	8	9	10	11
30/1	A	Burnley	1	Blacklaw	Angus	Elder	Adamson	Cummings	Miller	Connelly	McIlroy	Pointer	Robson	Harris (1)
37,932		Leyton Orient	1	George	Charlton	Lewis	Lucas	Bishop	Lea	White	Foster (1)	Dunmore	Graham	McDonald

FA CUP 4 Replay

Date	H/A	Team	Score	1	2	3	4	5	6	7	8	9	10	11
6/2	H	Leyton Orient	0	George	Charlton	Lewis	Lucas	Bishop	Lea	White	Foster	Dunmore	Graham	McDonald
31,000		Burnley	1	Blacklaw	Angus	Elder	Adamson	Cummings	Miller (1)	Connelly	McIlroy	Pointer	Robson	Harris

LEAGUE CUP 1

Date	H/A	Team	Score	1	2	3	4	5	6	7	8	9	10	11
11/9	A	Stockport County	0	Lea	Murray	Webb	Birch	Hodder	Porteous	Ward	McDonnell	Anderson	Murdoch	Partridge
7,615		Leyton Orient	1	George	Charlton	Lewis	Lucas	Bishop	Lea	White	Foster	Dunmore	Graham	McDonald (1)

LEAGUE CUP 2

Date	H/A	Team	Score	1	2	3	4	5	6	7	8	9	10	11
4/10	H	Blackpool	1	West	Arnfield	Martin	Hauser	Gatrix	Durrie	Horne	Peterson	Charnley	Parry	Oates (1)
9,910		Leyton Orient	1	George	Charlton	Lewis	Lucas	Bishop	Lea	White	Foster	Gibbs (1)	Graham	McDonald

LEAGUE CUP 2 Replay

Date	H/A	Team	Score	1	2	3	4	5	6	7	8	9	10	11
30/10	A	Blackpool	5	Waiters	Thompson	Martin	Crawford	Gatrix	Durrie	Hill	Peterson	Charnley (3)	Parry (2)	Horne
6,098		Leyton Orient	1	George	Charlton	Lewis	Lucas	Bishop	Lea	White	Foster	Dunmore	Newman	McDonald (1)

1962-63 MATCH-BY-MATCH

FOOTBALL LEAGUE DIVISION ONE

Date / Att		Team		1	2	3	4	5	6	7	8	9	10	11
18/8	H	Leyton Orient	1	Robertson	Charlton	Lewis	Lucas	Bishop	Lea	Deeley	Gibbs (1)	Dunmore	Graham	McDonald
26,300		Arsenal	2	McKechnie	Magill	McCullough	Brown	Neill	Snedden	Armstrong	Strong (1)	Baker (1)	Barnwell	Skirton
22/8	A	West Bromwich A.	2	Millington	Howe	G. Williams	S. Williams	Jones	Drury	Jackson	Burnside	Smith (1)	Kevan (1)	Clark
22,409		Leyton Orient	1	Robertson	Charlton	Lewis	Lucas	Bishop	Lea	Deeley	Gibbs	Dunmore (1)	Graham	McDonald
25/8	A	Birmingham City	2	Schofield	Lynn	Sissons	Hennessey	Smith	Beard	Hellawell (1)	Bullock (1)	Stubbs	Leek	Thwaites
23,500		Leyton Orient	2	Robertson	Charlton	Lewis	Lucas	Bishop	Lea	Deeley	Gibbs	Dunmore (1 pen)	Graham (1)	McDonald
29/8	H	Leyton Orient	2	Robertson	Charlton	Lewis (1 OG)	Lucas	Bishop	Lea	Deeley (1)	Gibbs	Dunmore (1 pen)	Graham	McDonald
17,289		West Bromwich A.	3	Potter	Howe	G. Williams	S. Williams	Jones	Drury	Jackson (1)	Hope	Smith	Kevan	Clark (1)
1/9	H	Leyton Orient	2	Robertson	Charlton	Lewis	Lucas	Bishop	Lea	Deeley	Bolland	Dunmore (1)	Graham (1)	McDonald
23,918		West Ham United	0	Leslie	Kirkup	Burkett	Peters	Brown	Moore	Dear	Woosnam	Sealey	Byrne	Crawford
5/9	A	Everton	3	West	Meagan	Thomson	Gabriel (1)	Labone	Harris	Bingham (1)	Stevens	Young	Vernon (1)	Morrisey
51,542		Leyton Orient	0	Robertson	Charlton	Lewis	Lucas	Bishop	Lea	Deeley	Bolland	Dunmore	Graham	McDonald
8/9	H	Leyton Orient	1	Robertson	Charlton	Lewis	Lucas	Bishop	Lea	Deeley	Bolland	Dunmore	Graham	McDonald (1)
24,901		Manchester United	0	Gaskell	Brennan	Dunne	Nicholson	Foulkes	Lawton	Moir	Setters	Herd	Law	McMillan
12/9	H	Leyton Orient	3	Robertson	Charlton	Lewis	Lucas	Bishop	Lea	Deeley (1)	Bolland (1)	Dunmore (1)	Graham	McDonald
21,756		Everton	0	West	Meagan	Thomson	Sharples	Labone	Harris	Bingham	Stevens	Young	Vernon	Morrisey
15/9	A	Burnley	2	Blacklaw	Angus	Elder	Walker	Talbot	Miller	Connelly	Pointer	Lochhead (1)	McIlroy (1)	Harris
24,978		Leyton Orient	0	Robertson	Charlton	Lewis	Lucas	Bishop	Lea	Deeley	Bolland	Dunmore	Graham	McDonald
22/9	H	Leyton Orient	2	Robertson	Charlton	Lewis	Lucas	Bishop	Lea	Deeley (1)	Bolland (1)	Dunmore	Graham	McDonald
20,125		Sheffield Wed.	4	Springett	Johnson	Megson	Eustace	Swan	Kay (1)	Young	Quinn (1)	Layne (1)	Dobson (1)	Holliday
29/9	A	Fulham	0	Macedo	Keetch	Langley	Mullery	Dodgin	Robson	Key	Cook	Brown	Henderson	Chamberlain
26,505		Leyton Orient	2	Robertson	Charlton	Lewis	Lucas	Clark	Lea	Deeley	Bolland	Dunmore	Graham (1)	McDonald (1)

				1	2	3	4	5	6	7	8	9	10	11
6/10	A	Manchester City	2	Dowd	Betts	Sear	Kennedy	Leivers	Benson	Young	Dobling	Harley (1)	Hannah (1)	Wagstaffe
19,706		Leyton Orient	0	Robertson	Charlton	Lewis	Lucas	Clark	Lea	Deeley	Bolland	Dunmore	Graham	McDonald
13/10	H	Leyton Orient	0	Robertson	Charlton	Lewis	Lucas	Clark	Lea	Deeley	Waites	Dunmore	Graham	McDonald
17,156		Blackpool	2	Waites	Armfiled	Martin	Crawford	Gatrix	Durrie	Watt	McPhee	Charnley	Parry (2)	Horne
20/10	A	Aston Villa	1	Sims	Neal	Aitken	Lee	Sleeuwenhock	Tindall	Ewing	O'Neill	Thomson	Wylie	Burrows (1)
29,370		Leyton Orient	0	Robertson	Charlton	Taylor	Gibbs	Bishop	Lea	Waites	Bolland	Dunmore	Graham	Deeley
27/10	H	Leyton Orient	1	Pinner	Charlton	Taylor	Lucas	Bishop (1 OG)	Lea	Deeley (1)	Bolland	Dunmore	Foster	McDonald
30,987		Tottenham Hotspur	5	Brown	Baker	Henry	Blanchflower	Norman	Marchi	Medwin (1)	White (1)	Allen (1)	Greaves	Jones (1)
3/11	A	Nottingham Forest	1	Armstrong	Wilson	Gray	Whitefoot	McKinley	Winfield	Hockey	Quigley (1)	Julians	Palmer	LeFlem
17,821		Leyton Orient	1	Pinner	Charlton	Taylor	Lucas	Bishop	Lea	Deeley	Bolland	Dunmore (1)	Foster	McDonald
10/11	H	Leyton Orient	1	Pinner	Charlton	Taylor	Lucas	Bishop	Lea	Deeley	Gregory (1)	Dunmore	Foster	McDonald
13,929		Ipswich Town	2	Bailey	Carberry	Malcolm	Baxter (1)	Nelson	Pickett	Stephenson	Moran	Crawford	Blackwood (1)	Leadbetter
17/11	A	Liverpool	5	Lawrence	Byrne	Moran	Milne	Yeats	Stevenson (1)	Callaghan	Hunt (3)	St. John (1)	Melia	A'Court
30,009		Leyton Orient	0	George	Charlton	Taylor	Lucas	Bishop	Lea	Deeley	Gregory	Dunmore	Foster	McDonald
24/11	H	Leyton Orient	0	George	Charlton	Lewis	Gibbs	Bishop	Lea	Dunmore	Taylor	Gregory	Lucas	Deeley
16,431		Wolverhampton W.	4	Davies	Showell	Thomson	Kirkham	Slater	Flowers	Wharton	Crowe (1)	Stobart (2)	Broadbent	Hinton (1)
1/12	A	Blackburn Rovers	1	Else	Bray	Newton	Clayton	Woods	McGrath	Ferguson	Lawther	Pickering	Douglas	Harrison (1)
15,593		Leyton Orient	1	Pinner	Charlton	Lewis	Lucas	Bishop	Lea	Deeley	Gregory	Dunmore	Graham (1)	McDonald
8/12	H	Leyton Orient	2	Pinner	Charlton	Lewis	Gibbs	Bishop	Lea	Deeley	Taylor	Dunmore (1)	Graham (1)	McDonald
9,874		Sheffield United	2	Hodgkinson	Caldwell	G. Shaw (1 pen)	Richardson	J. Shaw	Summers	Allchurch	Kettleborough	Pace (1)	Hodgson	Simpson
15/12	A	Arsenal	2	McClelland	Magill	McCullough	Barnwell	Neill	Sneddon	MacLeod	Strong	Baker (2)	Eastham	Armstrong
29,075		Leyton Orient	0	Pinner	Charlton	Lewis	Gibbs	Bishop	Lea	Deeley	Gregory	Bolland	Graham	McDonald
22/12	H	Leyton Orient	2	Pinner	Charlton	Lewis	Lucas	Bishop	Lea	Deeley	Gibbs	Bolland (1)	Graham	Musgrove (1)
11,646		Birmingham City	2	Withers	Lynn	Green	Hennessey	Foster	Smith	Hellawell	Bloomfield (2)	Harris	Leek	Auld

Date	V	Team	Sc	1	2	3	4	5	6	7	8	9	10	11
26/12	A	Leicester City	5	Banks	Sjoberg	Norman	McLintock	King	Appleton (1)	Cheesebrough(1)	Gibson	Keyworth (2)	Cross	Stringfellow
17,303		Leyton Orient	1	Pinner	Charlton (1 OG)	Lewis	Gibbs	Bishop	Lea	Deeley	Bolland	Dunmore	Graham	Musgrove (1)
16/2	H	Leyton Orient	1	George	Charlton	Lewis	Gibbs	Bishop	Lea	Deeley	Bolland	Dunmore	Graham (1)	Musgrove
17,132		Fulham	1	Macedo	Cohen	Langley	Mullery	Lowe	Robson	Leggat	Cook (1)	Brown	Hayner	Stratton
23/2	H	Leyton Orient	1	George	Charlton	Lewis	Lucas	Bishop	Lea	Deeley	Bolland	Dunmore	Elwood (1)	Musgrove
12,464		Manchester City	1	Dowd	Betts	Sear	Benson	Leivers	Oakes	Dobing	Kennedy	Harley (1)	Cheetham	Hannah
2/3	A	Blackpool	3	Waites	Arnfield	Martin	Crawford	Gatrix	Durrie	Lea	Quinn (1 pen)	Napier	McPhee (1)	Parry
11,732		Leyton Orient	2	Foster	Charlton (1 OG)	Lewis	Lucas	Bishop	Lea	Deeley (1 pen)	Gibbs	Dunmore (1)	Bolland	Elwood
9/3	H	Leyton Orient	0	Robertson	Charlton	Lewis	Lucas	Bishop	Lea	Deeley	Mason	Dunmore	Bolland	Musgrove
11,509		Aston Villa	2	Sidebottom	Fraser	Aitken	Tindall	Crowe	Deakin	Ewing	Baker	Woosnam (1)	Wylie (1)	Burrows
23/3	H	Leyton Orient	0	Robertson	Charlton	Lewis	Lucas	Bishop	Lea	Deeley	Mason	Dunmore	Bolland	Musgrove
14,079		Nottingham Forest	1	Grammitt	Wilson	Mochan	Whitefoot	McKinley	Winfield	Hockey	Addison (1)	Vowden	Quigley	Cobb
27/3	A	Tottenham Hotspur	2	Hollowbread	Hopkins	Henry	Marchi	Norman	Mackay	Saul	White	Smith (1)	Greaves (1 pen)	Jones
40,260		Leyton Orient	0	Pinner	Charlton	Lewis	Lucas	Bishop	Lea	Deeley	Mason	Dunmore	Graham	Musgrove
30/3	A	Wolverhampton W.	2	Davues	Showell	Thomson	Kirkham	Woodfield	Flowers	Wahrton (1)	Crowe	Stobart (1)	Broadbent	Hinton
13,739		Leyton Orient	1	Pinner	Charlton	Lewis	Lucas	Bishop	Gibbs	Deeley	Mason	Dunmore	Graham (1)	Musgrove
3/4	H	Leyton Orient	0	Pinner	Charlton	Lewis	Lucas	Bishop	Gibbs	Deeley	Mason	Dunmore	Graham	Musgrove
14,780		Leicester City	2	Banks	Chalmers	Norman	McLintock	King	Appleton	Riley	Cross	Keyworth	Hesth	Stringfellow (2)
12/4	H	Leyton Orient	0	Pinner	Charlton	Lewis	Lucas	Bishop	Gibbs	Gregory	Mason	Dunmore	Graham	Elwood
15,369		Bolton Wanderers	1	Hopkinson	Hartle	Farrimond	Rimmer	Edwards	Leonard	Birch	Russell	Davies	Hill	Butler (1)
13/4	H	Ipswich Town	1	Bailey	Carberry	Compton	Baxter	Nelson	Elsworthy	Stephenson	Moran (1)	Crawford	Phillips	Leadbetter
18,678		Leyton Orient	1	Pinner	Charlton	Taylor	Lucas	Bishop	Lea	Mason	Dunmore	Musgrove	Bolland	Elwood
15/4	A	Bolton Wanderers	0	Smirk	Hartle	Halton	Rimmer	Edwards	Leonard	Lee	Russell	Davies	Hill	Birch
16,649		Leyton Orient	1	Pinner	Charlton	Taylor	Lucas	Bishop	Lea	Mason	Dunmore (1)	Musgrove	Graham	Elwood

				1	2	3	4	5	6	7	8	9	10	11
20/4	H	Leyton Orient	1	Pinner	Charlton	Taylor	Lucas	Bishop	Lea	Mason	Dunmore (1)	Musgrove	Deeley	Elwood
8,724		Blackburn Rovers	1	Else	Bray	Taylor	McGrath	Woods	Newton	Douglas	McEnvoy	Pickering (1)	Ferguson	Harrison
26/4	A	Sheffield United	2	Hodgkinson	Badger	B. Shaw	Richardson	J. Shaw	Summers	Allchurch	Wagstaff	Pace	Jones (1)	Hartle (1)
20,703		Leyton Orient	0	Pinner	Charlton	Taylor	Lucas	Bishop	Lea	Mason	Dunmore	Musgrove	Deeley	Elwood
2/5	H	Leyton Orient	2	Pinner	Charlton	Taylor	Lucas	Bishop (1)	Lea	Mason	Deeley	Musgrove	Graham (1)	Elwood
8,273		Liverpool	0	Lawrence	Thomson	Byrne	Milne	Lawler	Stevenson	Callaghan	Hunt	St. John	Wallis	A'Court
4/5	A	Sheffield Wed.	3	Springett	Johnson	Megson	McAnearney	Swan	Young	Finney (1)	Quinn	Layne	Fantham (1)	Dobson (1)
20,762		Leyton Orient	1	Pinner	Charlton	Taylor	Lucas	Bishop	Lea	Bolland	Deeley	Musgrove	Graham (1)	Elwood
7/5	H	Leyton Orient	0	George	Charlton	Taylor	Lucas	Bishop	Lea	Elwood	Gibbs	Dunmore	Bolland	Musgrove
10,085		Burnley	1	Blacklaw	Angus	Elder	Adamson	Talbut	Miller	Meredith	Bellamy	Lochhead	Towers (1)	Harris
11/5	A	West Ham United	2	Leslie	Bond	Burkett	Peters	Brown	Moore	Brabrook (1)	Boyce	Sealey	Byrne	Scott (1)
16,746		Leyton Orient	0	Pinner	Charlton	Taylor	Lucas	Bishop	Lea	Mason	Gibbs	Musgrove	Bolland	Elwood
18/5	A	Manchester United	3	Gaskell	Dunne	Cantwell	Crerand	Foulkes	Setters	Quixall	Giles	Herd	Law (1)	Charlton (1)
32,759		Leyton Orient	1	George	Charlton (1 OG)	Taylor	Lucas	Bishop	Lea	Mason	Gibbs	Dunmore (1)	Bolland	Musgrove

CUP MATCHES

FA CUP

			1	2	3	4	5	6	7	8	9	10	11
FA Cup 3														
11/2 H Leyton Orient	1	George	Charlton	Lewis	Gibbs	Bishop	Lea	Deeley	Bolland	Dunmore	Graham	Musgrove (1)
9,757 Hull City	1	Williams	Davidson	Sharpe	Collinson	Garvey	McMilan	Clarke	Henderson	Chilton (1)	Cummins	McSeveney
FA Cup 3 Replay (AET)													
19/2 A Hull City	0	Williams	Davidson	Sharpe	Collinson	Garvey	McMilan	Clarke	Henderson	Chilton	Cummins	McSeveney
14,214 Leyton Orient	2	George	Charlton	Lewis	Gibbs (1)	Bishop	Lea	Deeley	Bolland	Dunmore	Graham	Musgrove (1)
FA Cup 4													
4/3 H Leyton Orient	3	Robertson	Charlton	Lewis	Lucas	Bishop	Lea	Deeley (1)	Gibbs	Dunmore (1)	Bolland	Elwood (1)
12,607 Derby County	0	Oxford	Barrowcliffe	Ferguson	Young	Moore	Waller	Stephenson	Parry	Curry	Hutchinson	McCann
FA Cup 5													
16/3 H Leyton Orient	0	Robertson	Charlton	Lewis	Lucas	Bishop	Lea	Deeley	Bolland	Dunmore	Elwood	Musgrove
25,769 Leicester City	1	Banks	Sjoberg	Norman	McLintock	King	Appleton	Riley	Cross	Keyworth (1)	Gibson	Stringfellow

LEAGUE CUP

			1	2	3	4	5	6	7	8	9	10	11
League Cup 2													
26/9 A Newcastle United	1	Hollins	Keith	McMichael	Neale	McGrath	Iley	Day	Hilley	Thomas	Hale	Fell (1 pen)
22,490 Leyton Orient	1	George	Charlton	Taylor	Lucas	Bishop	Lea	Deeley	Bolland (1)	Dunmore	Waites	McDonald
League Cup 2 Replay (AET)													
1/10 H Leyton Orient	4	Robertson	Charlton	Lewis	Lucas (10G)	Bishop	Lea	Deeley (1)	Bolland (1)	Dunmore	Graham (2)	McDonald
8,037 Newcastle United	2	Hollins	Keith	McMichael	Neale	Thompson	Dalton	Hilley	Suddick (1)	Thomas	Kerray	Fell
League Cup 3													
17/10 H Leyton Orient	9	Robertson	Charlton	Taylor	Gibbs	Bishop	Lea	Deeley (1)	Waites (3)	Dunmore (2)	Graham (3)	Wedge
7,428 Chester	2	Hardie	Molyneux	Flemming	Wilson	Butler	Curbishley	Gregson (1)	Myerscough (1)	Fitzgerald	Clarke	Jones
League Cup 4													
12/11 H Leyton Orient	3	George	Charlton	Taylor	Lucas	Bishop	Gibbs	Deeley	Gregory (1)	Dunmore	Foster (2)	McDonald
9,602 Charlton Athletic	2	Wakeham	Sewell	Hewie	Tocknell	Hinton	Bailey	Kennedy	Glover	Matthews (1)	Peacock (1)	Kinsey
League Cup 5													
3/12 H Leyton Orient	0	Pinner	Charlton	Lewis	Gibbs	Bishop	Lea	Deeley	Gregory	Dunmore	Taylor	McDonald
6,094 Bury	2	Harker	Robertson	Eastham	Turner	Stokoe	Atherton	Mayers	Jones (1)	Calder (1)	Beaumont	Bartley

THE BARGAIN BOOKSHOP
020 8524 9002
www.bookservice.biz

30/01/2007 13:04
000000#5180 CLERK 01   01

DEPT.02   *16.99
DEPT.01   *4.99
DEPT.02   *9.95
DEPT.13   R-5.00

ITEMS   30
CASH   *26.93

The Little Bookshop
with the Big Heart!
Thank You VAT 506364361